for beauty, and the urgent need to cleave to his presence among the trance
es of much of modern life. This is antidote to anyone perceiving Christianity
worn-out husk rather than a vessel of wonder and vocation. Dreher is holding
ght in the dark with this, maybe his most important, book.

—DR. MARTIN SHAW, author, *Smoke Hole: Looking*
to the Wild in the Time of the Spyglass

pocalypse comes cheap these days. You can find it prophesied in paperback at
any airport bookstand: the end of this, the crisis of that, the decline of the other.
Our sense of being drained—drained of spirit, of resources, of energy—is pervasive
enough that it has become a source of exhaustion in itself. We are weary of being
wearied, bored of the end of the world.

But Rod Dreher's *Living in Wonder* is apocalyptic in the true and costly sense
of the word. Which is to say it is a revelation. The light hasn't been sapped out of
the world, Dreher suggests, but out of us—by our distractions, by our technological ambitions, by the dull ache of our compulsive pleasures. "As a man is, so he
sees," wrote William Blake. Our highest imperative is to relearn how to really look
and really see.

Dreher walks with us as a fellow novice alongside unassuming masters of this
sacred practice: miraculously rescued former addicts, impish mystics disguised as
lawyers, grateful survivors of demonic possession. Like all works of true religion,
this book is not a didactic exercise in moralism but an adventure into endless mystery, an escape route from the dreary certainties of the disenchanted world.

—SPENCER A. KLAVAN, host, *Young Heretics* podcast;
author, *Light of the Mind, Light of the World*

Open this book and it gets real weird, real fast. Or don't ope[n] [...]
to get weird anyway. A society founded on the dogmatic exc[...]
that eludes reductive explanation will ultimately find itself at a l[...]
our situation. As the crisis of the West unfolds, we have begun [...]
that our picture of reality has been cramped and partial. The good [...]
bewilderment makes our time pregnant with the possibility of discov[...]
in Wonder, Rod Dreher tells us that "the world is not what we think [...]
more mysterious, exciting, and adventurous." Transcending cultural do[...]
Dreher achieves, and invites us to, a new freshness of spirit.

—MATTHEW B. CRAWFORD, *New York Times* bestselling [...]
The World beyond Your Head; Substack author, *Arch*[...]

Living in Wonder captures the tectonic shift happening deep under politics, [...]
ture, and, in many ways, religion. Dreher sees how the worldview set to repla[...]
Enlightenment rationalism is already here. This new world is full of living presence, glimmering with intelligences that act on and through us. Hopefully, with
his help, we can learn to discern the spirits.

—JONATHAN PAGEAU, host, *The Symbolic World*

The yawning gulf beneath the surface of our culture is becoming clearer every
day, but Rod Dreher shows us that it doesn't have to be this way. The world is
enchanted, magical, and soaked with God. Our ancestors knew it, here in the
West as elsewhere. Modernity has hidden this truth from us, but it can't be hidden
forever. *Living in Wonder* points the way out of the delusions of our modern dream
and back toward reality. This is an important book.

—PAUL KINGSNORTH, novelist; author, *The Abbey of Misrule*

It's thrilling to read an honest and courageous writer like Rod Dreher on the great
subject of the age: how to re-enchant our disenchanted world. God is not dead.
We have learned not to see him. Through books like this, we can learn to see truly
again. Timely, necessary, and wise.

—ANDREW KLAVAN, author, *The Truth and Beauty*

A brave, lucid, and absolutely compelling book. Dreher brings his substantial storytelling skills to a subject in turns both disturbing and visionary: the business of
enchantment. We live in a time of peril and opportunity, and Rod-as-guide leads
us through the swamps and snares of a world on fire. He reveals a God with a soft

LIVING
IN
WONDER

LIVING
IN
WONDER

Finding Mystery *and* Meaning *in a* Secular Age

ROD DREHER

 ZONDERVAN
BOOKS

ZONDERVAN BOOKS

Living in Wonder
Copyright © 2024 by Rod Dreher

Published in Grand Rapids, Michigan, by Zondervan. Zondervan is a registered trademark of
The Zondervan Corporation, L.L.C., a wholly owned subsidiary of HarperCollins Christian
Publishing, Inc.

Requests for information should be addressed to customercare@harpercollins.com.

Zondervan titles may be purchased in bulk for educational, business, fundraising, or sales
promotional use. For information, please email SpecialMarkets@Zondervan.com.

Library of Congress Cataloging-in-Publication Data
Names: Dreher, Rod, author.
Title: Living in wonder : finding mystery and meaning in a secular age / Rod Dreher.
Description: Grand Rapids : Zondervan, [2024]
Identifiers: LCCN 2024025252 (print) | LCCN 2024025253 (ebook) | ISBN 9780310369127
   (hardcover) | ISBN 9780310369134 (ebook) | ISBN 9780310369141 (audio)
Subjects: LCSH: Secularism—21st century. | Christianity—21st century. | Spirituality—
   History—21st century. | BISAC: RELIGION / Christian Living / Spiritual Growth |
   POLITICAL SCIENCE / Religion, Politics & State
Classification: LCC BL2752 .D74 2024 (print) | LCC BL2752 (ebook) | DDC 248—dc23/
   eng/20240701
LC record available at https://lccn.loc.gov/2024025252
LC ebook record available at https://lccn.loc.gov/2024025253

Cover design: Studio Gearbox
Cover photos: Shutterstock
Interior design: Sara Colley

Printed in the United States of America

24 25 26 27 28 LBC 5 4 3 2 1

To Luca Daum
and to the memory of Andrei Tarkovsky,
two artists who taught me to see comets

CONTENTS

TO SEE INTO THE LIFE OF THINGS

Hundreds of people can talk for one who can think,
but thousands can think for one who can see. To see
clearly is poetry, prophecy and religion, all in one.

—John Ruskin

The world is not what we think it is."

You know who told me that? A devout Christian lawyer whose descent into the bizarre reality just beneath the surface of things began when he saw a UFO hovering over a field, which now, years later, has him sorting things out with an exorcist. The man, whom I'll call Nino, believed in God, in angels, saints, demons, and all the rest before his experience. But then it became intensely real for him in ways he couldn't have foreseen.

It started in 2009, when teenaged Nino was motoring along a country lane not far from his house in rural New England. He spied a large obsidian-colored craft hovering silently over a field. Nino stared at it for a short time, then drove on. As Nino confided to me, "It was as if they planted a seed inside me for later." Afraid of mockery, he told no one.

Fast-forward to 2016. Nino was a law student in a major American city. One day, studying at his kitchen table, he saw the bare wall of his kitchen begin to swirl. "It was like a portal was opening," he told me. "The best way to put it is that two humanoid-like beings glitched into reality. They were made of light, but it was like running water. There was a thickness to the air in the room, like if you touched it, it would have made ripples."

The beings communicated with Nino telepathically. They told him a bird was about to land on his windowsill. Then it happened. Next they said that a car was about to backfire on the street below. That happened too. Then they disappeared.

Nino rushed himself to a nearby hospital and demanded an MRI and blood work. He feared he was losing his mind. But nothing was wrong with him.

The visitors have returned every year since then. After he married, his wife saw them, too, which was a relief, because he knew he wasn't hallucinating. What's happening to Nino isn't unusual. Many who have seen or interacted with UFOs report paranormal experiences in the wake— including visits from beings like the ones that appear to Nino. Some Christians to whom this has happened report that when they speak the name of Jesus in the presence of these beings, the beings vanish.

"Did you ever pray when you saw them?" I asked.

"Oh sure," Nino said. "Twice. They disappeared immediately."

"Did that not suggest to you that they might be demonic?"

"You know, I never thought of it that way," he said. "I kind of figured that they saw they had scared me and wanted to back off. I thought that if they were demons, they would have wanted to fight."

Nino, a solid, conservative young man with close-cropped hair and an aquiline nose he could have stolen from Dante had been struggling for years to reconcile these experiences with his Catholic faith. We first spoke in early autumn of 2023, not long after he and his wife returned from a trip to Colorado. They had rented a remote cabin. One night, the same thickness Nino experienced during the apparition of the humanoids manifested in the cabin, and all the electronics in the place went crazy.

"I don't know what this is," I told him, "but I believe you need to see an exorcist to talk about this."

The next time I saw Nino, he had been in touch with the official exorcist of his diocese, who suspected the lawyer might be demonically oppressed—not possessed, which is rare, but nevertheless afflicted by harassing demons. Sitting across from me in a hotel in his city, Nino told me he would soon have the church's required psychiatric evaluation to proceed with the exorcism. He was eager to begin and to make the bizarre visitations cease.

For a man who has been living with something pretty frightening for seven years, Nino struck me as unusually confident, even upbeat.

"If the purpose of these beings is to drive a wedge between me and Christ, they've failed," he said. "Not only did they not drive me away from Jesus, they've actually brought me closer to him. This whole thing has made me understand that materialism is false. The world is not what we think it is."

That phrase is at the core of this book. This is a book about living in a world filled with mystery. It is about learning to open our eyes to the reality of the world of spirit and how it interacts with matter. This is a world that many Christians affirm exists in theory but have trouble accepting in practice. It's too scary. Even good things that upset our sense of settled order unsettle us. After all, remember the first thing that angelic messengers tend to say to people in the Bible? *Do not be afraid!* It is natural for us to feel uneasy in the presence of those portions of the world that are normally unseen. And all the more so for us moderns—we prefer to keep God and his movement in the world safely sequestered within a rationalistic, moralistic framework. After all, can't that be controlled?

But as you will read in the pages ahead, that's not how the world truly is. It's more than what we can see. And control? Well, that's an illusion. Maybe something paranormal has happened to you or to someone you know. Something unsettling or even frightening, but not something you could explain away. And maybe you are like Nino when he first saw the UFO: believing that something real had happened but too afraid of being laughed at to tell anybody.

What happened to Nino terrified him and drove him to Christ to deliver him from evil. But of course this isn't the only way that our world is expanded by experiences of a larger reality. A man named Ian Norton had a positive encounter with the numinous—the mysterious—that drew him out of a pit of his own making and into the arms of Jesus.

Here's what happened. It was the day after Easter, in 2022, and I was in the Christian quarter of Jerusalem's Old City, looking for a special souvenir before I left for the airport later that afternoon. I had just experienced one of the most unforgettable seven days in my life—Holy Week in Jerusalem—and wanted something ancient to remember it by. "I know just the place," said Dale Brantner, an American pastor and trained biblical archaeologist.

He took me to Zak's, a narrow antiquities shop in one of the Old City's ancient streets. Dale said he has known Zak, a Palestinian Christian, for years. Good man. Loves Jesus. Honest. Sells genuine articles. We walked into the shop, but Zak wasn't there. At the far end of the room, behind a computer, sat a tough-looking white guy, middle aged, with a bald head, fading primitive tattoos on his forearms, and the kind of face that says *No funny business, pal.*

"Zak's on his way," said the man, in a rough Cockney accent belied by the gentleness of his voice. You don't expect to run into a working-class Londoner in the heart of Jerusalem. He was busy working on the store's accounts when we Americans walked in. While we waited for Zak, I asked the man—Ian Norton was his name—to tell me how on earth he found himself so far from home.

"I've been here thirty-two years," Ian said. "I was a junkie. I left London for Amsterdam, looking for stronger drugs. Then I heard the heroin was even better in Tel Aviv, so I went there. It was true. But one day I realized that if I didn't get off it, I was going to die. I went to rehab once, but it didn't work. I knew I had one last chance."

The addict found his way to Jerusalem, on a mission to save his own life. Somehow he acquired an English-language New Testament—a book he had never read—then headed out for the banks of the River Jordan. The

Cockney desperado vowed that come what may, he was not going to leave the river until he was delivered from the demon of drug addiction. This was a risky strategy. Acute heroin withdrawal can cause muscle aches, fever, chills, nausea, diarrhea, and other dire symptoms. If vomiting and diarrhea are sufficiently severe, patients can die of dehydration.

"I was anticipating the pains to start, and the pains were starting, from not having any heroin, no food, no money, no anything. I was like, *This is it, I've got to break through this addiction*," he recalled. "So I was sitting by the Jordan River, waiting for the pains to begin, and they were starting to increase. I was reading the book of Matthew for the first time in my life. I got to that point where Jesus was coming to John the Baptist."

That event, recorded in Matthew 3:13–17, took place at the same river where the suffering Ian sat shivering from withdrawal pains:

> Then Jesus came from Galilee to the Jordan to be baptized by John. But John tried to deter him, saying, "I need to be baptized by you, and do you come to me?"
>
> Jesus replied, "Let it be so now; it is proper for us to do this to fulfill all righteousness." Then John consented.
>
> As soon as Jesus was baptized, he went up out of the water. At that moment heaven was opened, and he saw the Spirit of God descending like a dove and alighting on him. And a voice from heaven said, "This is my Son, whom I love; with him I am well pleased."

Ian went on.

"Reading that part, this cloud just appeared. It was all around, coming closer and closer. It crossed the water first, and as it came nearer to me, it was becoming more and more condensed, more concentrated. At first you could just see it. Then it was something you could taste, and you could touch—and I realized that it had wrapped itself around me. It encompassed me, and pressed in. It held me. All I can say about it is that it was total purity, and peace. These wonderful things I had never felt before were just pressing in all around me and holding me in this state of pure love.

"After four days of being held there like that, without anything, it dissipated—and I was free from the struggle with heroin, just like that."

He staggered back to Jerusalem, weak from having not eaten. He sat on the street, begging, with a sign reading "Hungry and homeless," which was true. Christian believers came to Ian to share their testimonies. Eventually a pastor from a Messianic Jewish congregation invited the young beggar to live in the church and sort his life out. It was there, more than two decades ago, that he came to believe in Christ, accepted baptism, and started his new life.

Stunned by what I'd heard, I told him that I had just completed a life-changing week of miracle and wonder in Jerusalem, and that it had come to me as a gift of light and balm, just as my life had taken a dramatic, painful turn after my wife filed for divorce. Ian nodded. He got it. That's what Jerusalem, one of the thin places of the world, where the veil between the seen and the unseen is porous, does to you.

"The first thing you feel when you get here is separation," he says. "The things that separate us from our Creator, in Jesus, are the attachments we hold to the world. I was born in London, and coming out of London, everything is so worldly. Even if you're born again, and you've given your life to Yeshua Jesus, there's still that struggle with the things of the world pulling you back to it.

"You come to Jerusalem, and everything is God focused. You're wrapped in that spirit here. Everything is focused on continuing that journey toward him. Once you're separated from the things you hold dear, you're open to the Spirit calling on your heart."

It's true. I had just lived it. After only a week in the Holy City, a week of miracles, signs, and wonders, I was headed back to a life in the West that was uncertain, even scary, but also full of hope and renewal.

Things like that happenstance conversation with a shopkeeper make me wonder. How many times over the years, in all the places I have lived around the world, have I walked past people like Ian? Have I missed knowing their stories or, frankly, even caring to know—even though they had been touched in a jaw-dropping way by an encounter with the divine? How might my life have been different had I been open to noticing, with open eyes, open ears, an open mind, and an open heart?

I bet it's like this for you too. You want to believe that this kind of thing can happen—that the world is, in fact, enchanted, despite what many modern people say—but you find it difficult. Or maybe you believe it already, but God's presence seems far away. Maybe your faith has become dry, a thing held more in your head than in your heart—or felt in your bones. Whether you are a curious unbeliever, a half-hearted believer, or a believer who wants to explore deeper this world of wonders but don't know how, this book is for you.

One autumn night in the Hungarian city of Debrecen, a young evangelical man approached me and asked for a word. He was an American exchange student at the local college and had read some of my previous books. "I'm a conservative evangelical and have been all my life," he told me. "But I'm dying. I mean, I'm like a fish lying on a riverbank, gasping for air. I believe it all, but I am desperate for a sense of enchantment. I'd like you to tell me about Orthodoxy."

He was talking about Orthodox Christianity, my own faith tradition, to which I converted in 2006. The young man discerned from my writing that Orthodoxy, largely unchanged from the patristic era, with its ancient rituals, ceremonies, candles, incense, and way of seeing the connection between matter and spirit, offers the enchantment he craved. He was right, I think; we have entered an era in which the Western church desperately needs to taste the medicine preserved in the Eastern church.

We will get into that later. But this is not really a book about Orthodoxy. It's rather a book about the profoundly human need to believe that we live and move and have our being in the presence of God—not just the *idea* of God, but the God who is as near to us as the air we breathe, the light we see, and the solid ground on which we walk.

As I mentioned, this way of seeing and living the faith is more common today among the Orthodox, who for various historical reasons escaped the passage to modernity, but this experience was standard for Christians in ages past. C. S. Lewis wrote of the mental model of medieval Christians.[1] In the medieval model, everything in the visible and invisible world is connected through God. All things have ultimate meaning because they participated in the life of the Creator. The specifics of that participatory relationship were matters of dispute among theologians, but few if any doubted that this was how the cosmos worked.

This is what sociologists and religion scholars mean when they say the world of the past was enchanted. Yes, the Middle Ages were a time of kings and knights, of castles and tournaments, of sorcerers and superstition and all of that. It was also a time of war, famine, cruelty, and suffering of the sort that we don't see in Disney versions of the past. But to call that age "enchanted" in the academic sense—and in the sense I mean in this book—is to refer to the widespread belief that, in the words of an Orthodox prayer, God is everywhere present and fills all things. To say this world is enchanted is to say that we live in a world of beautiful and terrible wonders—things that fill us with awe and call us out of ourselves in recognition of a higher and greater reality.

The religion scholar Charles Taylor described the experience of enchantment like this:

> We all see our lives, and/or the space wherein we live our lives, as having a certain moral/spiritual shape. Somewhere, in some activity, or condition, lies a fullness, a richness; that is, in that place (activity or condition), life is fuller, richer, deeper, more worthwhile, more admirable, more what it should be. This is perhaps a place of power: we often experience this as deeply moving, as inspiring. Perhaps this sense of fullness is something we just catch glimpses of from afar off; we have the powerful intuition of what fullness would be, were we to be in that condition, e.g., of peace or wholeness; or able to act on that level, of integrity or generosity or abandonment or self-forgetfulness. But sometimes there will be moments of experienced fullness, of joy and fulfillment, where we feel ourselves there.[2]

We typically experience this fullness, says Taylor, in "an experience which unsettles and breaks through our ordinary sense of being in the world, with its familiar objects, activities and points of reference." This is what we call awe, or wonder. It is a primal experience on which all true religion depends. "We feel ourselves there."

Nobody can live forever awestruck. In its rituals and trappings, religion is largely an attempt to capture that primal experience of wonder, to make it present again in some way so that its power can penetrate our everyday lives. We want this encounter with a power greater than ourselves to draw us out, to change us, to make us better—to make us, dare we say, holier.

Life ebbs and flows. We feel closer to God in some seasons than in others. Yet in an enchanted society, it is easier to believe in God, to always feel his presence nearby. We are more capable of perceiving meaning in the world, of sensing moral structure that gives our own lives purpose.

Taylor's take on the medieval model is close to Lewis's. In the premodern past, people (not only Christians) took for granted that the natural world testified to the existence of God, or the gods. They believed that society was grounded in this divine reality. They believed that spirit was real—not only the souls of men and women, but also angels, demons, and perhaps other discarnate beings. Everything was bound together in a coherent model—a symbol—that gave meaning to our joys and our sorrows in this life.

The social world that sustained this everyday view of enchantment has disappeared. This is not to say that no one still believes in God. It is to say, however, that even for many Christians in this present time the vivid sense of spiritual reality that our enchanted ancestors had has been drained of its life force. Instead, many of us experience Christianity as a set of moral rules, as the bonds that hold a community together, as a strategy for therapeutic self-help, or perhaps as the ground of political commitment. And, yes, it is all of those things. But without the living experience of enchantment present and accessible, and at the pulsating center of life in Christ, the faith loses its wonder. And when it loses its wonder, it loses its power to console us, change us, and call us to acts of heroism. Slowly, imperceptibly, the vibrant life of the spirit ebbs away, and with it ebbs our confidence in ultimate meaning. Maybe even our hope for the future.

That American student in Debrecen knows his Bible. He has all the arguments for the faith clear in his head. But he craves an experience of the "deep magic" of the Christian faith. He longs for a faith like that of the apostle Paul and his team, who traveled through the Mediterranean casting out demons, healing the sick, and defeating unclean spirits and pagan deities by the power of the true God. We read these stories in the book of Acts and marvel at the signs and wonders that were common in the early church.

On summer vacations, Americans sometimes venture to Europe, visit the great medieval cathedrals, and wonder about the kind of faith that could raise such temples to God's glory from societies that were poorer than our own. We read old tales of miracles, visions, pilgrimages, and religious feasts and feel the poverty of our own religious experience. We dutifully drag ourselves to church on Sunday, we read our Bibles, we follow the law, we work to serve our nation or our community, we stay current with our reading, but we still may wonder, Is this all there is?

No, it's not. There's so much more. Ian in the Holy Land knows that. So does Nino in America. So do others you will meet in these pages, who came to Christ through experiences of awe—mostly by meeting Christ or his messengers, or in some cases through encounters with demons or other experiences that sent them running to Jesus for refuge.

The stories are credible, weird, and powerful. The truth, however, is that most of us won't experience something like what happened to Ian, the strung-out drug addict, or to Nino, the UFO-haunted lawyer. We might not ever meet somebody who has had their world rocked by the supernatural. In fact, most of us will probably carry on through life without witnessing a miracle or some other manifestation of the numinous, and, in any case, we can't make them happen. And that's okay. We don't have to have a close encounter with angels and miracles to experience enchantment. That's not how God works.

If the cosmos is constructed the way the ancient church taught, then heaven and earth interpenetrate each other, participate in each other's life. The sacred is not inserted from outside, like an injection from the wells of paradise; it is already here, waiting to be revealed. For example, when a priest blesses water, turning it into holy water, he is not adding something to it to change it; he is rather making the water more fully what it already is: a carrier of God's grace. If we do have an experience of awe, a moment when the fullness of life is suddenly revealed to us in an extraordinary way, it is more likely to be far more ordinary than a mystical cleansing cloud blowing in from the River Jordan.

We might be like the Austrian Jewish psychiatrist and Holocaust survivor Viktor Frankl, who, as a ragged inmate digging a trench in a German concentration camp, tried to drive away the despair engulfing him by thinking of his faraway wife. Frankl writes that he suddenly "sensed my spirit piercing through the enveloping gloom. I felt it transcend that hopeless, meaningless world, and from somewhere I heard a victorious 'Yes' in answer to my question of the existence of an ultimate purpose. At that moment a light was lit in a distant farmhouse, which stood on the horizon as if painted there, in the midst of the miserable grey of a dawning morning in Bavaria. 'Et lux in tenebris lucet'—and the light shineth in the darkness."[3]

Dr. Frankl found the strength to go on that day—and later in his life, to help untold millions through his books about finding meaning in suffering.

Or we might have an experience like the Soviet spy Whittaker Chambers did in the late 1930s, which ultimately led him out of the Communist underground. He was at home watching his adored baby daughter eating in her high chair. "My eye came to rest on the delicate convolutions of her ear—those intricate, perfect ears," Chambers wrote. "The thought passed through my mind: 'No, those ears were not created by any chance coming together of atoms in nature (the Communist view). They could have been created only by immense design.' The thought was involuntary and unwanted. I crowded it out of my mind. But I never wholly forgot it or the occasion. I had to crowd it out of my mind. If I had completed it, I should have had to say: Design presupposes God. I did not then know that, at that moment, the finger of God was first laid upon my forehead."[4]

In my own far more homely case, I owe my faith to walking into an old French church on a summer's day in 1984. I was a bored seventeen-year-old American, the only young person on a coach full of elderly tourists, and I could barely stand the tedium of the long bus ride to Paris. I followed the old folks into the church, because the prospect of sitting on the bus was even more dull.

The church was the Chartres Cathedral, the medieval masterpiece that is one of the most glorious churches in all of Christendom. But I didn't know that at the time. I stood there in the center of the labyrinth on the nave gazing up at the soaring vaults, the kaleidoscopic stained glass, and the iconic rose window and felt all my teenaged agnosticism evaporate. I knew beyond a shadow of a doubt that God was real, and that he wanted me. I remember nothing else about the entire vacation, which was my first trip to Europe, but I can never forget Chartres, because it was where my pilgrimage to a mature faith in God began.

In these three cases, three very different men met the transcendent at the borderline of the material world. A spark crossed the barrier, signaling to the watchers that there was something beyond what could be seen, touched, and heard. It changed their lives.

Enchantment is not about having bespoke mystical experiences. It's not learning how to ensparkle the mundane world with mental fairy dust to make it more interesting. It's more than a way to escape the sense of alienation and displacement that many people today feel. Those are all superficial approaches, ones more likely to lead us into deception at best, and at worst—as has happened to curious seekers who have given themselves over to the occult or other distractions and deceptions—spiritual captivity.

No, true enchantment is simply living within the confident belief that there is deep meaning to life, meaning that exists in the world independent of ourselves. It is living with faith to know that meaning and commune with it. It is not abstract meaning, but meaning that lives in and through God, and in his Son, the Logos made flesh. We can know in our bones that life is good, purposeful, and worth living—but also that spiritual evil and forces of chaos exist as well, and we must prepare to battle them, for daily life requires spiritual warfare. For Christians, this is about learning how to live as if what we profess to believe is true. It is also about learning how to perceive the presence of the divine in daily life and to create habits that open our eyes and our hearts to him, as our fathers and mothers in the faith once did.

That was then, but despite the spiritual desert made by modernity, it is also now. You will notice that the manifestations of the awesome of which I've spoken so far happened not in the distant fairy-tale past but in our time, in an era of disenchantment, when things like this are not supposed to happen. But they still do. The world has never been truly disenchanted. We modern people have simply lost the ability to perceive the world with the eyes of wonder. We can no longer see what is really real. The hunger for enchantment has not gone away, because the hunger for meaning, connection, and the experience of awe is part of human nature. But in the absence of trust in tradition, and inside an antinomian culture that effectively denies any transcendence or structures of truth outside of the choosing self, we no longer know where to look, or how.

The point cannot be overstated: the world is not what we think it is. It is so much weirder. It is so much darker. It is so, so much brighter and more beautiful. We do not create meaning; meaning is already there, waiting to be discovered. Christians of the first millennium knew this. We have lost that knowledge, abandoned faith in this claim, and forgotten how to search. This is a mass forgetting compelled by the forces that forged the modern world and taught us that enchantment was for primitives. Exiled from the truths that the old ones knew, we fill our days with distractions to help us avoid the hard questions that we fear can't be answered. Or we give ourselves over to false enchantments—the distractions and deceptions of money, power, the occult, sex, drugs, and all the allure of the material world—in a vain attempt to connect with something beyond ourselves to give meaning and purpose to life.

Very well: this book will show you how to seek, and how to find. It will help you regain the ability to read signs that reveal the map of the Way to us, and to walk that well-worn path. It is a book about recovering the deeper and richer dimensions of our lives that have been obscured in modern times, because we have forgotten how to see the world as it really is. This will be a work of remembrance, recovery, and healing. To borrow a metaphor from Dante, the supreme Christian poet, this is how we escape the dark wood of late modernity, with its death, depression, and nihilism, and find our way back to the straight path: the same pilgrim trail to God that many centuries of Christians before us walked.

This is not a story about sorting ourselves out in a legal proceeding and rightly ordering our lives according to a plan, to live by the law. There's nothing wrong with wanting to bring order to a messy life to align it with purpose. For some, it might be the first step toward re-enchantment, but it's not the same thing as re-enchantment. No, what we are looking for is more akin to breaking down a dam that prevents living water from flowing to a parched and withered garden and restoring it to a flourishing life.

The psychiatrist Iain McGilchrist, one of the heroes of this book, claims that the very skills and habits that led modern Western man to such material success have radically impoverished him spiritually and emotionally. They have washed away our sense of living in a world of wonder, meaning, and harmony, and made us miserable.

"Indeed, if you had set out to destroy the happiness and stability of a people, it would have been hard to improve on our current formula," he writes—a formula that includes rejecting all transcendent values and even the possibility that they might exist. Yet we moderns still insist that our scientific, materialist way of knowing, a way that has brought us far more control over our lives, is the only valid way—a grave mistake that prevents us from doing what we must to restore ourselves to health. McGilchrist puts it like this: "We are like someone who, having found a magnifying glass a revelation in dealing with pond life, insists on using it to gaze at the stars—and then solemnly declares that if only people in the past had had such a wonderful magnifying glass to look through, they'd have known that, on closer inspection, stars don't actually exist at all."[5]

Some Christians are suspicious of the word "enchantment" because of its magical overtones. If this is you, put your mind at ease. The literary theorists Joshua Landy and Michael Saler, editors of an academic essay collection exploring re-enchantment from a completely secular angle, say any meaningful form of re-enchantment will recognize that the world holds these realities:

- Mystery and wonder
- Order
- Purpose
- Meaning, as a "hierarchy of *significance* attaching to objects and events encountered"
- The possibility of redemption, for both individuals and moments in time
- A means of connecting to the infinite
- The existence of sacred spaces
- Miracles, defined as "exceptional events which go against (and perhaps even alter) the accepted order of things"
- Epiphanies, which are "moments of being in which, for a brief instant, the center appears to hold, and the promise is held out of a quasi-mystical union with something larger than oneself"[6]

This, within a thoroughly Christian context, is our goal. If you are not a religious believer, you may think this is impossible. The good news is that you are wrong—and I'm going to tell you why in the pages that follow. And if you are a religious believer who reads this list and sees its goals as far from the dry or shallow kind of Christianity with which you're familiar, well, read on: you will discover that deep within the traditions of the Christian faith are resources that can illuminate your religious imagination and renew your soul.

My hope is that when you have finished this book, you will undertake a search, or that you will take up again a search that you had put aside. Though I first found Christ as a Roman Catholic, my own quest led me to Orthodox Christianity in 2006, where I came even more strongly to believe that we are all on a path either toward or away from the God who revealed himself in the Bible. Faithful, practicing Christians of all traditions can learn from this book how to deepen their own awareness of God, who fills all things. Lapsed or uncertain Christians can find in this book reasons to give the faith a second look, because it's weirder and more wonderful than they think. The Christian churches of the East—the Orthodox, and the so-called Oriental Orthodox—have maintained a distinctly more mystical character than their Western brethren. Now, at the end of the Christian age in the West, an infusion of authentic, time-tested mysticism is a gift from the Eastern churches to the suffering West. The young evangelical in Debrecen senses this, which is why he sought me out.

As with my last two books, adherents to non-Christian faiths may not be able to accept all the Christian claims here, but I believe they will nevertheless find much of value that resonates with their own traditions' teachings. Unbelievers will struggle with parts of this book, but I hope they will at least come away from it with minds more open to the possibility that God exists and that there really is a transcendent realm. All readers of this book should come away with eyes that can see more deeply into the world, beneath the surface, into the truth of things.

A friendly warning: learning how to see for enchantment is not going to be easy. It is going to cost you something. In fact, it has to. In the medieval masterpiece *The Divine Comedy*, the greatest story of Christian re-enchantment ever told, the pilgrim Dante can't escape the prison of the dark wood without putting himself in the hands of a trustworthy guide. That guide, the poet Virgil, takes him on a long and arduous pilgrimage of repentance and rebuilding the inner life so that Dante can bear the weight of God's glory. Repentance begins with the sacrifice of control—and that can be frightening.

The thing is, enchantment that doesn't compel you to change your life is not enchantment at all. It's going to be hard to make this journey back to a richer and more vital understanding of our spiritual lives, but what else can we do? As Virgil says to Dante when they first meet in the forest clearing, if you stay here, you're going to die. I am convinced that the only way to revive the Christian faith, which is fading fast from the modern world, is not through moral exhortation, legalistic browbeating, or more effective apologetics but through mystery and the encounter with wonder. It's not going to come quickly or without struggle. A pilgrimage is not the same as a three-hour tour.

The philosopher Elaine Scarry says that education is the process of training people to be looking at the right corner of the sky when the comet passes. This book is what I worked on while I waited, hoping that through the things I would discover along the way I would learn how to see what is right in front of me—which is to say, to perceive in the everyday and the commonplace the comet blazing across the night sky.

The world is not what we think it is. It is far more mysterious, exciting, and adventurous. We have only to learn how to open our eyes and see what is already there.

EXILE FROM THE
ENCHANTED GARDEN

2

Fate would be fated; dreams desire to sleep.
This the forsaken will not understand.
Arthur upon the road began to weep
And said to Gawen, "Remember when this hand
Once haled a sword from stone; now no less strong
It cannot dream of such a thing to do."

—Richard Wilbur, "Merlin Enthralled"

For many years I have been thinking about the story told by linguist Daniel Everett about the time he lived with his family deep in the Amazon jungle. He was a Christian missionary sent to convert the Pirahã, a tribe that had been notoriously unaccepting of the gospel. His goal was to learn their language, translate the New Testament into their tongue, and, he hoped, lead them to conversion.

One morning, as Everett and his family slept in their hut, they awoke to the clamor of the tribe rushing down to the river. When he and his young daughter followed, they found the excited natives shouting and pointing to the sandy beach a hundred yards away. The Pirahãs were shouting and pointing at something they called Xigagai—their name for a hostile jungle god. The Everetts saw nothing, but the natives insisted that Xigagai was actually present—that they were witnessing what theologians call a "theophany," or a revelation of a god.

"What had I just witnessed?" Everett wrote later in his memoir of his Amazon experience. "Over the more than two decades since that summer morning, I have tried to come to grips with the significance of how two cultures, my European-based culture and the Pirahãs' culture, could see reality so differently."[1]

Everett eventually left the jungle, lost his faith and his marriage, and returned to the United States to teach linguistics. Though he now considers himself an atheist, he is still mystified by what happened on that Amazon beach. Everett is not willing to say that the Pirahãs saw a demonic jungle god—but he's not willing to say that the Pirahãs hallucinated it either. It is a mystery that may never be solved.

When scholars speak of the world as "disenchanted," they mean that in modern times, with the advance of science and secularism, people no longer perceive the presence of spiritual things as they once did. Even many Christians, though professing belief in God and a transcendent realm, have come to regard the faith as primarily a source of morals and ethics and an impetus for social change. Talk of signs, wonders, miracles, and suchlike things makes them uncomfortable because it hearkens back to a superstitious age beyond which humankind is supposed to have progressed.

But what if we in the modern West have not progressed but actually regressed? That is, what if we have made ourselves blind and look down on the rest of the world for their seemingly childish, simplistic belief in light?

Here's what I'm talking about. Back in 2010, a team of psychological researchers published a startling finding. They noted that almost all the research in the field had been done on subjects from Western culture, resulting in a baseline of knowledge that they took as representative of humans the world over. But this, the researchers found, is quite wrong.

Harvard anthropologist Joe Henrich and his colleagues discovered that in terms of psychology Western people are far outliers on the spectrum of human experience, both historically and geographically. The way we see the world is very different from the way our own premodern ancestors saw it and the way the vast majority of people on the planet today experience it. They cleverly tagged us as WEIRD: Western, educated, industrialized, rich, and democratic.

Henrich and his colleagues suspect that what scientists thought was universally valid for all humans might instead be culture bound. It's not simply a matter of different values between the West and the Rest. It has to do with visual perception, spatial reasoning, and modes of moral reckoning. WEIRD people—and no people on earth are WEIRDer than Americans, says Henrich—are more individualistic, analytic, impersonal, and much less connected to the natural world than others.

We moderns are so bound to the myth of progress, which teaches that the contemporary West, with all its scientific and technological knowledge, is at the apex of human discovery. We might be disenchanted, we tell ourselves, but at least we live in the truth, unlike all of those superstitious people in the past and in non-Western cultures today.

When he was an Amazon missionary, Everett, a believing Christian, in some sense lived in an enchanted world—a world in which God was present. So did the Amazon tribespeople, though they had different ideas about religion. There's something else interesting about the Pirahã that has to do with enchantment. Living with the tribe, Everett finally figured out why they could not accept the gospel. In their cultural epistemology—how they determine what is true—the Pirahãs refused to believe anything that was not seen directly by a living person or was not related by a living person who had heard it from another living person. The idea that events recounted in the Bible—or events that happened that very day in Paris—might be true was inconceivable.

The Pirahãs were blinded by the mental construct they used to make sense of the world. Here's the thing: in that, these Amazon primitives are not so different from us moderns. As the atheist Everett has the intellectual humility to admit, we would be presumptuous to declare that we, with our materialist assumptions, have a more accurate take on reality than the jungle tribe does.

To be clear, it is not the case that either the world is wholly explained by materialism or there are angry jungle demons haunting Amazonian sandbars. Both could be false. The point is that we err in assuming that we modern Westerners uniquely possess the capabilities of seeing with clarity and accuracy and that anyone whose perceptions differ can only be fools or frauds. To open one's mind to the possibility of enchantment is, in fact, a reasonable thing to do.

HOW THE WEST GOT WEIRD

Joe Henrich does not use WEIRD as an insult. He's trying to understand something about epistemology, which is the study of how we know what we know. "Culture can and does alter our brains, hormones, and anatomy, along with our perceptions, motivations, personalities, emotions, and many other aspects of our minds," Henrich writes.[2]

When did the West branch off from the rest of the world, and even from its own history, to walk the way of the WEIRD? In Henrich's telling, it had to do with two basic events. The first was the collapse of the Roman Empire in western Europe, which left the Catholic Church as the main authority there. The Latin church authorities instituted rules of marriage that broke up barbarian clans and over time led to the rise of individualism and more flexible societies. The second was the rise of mass literacy after the Reformation, which eventually changed cognitive behavior to reward and promote analytical modes of thinking.

These two fundamental factors, argues Henrich, is ultimately why science, capitalism, political liberalism, and other phenomena associated with modernity emerged in the West and nowhere else—not even in the Christian East, where the Roman Empire continued for another thousand years.

RELIGION IN ANCIENT TIMES

Let's go back to premodern times and think about humankind's *phrone-ma*—a Greek word meaning "mindset"—toward sacred matters for most of its history.

The great scholar of religion Mircea Eliade taught that modern man has a radically impoverished idea of religion, at least compared to archaic man and even Christians of the premodern era. In his classic work *The Sacred and the Profane*, Eliade writes that, to the religious man, experiencing the "living God" is not like encountering the God of the philosophers. "It was not an idea, an abstract notion, a mere moral allegory. It was a terrible *power*, manifested in the divine wrath."[3]

This holy terror, this fear of God, is not like what it means to be scared by an encounter with a bear in the woods. It is more like what one feels when one is confronted with an overwhelming manifestation of power, mystery, majesty, "in which the perfect fullness of being flowers."[4]

The sacred, in this sense, is a manifestation of "a reality of a wholly different order from 'natural' realities."[5] Eliade prefers the term *hierophany*—meaning "manifestation of the sacred"—to refer to this phenomenon. So, for traditional man, the material world can be saturated with divinity and becomes something else while remaining itself. In other words, a sacred grove is indeed a grove like any other to outward appearances, but to those who hold it to be holy, it is also grounded in transcendent reality. To traditional man, the entire cosmos can become a hierophany.

Translated into Christian language, the universe and everything in it is sacramental—it is a symbol of a spiritual reality that both points to transcendent reality and participates in it. Christians use the term customarily with reference to the Eucharist, baptism, and other sacraments. These are special instances in which God's power and being is made manifest within the life of the church. To call the cosmos sacramental means that, in a mysterious way, all created things bear divine power and participate in the life of God.

All Christians of the first 1,300 years of the faith generally shared with the pagans this sacramental vision: a material world saturated with spiritual meaning and power.* Indeed, historian Robert Knapp argues that a main reason the early church succeeded in winning so many converts in the Greco-Roman world is that the "magic" of the Christians was more powerful than the magic of the pagan priests and sorcerers. The Gospels show Jesus of Nazareth working healings and casting out demons. The book of Acts records the apostles doing the same things, in Jesus' name. Holiness radiated through Paul so profoundly that "even handkerchiefs and aprons that had touched him were taken to the sick, and their illnesses were cured and the evil spirits left them" (Acts 19:12).

The place is a ruin now, but at the dawn of Christianity, Ephesus was one of the most important cities of the Roman world. The coastal port city in Asia Minor was home to one of the seven wonders of the ancient world: the vast Temple of Artemis, the goddess of the hunt. There was a small Christian community there. Paul preached there, and his letter to the church in Ephesus was included in the New Testament canon. What modern Christians may not know is that ancient Ephesus, during the time of the early church, was an intense spiritual battleground between the first Christians and the pagans, who were just as aware of the reality of the supernatural as the Jesus followers were.

None of them would have regarded "the supernatural" as a separate category. As Knapp writes,

> We are used to thinking of the natural world and the supernatural world as distinct although they interpenetrate at times. In the ancient world, people did not perceive things that way. Rather, the operational realms were not separate, sealed off from each other, with some communication, but not a regular intertwining. Rather, they were a single entity. There was not a "natural" sphere distinct from a "super-" or "supranatural"

---

* To be clear, Christianity is far more than a variation of pagan metaphysics. The important point here is that nearly all ancient peoples believed that spirit and matter existed in some kind of relationship.

sphere. There was, however, despite their human-ness, a sense of other-ness with regard to the unnatural world. The powers that inhabited this sphere surpassed human capabilities, often defying human comprehension, and dwelt not only in the human sphere but in their own discrete realms inaccessible to humans.[6]

The faith framework of the Greco-Roman world was one in which the exchange between the world of gods and men was a daily occurrence. "Everything had a sort of electrical charge that could power results in the natural world," Knapp continues. "Everything was pregnant with that power, waiting for the occasion to act."[7]

If you have the idea that evangelism in Ephesus was merely a matter of presenting the gospel rationally and inviting unbelievers to make up their minds, you badly misunderstand the world into which the Christian faith appeared. Magic was everywhere. Yes, everybody, with the notable exception of the Jews, believed in a panoply of gods, but even some Jews, despite the religious taboo against it, dabbled in magic. Paul and the early Christians found themselves in a situation like the prophet Elijah faced against the priests of Baal: compelled to demonstrate that the power of their God was greater than the power of his rival. The book of Acts, chapter 19, records Paul's visit to Ephesus, which included preaching but also casting out demons and working miracles.

Acts 19 gives us a powerful sense of how dangerous it was to believe in Jesus back then. To turn from the pagan gods and follow Christ meant radically revising not only your sense of reality but your relationship to your society. Had Jesus been an ordinary god, it would have been easy for the polytheists to add him to their roster. But Jesus was the second person of the Trinity, the same God who revealed himself to Moses on Sinai and commanded the ancient Israelites to worship him exclusively. To become a Christian was to renounce paganism. There was no middle way.

Greco-Roman polytheism tolerated the Jews living among them, for even though the Jews were monotheists, pagans understood that it was normal for gods to be particular to distinct peoples. Christianity, however, was universalist. It sought converts. And that threatened the social and economic order of the empire.

In Acts 19, an Ephesian silversmith named Demetrius recognized that if Christianity spread, craftsmen like him, who made a living creating small idols of Artemis, would be out of business. He roused a mob and tried to incite a pogrom against the Christians. The mob seized two of Paul's traveling companions and hauled them off to the city's theater, where for two hours the crowd wailed and bayed praises to Artemis, working itself up into a frenzy from which the evangelists Gaius and Aristarchus barely escaped.

It is one thing to read that story in the New Testament. It is another to stand in the well of the Great Theater of Ephesus, as I did on an early winter morning, imagining that you were Gaius or Aristarchus, looking up at a steep stone terrace filled with enraged religious fanatics stoking their rage waiting for a chance to get at you. It was there that I understood how much a pagan had to sacrifice, and the risk one was prepared to take on, to accept Christ.

Why would they do it? According to Knapp, for most people it wasn't because of the excellence of the evangelists' preaching. It was the signs, wonders, and miracles the apostles worked—deeds that demonstrated that the power of Jesus was greater than the power of the pagan gods. When the evangelists faced the pagan crowds and healed the sick, cast out demons, or performed other wonders, writes Knapp, "the demonstration of power validated the message [they] sought to convey."[8]

We know from writings from the early church that miracles, not message, were the prime motivator for the conversion of the first Christian generations. No wonder, given how radically different Christianity was to paganism and the difficulties accepting the new minority religion would bring and the danger into which it would put you. Writes Knapp, "To convert people, deeds would need to be many and great."[9]

"While it is true that there are examples of polytheists or Jews converting through persuasion alone to Christian thinking," he wrote, "they were far outnumbered by examples of a supernatural event impelling that fundamental reorientation."[10]

Celsus, the pagan philosopher and opponent of the early Christians, affirmed that miracles established Christianity in the minds of the pagan masses. Origen, the Alexandrian theologian who became Celsus's chief opponent, agreed: "And I shall refer not only to his miracles, but as is proper, to those also of the apostles of Jesus. For they could not without the help of miracles and wonders have prevailed on those who heard their new doctrines and new teachings to abandon their national usages, and to accept their instructions at the danger to themselves even of death."[11]

Even after the triumph of Christianity and the vanquishing of Greco-Roman paganism, Christians did not make a sharp distinction between the natural and the supernatural. All reality was one in God, whose relationship with his creation was both transcendent and immanent. The fabric of reality, seen and unseen, was tightly wound in what Anglican theologian Hans Boersma calls a "sacramental tapestry."[12] The entire material world was both a symbol of God—that is, a participant in the divine reality—and a sign pointing us to deeper communion with the Creator.

The world, then, was a mystery (from the Greek word for "sacrament"), a sacred reality that we could not hope to comprehend but in which we could participate. The French language helpfully has two verbs for "to know": *savoir*, which means knowing facts intellectually, and *connaître*, which entails personal knowledge. We can never hope to bound the ultimate mysteries of God and creation with our minds (*savoir*), but we can relate to them—primarily through our hearts, that part of the human person open to spirit (*connaître*). In the premodern world, Christians used holy rituals, created sacred spaces, went on pilgrimages, and in other ways participated in this divinely ordained absolute reality and integrated the material world into it.

THE WEST MOVES TOWARD THE MIND

When did this vision begin to break apart? It's hard to say precisely, but as good a date as any is the year 1054, when the Great Schism separated the

Western church, headquartered in Rome, and the Eastern church, scattered in patriarchies around the Mediterranean. Around this time, theologians in the Latin church began to absorb the texts of Aristotle, which had been transmitted to them from antiquity through Arab scholars. Boosted by the encounter with Aristotle, Latin theology reached new heights of complexity in the work of the Scholastics, the greatest of whom was Saint Thomas Aquinas (1225–1274). Scholasticism taught what we would later call "metaphysical realism," a concept holding that all things in the material world are connected in a true sense to the transcendent realm.

Eastern Christianity also taught this, broadly speaking, so what's the difference? East and West diverged on how man is rightly to know God and his relationship to creation. To oversimplify, the scholastic West, having imbibed Aristotle, leaned heavily into an intellectual approach to the divine, one rejected by the Eastern church, which stuck with a more spiritual, or "noetic," way.

Of course, the Scholastics believed, as the Easterners did, that the material world was enchanted, in the sense that it was charged with spiritual force. The key difference between East and West was in how humankind is to know God. In the High Middle Ages, the mind of the Latin Church began to separate "nature" and "supernature." Nature becomes supernature when it is charged with God's grace. The word *symbol* started to take on the meaning we use today. For the East, God could not be grasped simply through rational contemplation of Scripture and the natural world but had to be known primarily through participation, via prayer, liturgy, and so on. In the view of Eastern Christians, the Scholastics, without meaning to, construed the world as an object to be contemplated, not a subject to be integrated through the spiritual penetration of the divine energies.

In time, the medieval Franciscan friar William of Ockham (c. 1287–1347) feared that the Schoolmen were putting God in a rationalist box, binding him by the rules of logic and dangerously limiting his sovereignty. Ockham taught that the material world did have meaning, but to say that meaning was intrinsic—bound up in the very existence of phenomena—was to limit God. Ockham was what we now call a nominalist, from the Latin word for "name." He said that material phenomena were neutral and had meaning only because God said they did. For Ockham, the world meant something not because the transcendent God was somehow entangled with it but because God exercised his sovereign will imputing value to it.

It may seem absurdly subtle to us, but it was a revolution at the time. Nominalism had the effect of separating God metaphysically from creation and its design—of making explicit what the Christian East said was implicit in Scholasticism. God was no longer mysteriously both transcendent and immanent but located radically outside of his creation, which he observed from afar, and upon which he imposed his will. Scholastics believed that all things in the natural world pointed to God; to nominalists, that was nonsense.

In the great late-medieval intellectual showdown, the God of the nominalists defeated the God of the Scholastics. It is quite likely that the horrors of the fourteenth century—the wars, the Black Death—had something to do with that too. The era's chaos and suffering made it harder to believe in a rational deity presiding over an ordered universe. The metaphysical baggage carried by the elaborate systematic theology of the Scholastics did not make it through the bumpy passage across the fourteenth century.

"The God that Aquinas and Dante described was infinite, but the glory of his works and the certainty of his goodness were everywhere," writes the historian and philosopher Michael Allen Gillespie. "The nominalist God, by contrast, was frighteningly impotent, utterly beyond human ken, and a continual threat to human well-being."[13]

Sacramental religion did not disappear. That would happen in much of Europe later, with the Reformation in the sixteenth century, provoked in part by a succession of corrupt Renaissance popes, though it's important to note that even today's Lutherans profess a relatively modest form of sacramentalism. Nevertheless, the natural-versus-supernatural model made it easier to conceive of the natural world as existing on its own terms, entirely self-sufficient. This opened the door for the Scientific Revolution—which, not coincidentally, began nearly simultaneously with the Reformation. Though the early scientists were not atheists, they no longer believed that one had to refer to God to explain nature.

THE DISENCHANTING REFORMATION

It is impossible to discount the role that the Reformation played in exiling the numinous from the collective consciousness of Western Christianity. Yale historian Carlos Eire describes the "earth-shaking paradigm shift" brought about by Protestantism, one that overturned the spiritual and metaphysical model that had been uncontested in Christianity, both Eastern and Western, since the beginning. Writes Eire, "It gave rise to a disparate mentality that still saw reality in binary terms but drew the line between religion and magic differently, rejecting the intense intermingling of the natural and supernatural as well as of the material and the spiritual, thus placing much of Catholic ritual and piety in the realm of magic. Moreover, this Protestant mentality also involved a redefinition of the concepts of holiness and sainthood, and a rejection of the assumption that self-denial and virtuous behavior could allow human beings to be gifted with supernatural powers."[14]

Miraculous events, such as levitations, were still observable, says Eire, and in fact there are many written records attesting to these phenomena. Protestants, though, chalked them up entirely to the devil. As Eire writes, "Protestants stripped God's agency from all such Catholic miracles and gave credit to the devil instead."[15]

Leading contemporary scholars like Eire and Rice University's Jeffrey Kripal note that the modern West—that is, culture dominated by the Reformation and its secular successor, the Enlightenment—established a rigid framework within which numinous phenomena are to be evaluated. If they cannot be verified according to the scientific method, they cannot be counted as real. Thus, a large body of written testimony in modern times by people who witnessed and experienced uncanny events has been cast out by materialist fundamentalists. After all, as religion scholar Diana Pasulka puts it, "one cannot put an angel under a microscope."[16]

It is not hard to understand why scientists have done this. But why have Christians gone along with it? Many theologically conservative Christians today who profess a basic supernatural outlook have denatured it under the weight of modernist presuppositions. Modernist Catholics find talk of angels, demons, and miracles to be superstitious and embarrassing. Theologically conservative Catholics may confess belief in these things but prefer to avoid thinking too much about them, while theological liberals lean hard into good works and political change.

On the evangelical side, Bible scholar Michael Heiser devoted the last years of his life to teaching his fellow evangelicals how to recover the "supernatural" worldview of the ancient Israelites—a view entailing vigorous belief in angels, demons, and other entities. Heiser contended that modern Protestants process their experiences "through a mixture of creedal statements and modern rationalism," in a way that leads them to a "selective supernaturalism" that is unfaithful to the Bible's actual teaching about the strangeness of creation.

"The truth is that our modern evangelical subculture has trained us to think that our theology *precludes* any experience of the unseen world," he writes. "Consequently, it isn't an important part of our theology."[17]

Though Orthodoxy in principle retains all the old beliefs, far too often we Eastern Christians live as if we didn't. For example, in the United States, I know of only two Orthodox exorcists—and one of them, a friend of mine, had to go to Rome for training. Our clergy will speak of the reality of demons but are content to let news of spiritual warfare remain a rumor.

SCIENCE AND MODERNITY

The first philosopher of the modern age was René Descartes (1596–1650), a Catholic who lived and thought during the worst of the European Wars of Religion, a gruesome series of conflicts, sparked by the Reformation, that shredded the European political and social order. He hoped to create a more rational basis for understanding God's universe, one that was not subject to the passionate and capricious deity of the nominalists and their heirs, the Protestants. Inadvertently, though, Descartes laid the groundwork for further secularization.

The French-born mathematician and philosopher is best known for his concept of mind-body dualism. That's the view that the mind—that is, consciousness—is wholly separate from the body. It is hard to overstate the importance of this concept. One clear implication of this theory is that the material world exists separately from the human person and can be experimented on, and manipulated, at will.

Though Descartes professed the Christian faith, his thought effectively made the reasoning individual the master of the world and served the cause of liberating man to be the absolute master of nature. The material world, then, further lost its sacramental value, becoming mere stuff in the hands of men, who, like the God of the nominalists, were free to impose their own will on it, for the greater good of all.

The achievements of the Scientific Revolution—particularly the advances of Isaac Newton in physics—further desacralized the world by revealing the workings of the universe without needing the light of philosophy. Though himself a Christian, indeed one preoccupied with occultism in the form of alchemy, Newton's thought gave rise to the "watchmaker God" model, in which the deity created the cosmos but then stepped away from it to watch it from afar. Science progressively demystified the natural world.

Meanwhile, progress in technological development sparked by the Scientific Revolution opened the door to the Industrial Revolution and the birth of modern capitalism—with powerful effects on the abilities of modern people to perceive the sacred in the material world. The philosopher Karl Polanyi said that while most accounts of modern disenchantment blame (or credit) science, the true engine of desacralization was, believe it or not, capitalist economics.

THE DISENCHANTMENTS
OF CAPITALISM

What does the way we get and spend have to do with the loss of a sense of the holy? Well, about thirty years ago, a friend who was at the beginning of her journalism career told me why she had switched from covering politics to the economy.

"I used to think the decisions made by politicians were what ultimately mattered," she said. "Then I was assigned to cover the international currency markets, and I learned quickly that politicians are nothing compared to the power of money."

She stayed with financial journalism, because that's where the real action was, and eventually rose to the top of her field. My friend divined that in the capitalist world what people really worshiped was money. The Bible tells us that "the love of money is a root of all kinds of evil" (1 Tim. 6:10). Saint Augustine understood in the early centuries of Christianity that we become what we love most of all. Therefore, the great mover of history was not belief in God, or even faith in politics, but the pomps and works of mammon.

The Catholic historian Eugene McCarraher argues that the rise of capitalism has not really disenchanted the world so much as it has replaced old Christian enchantment with a religion of money. It has redirected the old Christian sense that grace is transmitted, or at least revealed, in consecrated material objects to the sacralization of money. To McCarraher, the worship of money has become "a parody or perversion of our longing for a sacramental way of being in the world."

Its animating spirit is money. It's theology, philosophy, and cosmology have been otherwise known as "economics." Its sacramentals consist of fetishized commodities and technologies—the material culture of production and consumption. Its moral and liturgical codes are contained in management theory and business journalism. Its clerisy is a corporate intelligentsia of economists, executives, managers, and business writers, a stratum akin to Aztec priests, medieval scholastics, and Chinese mandarins. Its iconography consists of advertising, public relations, marketing, and product design. Its beatific vision of eschatological destiny is the global imperium of capital, a heavenly city of business with incessantly expanding production, trade, and consumption. And its gospel has been that of "Mammonism," the attribution of ontological power to money and of existential sublimity to its possessors.[18]

Put more plainly, we in the wealthy modern world have built a vast and bustling stockyard of golden calves. It is sometimes said that you can tell what is most important to a society by which buildings are its tallest. In the medieval era, the spires of cathedrals towered over the cities of the West. Today, skyscrapers of banks and corporations stand like giants watching over our metropolises. Our buildings tell the true tale of who and what we worship.

The Reformation made us all rich. How? It's not that Protestantism caused capitalism. Modern banking practices began in Renaissance Italy, long before the Reformation, and the notorious luxury of the era's popes is well known. Even so, says McCarraher, by taking down the "sacramental architecture that sacralized medieval society, Protestantism made possible the transvaluation of values that culminated in capitalist enchantment."[19] When everything can potentially be put on the market, the only enchantment left is the magic of monetary value.

The surge of worldliness, the turning away from the world of the spirit to celebrate humanity, which began with the Renaissance in Catholic Italy, took on a new form in post-Reformation Europe. Why? Consider this: If the value of the material world depends not on its intrinsic qualities but rather on esteem projected from without, then it's easy to think of the world around us as mere material that can be molded and exploited according to human will. If nature is not sacramental, then there are in principle no limits built into the material world that could stay the creatively destructive hand of Promethean moderns. In other words, if nothing has intrinsic sacramental value, then the best way to measure the value of things is by putting a price tag on them.

Capitalism is not evil; it has lifted countless millions out of abject poverty—in some cases, as in China, a poverty to which Communism condemned them. But it must be strictly bound by ethical standards that restrain its most destructive instincts. In the modern age, capitalism has, in many ways, subdued Christianity. And part of the way it has done this is by cheapening the whole world into something that can be bought and sold.

After all, if, contrary to Christian teaching about the world, there is no intrinsic meaning to our bodies or to the sexual act, aside from the meaning that individuals assign to it, what is wrong with consenting adults treating the most intimate of human exchanges as a commodity? If we believe in markets for everything, what is wrong with a transaction in which a mother consents to conceive a child, carry her to term, and sell her to a wealthy couple to fulfill a contract? What is wrong with a woman choosing to rent out her body to men for sexual pleasure? This kind of exchange was unthinkable in Christian society. Today, though, neither the sexual integrity of the person nor the mother-child bond is sacred; cash and contracts are.

THE INTERNET AS DISENCHANTMENT MACHINE

But there's one more vital aspect to the disenchantment story: technology, especially the various information technologies born in the twentieth century, which have become so dominant that we now live in the so-called Information Age.

Note that the brain is not the same thing as the mind. Rather, the brain is the means through which the mind (consciousness) relates to the world beyond the body. The internet is a technology that, for all of its many blessings, is re-forming our neurological architecture to make it difficult to perceive the truth of things, spiritual and otherwise. The internet can be thought of as a vast disenchantment machine.

It is a truth well established, but not widely appreciated, that our technologies change the way we perceive the world. Many people believe that the internet is nothing more than an information-delivery device. Not true. As media theorist Marshall McLuhan famously said, "The medium is the message."

He means that the means by which we receive information matters more, on the whole, than the information received. Why? Because the medium determines "patterns of perception," the mental framework with which we take in the information. The invention of mechanized printing, for example, trained the Western mind in linear ways of thinking that had both positive and negative effects over the centuries.

"All technologies are extensions of our physical and nervous systems to increase power and speed," says McLuhan.[20] If, say, the invention of a mechanical digger extends the power of our hands, or the invention of the automobile magnifies the power of our feet to provide locomotion, then, argues McLuhan, the advent of electronic media amounts to externalizing our entire nervous system. If so, we are all extraordinarily vulnerable to outside manipulation.

McLuhan, who died in 1980, did not live to see the internet, though it is a fulfillment of his prophecies. In his classic 2010 book *The Shallows*, journalist Nicholas Carr observes that since he began relying on the internet, he has suffered a diminished ability to concentrate, an experience familiar to many of us. There are neuroscientific reasons for this, Carr found.

Though most of our brain's structure comes to us from our genetic code, that's not the whole story. Neuroplasticity is a biological fact. The brain is malleable, within limits (it is not elastic), and can change depending on the environment in which an individual lives.

For example, people who go deaf develop other senses in their brains to help compensate for the loss of hearing. People who speak different languages have slightly different brains, likely owing to the particularities of a language's structure and orthography. In one experiment, scientists found that the brains of London cabbies, who are required to memorize the entire streetscape of the British capital, are anatomically different from normal brains, in that they have more space devoted to the capacity to store spatial memory. This is what Harvard's Joe Henrich means when he says mass literacy after the Reformation altered the way Western man's brain worked.

Our brains were not made to function with internet technology. It renders the task of understanding what we perceive much more difficult. Writes Carr, "It takes patience and concentration to evaluate new information—to gauge its accuracy, to weigh its relevance and work, to put it into context—and the internet, by design, subverts patience and concentration. When the brain is overloaded by stimuli, as it usually is when we're peering into a network-connected computer screen, attention splinters, thinking becomes superficial, and memory suffers. We become less reflective and more impulsive. Far from enhancing human intelligence . . . the internet degrades it."[21]

It's not just the internet but the ubiquitous way most of us access it: through the smartphone. Neuroscientists have found that the constant bombardment of information coming through the black-mirrored devices blitzes the prefrontal cortex, where most of our reasoning, self-control, problem-solving, and ability to plan takes place. The brain's overwhelmed frontal lobes wind down higher-order cognition and defer to its emotional centers, which spark a cascade of stress and pleasure hormones.

Because the internet produces exactly the kind of stimuli that quickly and effectively rewire the brain, Carr says that it "may well be the single most powerful mind-altering technology that has ever come into use."[22]

Fine, but why is it a disenchantment machine? Because the internet destroys our ability to focus attention. The unruly crowd of competing messages jostling for the attention of our prefrontal cortex not only makes it harder for our brains to focus but also renders it far more difficult for us to form memories. This is because, for lasting memories to lodge in our minds, we need to process the information with sustained attention. Using the internet creates brains that cannot easily remember. As we will see later in this book, it also creates brains that cannot easily pray, which is the main and most important way we establish a living connection to God.

THE SELF IN THE INTERNET AGE

The internet is the greatest machine humanity has ever built, and it is on the verge of conquering its creators, who have no idea what's happening to them.

Technology is not a neutral tool. Our technology inevitably shapes the way we see the world: what counts as meaningful, what counts as possible, and how we relate to these things. The internet trains us to conceive of the self as fluid and fragmented, like the experience of the web itself. It makes us prisoners of our passions and deludes us into thinking that not only can we fully construct ourselves through the exercise of personal choice but that self-definition is a metaphysical right. The ways of the web design the culture in which we live and our very selves. For a self formed by the internet, the world and everything in it—including, of course, the self itself—is nothing but stuff waiting to be fashioned by the will of individuals.

We have stumbled into a tech-driven form of the ancient Gnostic heresy. The Gnostics were a sect in early Christianity. They taught that the body was a prison in which the soul was trapped. The church fathers, by contrast, upheld the teaching that the body was created good and that the body and the soul were an ontological unity, separated only at death and destined to be reunited at the end of time in the general resurrection. What the modern gnostics have done—most shockingly in the rise of gender ideology, which denies that the body has anything to do with one's sex—is to separate humanity radically from the material world. To these true believers, the self is defined entirely by the mind; the body is irrelevant. The next step beyond transgenderism is transhumanism, which means the assimilation of the human into the wholly controllable realm of technology. Having rejected the classical metaphysics that undergird Christianity, modern man is preparing himself to become a machine.

The English writer Paul Kingsnorth, whom you will meet again later in this book, has emerged as one of the most articulate prophetic voices railing against the idol of our age, which he identifies as, simply, the Machine, with a capital *M*. What does the Machine want? He writes, "Conquest and expansion are the essence of the Machine. If it could be said to have an ideology, it would be the breaking of bounds, the destruction of limits, the homogenization of everything in its pursuit of its continued growth. The end result of this is the flattening of the world—cultures, ecosystems, landscapes, traditions: any forms of resistance which limit the scope of its kingdom. The Machine is, to its core, anti-limits and anti-form: which means anti-nature, and thus anti-human."[23]

For Kingsnorth, the Machine world creates mass bureaucratized society and global markets, all of which depend on the Machine for their survival. It uses mass media, as well as social media, to propagandize the captive population, and technology to monitor and control it. The ideology of the Machine teaches that progress, defined by the further conquest of nature and the abolition of limits to the expression of will, is inevitable. Humankind will be free only when the Machine and its values are universally realized. The market is the measure of all things, with frictionless economic exchange considered a core aspect of liberty. The choosing individual—as distinct from the family, the congregation, the labor union, the village, the nation, or any other collective—is the basic unit of society. Science and technology, not traditional religion or moral systems, are believed to be neutral and objective and define right and wrong. The past is at best useless and at worst a source of evil; only the future matters.

THE ABOLITION OF MAN

We began this narrative around one thousand years ago, in a Christian culture that regarded the world as filled with spiritual force and guided by spiritual, contemplative pursuits. We sojourned through a period in which we steadily cast off the links with God and the natural world, for the sake of extending our dominion over that world and becoming masters of our own fates. Now we end with a world in which humanity has been liberated by technological advances and de-Christianization to become its own god—and with each passing day, the Machine moves ever closer to the abolition of man.

What makes modern Western man WEIRD is that he is psychologically very different from other peoples around the world who have not undergone this long path to modernization. It remains to be seen whether the coming of technology, especially information technology, to diverse peoples globally will disenchant them as it has us. For now, though, we can say without a doubt that disenchantment is a Western phenomenon.

That should give us hope, actually. Why? Think about it: Is it really the case that the worldview developed by a people living in one part of the planet, over a relatively short historical period, is likely to be more accurate about the nature of reality than the wisdom of countless cultures outside the West—and even of the West itself in the premodern era?

This is not to diminish the accomplishments of the West and is certainly not to say that the opinions of Amazon tribesmen about the moon and stars are of equal weight as the findings of astronomers and astrophysicists. It is only to say that we in the West should approach these questions with more humility than we have shown. If you have dismissed the idea of enchantment because you think that science has proven it to be impossible, well, think again. It's a lie, and a lie that has led us down a cul-de-sac.

The good news is that we don't have to stay here.

But we do have to change our minds.

ENCHANTED MIND, ENCHANTED MATTER

Sweet is the lore which Nature brings;
Our meddling intellect
Mis-shapes the beauteous forms of things:—
We murder to dissect.

—William Wordsworth, "The Tables Turned"

Wordsworth addresses in his poem a friend weighed down with "toil and trouble" because he is lost in studying his books. The poet beckons his sad companion to close the books and go outside. "Come forth into the light of things," says the poet. "Let nature be your teacher."

Wordsworth speaks to me, though, as an avid indoorsman, I mount a fierce resistance. It's easy to stand up to an English Romantic poet; it's rather more difficult to resist driving with an exuberant Italian lawyer on one bright summer afternoon.

On that day, I crossed over the spine of Italy's Sibylline Mountains with my good friend Marco Sermarini. Marco and I had both become single men recently. My wife was in the process of divorcing me; his had recently died of cancer. I was struggling with depression; Marco was overflowing with joy. There, splayed in front of us, was the breathtakingly beautiful plateau the Italians call the Piano Grande di Castelluccio. It was a lake of velvety green grass in the chalice of an extinct volcano, speckled with brightly colored wildflowers in pink, salmon, lilac, blue, gold, and seemingly every shade in between.

"To be in this place for only one hour, you will recover a sense of life that is based on the sense of wonder," Marco said, as he motored down toward the bottom. "When I come here, Rod, for me, the clouds are enough. I sit at my window and I see the sky, the clouds, and I say, 'How is it possible? This is magic.'

"G. K. Chesterton said, 'If there is magic, then there is a magician,'" he continued. "So, if you want to keep yourself sane, you have to regard all of this as if it were a gift for you. If there is a gift, there is love. If there is love, there is the lover. If there is the lover, there is life. It's simple. So, you can start every day with this idea."

As Marco's car climbed the far side of the Piano Grande, he still talked about Chesterton and how one needs to cultivate humility to see the world with wonder. "Chesterton said that from the mountaintop everything looks small. It's better to stay in the valley, because from there you can only see great things.

"Ah! The *coniglio*!" he suddenly exclaimed, pointing to the tall clover on the shoulder of the mountain road. "The rabbit! *Ah, bellissimo!* A wild rabbit!"

This is how it is to be with Marco Sermarini, a practicing attorney who lives besotted with effortless joy, in a most unlawyerly wonderland. With him, the whole world stops in a flash to behold the appearance of a jackrabbit and to call it the most beautiful thing ever.

"While we are living, we have to remain alive," Marco said. "In Italian, we say that middle-class ideals are the death of life. If you can't control everything, you are unhappy, you are sad. If you try to control it all, you will be unhappy."

He cut loose with merry laughter.

"You have to live—and that means giving up control!"

I sat quietly marveling at the happy genius of my friend, knowing that if I were ever to lose the sorrowful cataracts that blurred my vision in this unhappy time, I would have to work to see the world as clearly as my enchanted widowed friend Marco does.

Christian re-enchantment is not about imposing fanciful nostalgia onto the world, like coating a plain yellow cake with pastel fondant frosting. Instead, it is about learning how to perceive what already exists and reestablishing participatory contact with the really real. God has already enchanted the world; it is up to us to clear away the scales from our eyes, recognize what is there, and establish a relationship with it.

The mental framework through which you view the world determines what you see—and what you miss. Mind and matter are more closely related than we might think. The tragedy of Western man is that the same mental shift that brought us great wealth and enormous mastery of the natural world has also alienated us from it and, crucially, convinced us to accept partial truths as the whole thing.

The good news, though, is that the ability to recover a more accurate vision is within our own brains, and therefore within our capacity to achieve. His understated tweedy demeanor belies the fact that Iain McGilchrist, a white-bearded British psychiatrist and literary scholar, is leading a quiet revolution in consciousness. For an increasing number of readers of his books and subscribers to his YouTube channel, McGilchrist is a genial Virgil rescuing lost moderns from the dark wood of their brain's left hemisphere.

PRISONERS OF THE LEFT BRAIN

As a cultural critic trained in neuroscience, McGilchrist argues that we in the modern world distort our relationship with reality by depending too much on the representation of the world provided by our brain's left hemisphere.

Neuroscience knows that the brain's left side is where abstract reasoning happens, while its right hemisphere is where we receive pure experience and where our capacity for intuition and empathy resides (the biblical term for this faculty of noetic knowledge is "the heart"). In a healthy brain, both hemispheres work together to give a person a more-or-less accurate picture of reality. To put it crudely, the right brain receives information, sends it to the left brain for analysis, receives the left brain's report, and integrates it into a holistic picture of the world.

"You could say, to sum up a vastly complex matter in a phrase," McGilchrist writes, "that the brain's left hemisphere is designed to help us *ap*prehend—and thus manipulate—the world; the right hemisphere to *com*prehend it—see it all for what it is."[1]

It's an exaggeration to say that the left brain is analytical and the right brain emotional. Nevertheless, it is true that the most important difference between the sides of the brain is how they attend to the world. The left brain picks things apart to analyze them, and the right brain puts them together again. Both cerebral hemispheres are necessary for the healthy functioning of the brain—but the left must never dominate the right, because the left brain makes a good servant but a poor master. This is in part because the left hemisphere is domineering by nature and doesn't know what it doesn't know. The left brain is intelligent, but it is not wise.

In the modern world—that is, during the past five hundred years—we in the West have privileged the left-brain way of knowing. We have prioritized the abstract over the concrete, diminishing right-brain methods of knowledge as subjective and therefore second-rate. Science, mathematics, and empirical reasoning (left brain) have crowded out poetry, art, and religion (right brain) as ways of knowing.

This has given the West immense advantages, as we discussed in the previous chapter. But there is a price. The left brain believes it lives in reality and that anything added to its perception is secondary, only so much emotional window dressing. But this is a lie—a lie that led over the centuries to the dismissal of experiences that did not conform to the left brain's hyperrational protocols.

All societies must exist based on certain things that cannot be known through reason alone. It is characteristic of the left-brain way of thinking to cast aside things it cannot understand. The left brain seeks mastery and control of the world; it regards as the enemy anything that insists on the irreducibly mysterious aspects of our existence or denies that the world can ultimately be brought under man's dominion.

As we saw in our account of the West's progressive disenchantment since the High Middle Ages, the Franciscan friar William of Ockham is a key figure. Though the father of nominalism, he is known by most people today because of the term "Ockham's razor" (sometimes rendered as "Occam's razor"). It is a principle of problem-solving that says the simplest explanation is probably the true one. This helpful tool has been construed as dogma in modernity and has vastly oversimplified the complexities of the real world. We labor under the false belief that the most reductive account of a phenomenon must be the best one.

Ockham's razor is a useful principle, but a limited one. It distills the left brain's way of knowing, while dismissing the right brain's way of knowing as deception. When confronted with a phenomenon that can't be properly understood by following the rules and logic of a theory, Ockham's razor is not only unhelpful, but it can send us in the wrong direction. This is why the right brain, which perceives more subtle forms of meaning, is important to our understanding.

To a person, and to a culture, unhealthily dominated by the brain's left hemisphere, the world appears to be a giant mass of disconnected things. There is no intrinsic horizontal link between phenomena and no vertical link to a higher world. There is no higher truth, only power relationships and personal preferences grounded in nothing but individual desire. Worse, those stuck in this cognitive and perceptual trap believe that there is nothing more to be seen or known.

It's like this. Modern physics tells us that light is both particle and wave. If you stop the motion of light—to use the language of physics, to collapse its wave function—you will see it as a photon particle. But stopping its motion causes it to lose its ability to illuminate. To regard the phenomenon of light as it is requires accepting that to freeze it, to isolate a particle of light from the flow of the whole, is in a sense to kill it.

Our problem is that we have dissected the world to understand it rationally, to gain power over it, and have blinded ourselves to the complementary truth that reality is also—and even primarily—made of flow. To forget this is to mistake the representation of reality provided by the left brain for reality itself. And it is to court civilizational catastrophe. The great twentieth-century economist Friedrich Hayek makes this point: "The most dangerous stage in the growth of civilization may well be that in which man has come to regard all these beliefs as superstitions and refuses to accept or to submit to anything which he does not rationally understand. The rationalist whose reason is not sufficient to teach him those limitations of the powers of conscious reason, and who despises all the institutions and customs which have not been consciously designed, would thus become the destroyer of the civilization built upon them. This may well prove a hurdle which man will repeatedly reach, only to be thrown back into barbarism."[2]

This is what has happened to us. McGilchrist speculates that it's no coincidence that we are witnessing a sharp rise in dissociative disorders, with their accompanying loss of personal identity, given that the hyperrational, analytical stance that has become standard for contemporary Westerners mimics schizophrenia. We have cast the mind out of the world and have made it insane.

McGilchrist is by no means a lone heterodox voice crying in the materialist desert. The eminent philosopher of consciousness Thomas Nagel shocked his colleagues a few years back when he published a book explaining why he did not believe the standard reductionist account of the world, which says everything can be explained entirely through materialistic causes. Nagel is not a theist but says simply that the disenchanted "just dead stuff" view of reality is no longer credible. According to Nagel, the more we learn about the nature of reality, the more reason we have to believe that the mind is an inherent part of it.

Nagel even goes so far as to say that there may be purpose and meaning woven into the fabric of reality, not simply imposed by humans from outside. This claim, he says, "will strike many people as outrageous, but that is because almost everyone in our secular culture has been browbeaten into regarding the [reductionism] as sacrosanct, on the ground that anything else would not be science."[3]

It's important that men of science like Nagel and McGilchrist raise their voices against the gnostic materialism of the Machine. Poets and priests do so all the time, but given the preeminent authority science has had since the nineteenth century, people who intuit that there must be more to the world than materiality can gain confidence from the fact that some top scientists agree.

The path away from barbarism and back to reality is to change our minds—literally. Those who want to rescue themselves from the prison of unreality should reject the twin doctrines of nominalism and mind-body dualism, which erect barriers between matter and spirit. They should open themselves to art, poetry, music, and religion as ways of knowing—not simply as pleasant decorations and diversions from the real business of life, which is scientific and rationalist, but as complementary sources of information and insight into the nature of reality.

More precisely, we should use these ways of knowing not simply to tell us about the world but to draw us more intimately into relationship with it. To know the world not as a scholar knows the library but as the lover knows the beloved. This is what it means to live in wonder—to live within enchantment.

THE RESONANT MIND

The disenchanted mind regards itself as separate from the rest of the world. The enchanted mind, by contrast, recognizes that it is part of the world and in relationship with it. But what does that mean?

A few years ago, I was on vacation with my family in the Azores, the Portuguese islands in the North Atlantic. We went walking in a forest of

Japanese redwood trees, a non-native species that had once been introduced to the islands. Maybe it was because I grew up in the sweat-sodden subtropics, where the outdoors is the domain of snakes, alligators, and mosquitoes, but I don't much care to be out in nature. Oh, but that day in those North Atlantic islands there was something about these redwood groves that seized my imagination, in a way I can't explain. I felt so at home there that for days afterward I fantasized about living in a hut deep in the enchanted Japanese redwood forest, like a hermit at peace with the world.

The unexpected sense of oneness I felt inside the Japanese redwood forest, and what Marco Sermarini experiences every time he visits the Piano Grande di Castelluccio, is what the German sociologist Hartmut Rosa calls "resonance." The word refers to the reciprocal relationship between the self and the world beyond it. A person who experiences resonance feels positively connected to the world outside of his head, and if, as Marco advises, he allows himself to begin making connections, he may experience a revivifying sense of wonder. To lose a sense of resonance with the world, however, is to regard it as meaningless and disenchanted.

What Marco Sermarini intuits from his life experience, Hartmut Rosa has validated in his research. For Rosa, the most important cultural force in the modern world is "the idea, the hope and desire, that we can make the world *controllable*."[4] Indeed, modern thinkers have linked the cause of human freedom to the world's controllability—which entails the ability to prevent bad things from happening. Aldous Huxley's novel *Brave New World* presents a technocratic dystopia in which no one ever has to worry about boredom, discomfort, or unpredictability. Yet the price for achieving this state is one's own humanity.

We crave control, says Rosa, "yet it is only in encountering the *uncontrollable* that we really experience the world. Only then do we feel touched, moved, alive."[5] In our relentless desire to control our experience, we diminish the aspects of the world that give us meaning, joy, resonance—and enchantment. We WEIRDos are proud of our mastery of the material world, but it has made us miserable, because we no longer feel at home here.

Rosa says there is a four-part process to losing resonance:

- Make the world visible. Identify a thing that interests you.
- Make the visible world accessible. Establish a relationship to it.

So far, so good. But then modern man makes a wrong turn.

- Make the visible, accessible world manageable. Act in ways that stand to increase your control over it.
- Make the visible, accessible, manageable world do what you want it to do.

Nihilism—the belief that there are no truths and that nothing ultimately matters—is inevitable for those who lose their sense of resonance. Worse, our secular materialistic culture has formed us—or, rather, deformed us—so that, in Rosa's estimation, "modernity has lost its ability to be called, to be reached."[6] To restore resonance—or, I would say, enchantment—one has to open oneself to the call. One has to be willing to be surprised by mystery—and be prepared to respond to it.

This requires a renunciation of the compulsion to control everything. There is no five-step formula to create resonance between oneself and the world. It requires simply cultivating a disposition to be called—to be reached by something outside oneself. To learn how to read signs and to respond to them. Once again, it's a question of mental framing: if you do not believe there is a world beyond your head, you will not be able to be called. To bring the world inside your head, so to speak, is to render it fully controllable. But that guarantees disenchantment, a loss of resonance.

"My argument is that, if I could make it snow at will, then I could never experience being called by the falling snow," writes Rosa. "If my cat were a programmable robot that always purred and wanted to be cuddled, she would become nothing to me but a dead thing."[7]

In other words, if you don't believe that there is a fundamentally mysterious dimension to existence—one that you can never fully know in the intellectual sense but that you can know in the relational sense—you will never know enchantment. You must begin from a position of faith, of openness to the possibility that there is God, or at least there is meaning, beyond your head.

And you must make yourself vulnerable enough to trust the other, to enjoy the relationship for its own sake. This is the basis of love—and, says Rosa, the basis for true prayer. Alchemy and magic are attempts to tap into supernatural power and bend it to human use. To pray, though, is to approach God out of love, not out of a sense of what God can do for you.

MIND, MATTER, AND METANOIA

The Greek word for "repentance" is *metanoia*, which means "to change one's mind." But the Greek word conveys deeper meaning, implying that the change of mind must be profound, such that it grants one a new outlook on life. If it's true that we moderns have embraced, however unconsciously, a frame of mind that has disenchanted us and is leading to our spiritual death, then if we want to live, we will have to seek metanoia.

So far, we've talked about the importance of understanding that the right-brain way of knowing—through art, music, poetry, and so forth—is as important for an accurate view of reality as the left brain's more analytic frame. We have also seen that enchantment requires resonance with the world outside our heads, and that means we have to surrender the modern urge to control the world and our experience of it.

The deepest metanoia, though, is a radical change in how we relate to God, which is necessary to establish a right relationship to material reality. The work of contemporary secular scholars like McGilchrist and Rosa, and the late Marshall McLuhan, sheds new light on ancient Christian teaching, revealing how premodern followers of Christ can help us to see the wonder-filled world as it really is.

Back in the seventh century, at the end of the patristic era, Maximus the

Confessor, saint and theologian, taught that all created things are connected to the divine Logos. If we want to perceive that reality, we need to learn to see it with the eyes of the purified heart.

What could this mean? In biblical language, the heart is the faculty of perception that allows a person to access spiritual realities. It is the eye of the soul that receives illumination from God. Eastern Orthodox Christianity calls it the *nous* (pronounced "noose") and holds it to be the way of knowledge through spiritual intuition, as distinct from the way of knowledge through conceptual analysis. (The comparison to McGilchrist's left-brain / right-brain model is clear.)

From an Eastern Christian point of view, the fall of man entailed the darkening of the nous. It damaged—but did not destroy—the part of our souls that allowed us to commune directly with God and with the world of spirit, of transcendence. Before that, man's relationship with the Creator was one of perichoresis—an idea derived from the Greek word for rotation, describing a constant flow of love and spiritual energy among the persons of the Godhead and between God and individual people. Without that flow, we dwell in the darkness, and like a plant stored in a windowless shed, we eventually die spiritually.

Most of us live with varying degrees of damage to our nous. The purpose of the spiritual life is to restore our transformative relationship to Christ, resulting eventually in *theosis*—that is, to become fully united with God while remaining oneself.

Theosis is a word and a concept common in the East but less well known in the West. But it is by no means heterodox. Dante's *The Divine Comedy* is about a journey to theosis, as the pilgrim Dante within the poem repents of his sins and slowly but steadily becomes regenerated by the light of the Holy Spirit. In more modern times, C. S. Lewis's *The Great Divorce* showcases theosis, and Lewis's fellow Inkling Charles Williams wrote favorably of the concept, translating it as "inGodding."

Again, perichoresis describes the flow of transforming grace from God to individuals, which is returned to God as love. The degree to which we can receive God's grace is governed by the transparency of one's nous. The clearer one's nous becomes (through prayer, fasting, obedience, and works of love), the more grace flows into one's soul, purifying it and drawing it closer in unity with God.

If this sounds strange to you, consider that it would not have sounded that way to Christians of any era until the close of the medieval period. Believers of ages past had a far more sacramental vision of the relationship between God and creation, including humankind, the pinnacle of God's artistry. They believed in a much closer metaphysical connection than most Christians do today—hence their ease of experiencing enchantment, relative to us moderns.

Still, the sacramental churches of the West, especially the Catholic Church, align with the Orthodox churches of the East in recognizing that God's grace, in some form, comes to us in part through created things. Relax, Protestants: It's probably overstated to say that a contemporary Christian must join a sacramental confession or they will never experience re-enchantment. But it becomes far easier to experience wonder if one espouses a sacramental framework—which, don't forget, is how all of the world's Christians lived, thought, and prayed until the Renaissance and the Reformation.

The kind of metanoia needed for modern man to return to enchantment entails, once again, abandoning both nominalism and the mind-body separation, in whatever Christianized form it may have taken, and learning to perceive the world in a more noetic way. We cannot think our way back to enchantment or unity with God. We can find it only by participating in his life. Thinking—which entails studying and theologizing—is important, but it is only significant as a map back to God. Information is not the whole of reality; studying the map is not the same as crossing the territory. We can return to God only by using our entire selves: our minds, our bodies, and, by exercising our noetic faculties, our spirits.

Learning to see for enchantment is not like learning proofs for God's existence or the meaning of covenant theology. It's more like learning how to play the violin. You learn it by practice—and, even then, it's not a process that can be controlled. That's not how wild grace works. The lives of the saints testify to how God can withdraw from us for a time for our own spiritual good. To find re-enchantment we have to get out of our heads and take up the practices that lead to theosis.

The lesson here is that enchantment is not a permanent state of existence; the best we can do is live within a framework—mental and spiritual, and within the home we build for ourselves—that keeps us open to it and also sustains us in stability until the comet returns, so to speak. You can have a mindset that cherishes enchantment, but if you don't have a mindset that can sustain enchantment's eclipse, it will do you no good. You will be no better than a shallow aesthete, chasing thrills but remaining spiritually immature.

THE RECEPTIVE MIND

A mind that is able to be changed has to first be receptive to facts that falsify what it once thought to be true. An open mind requires a heart humble enough to admit error and brave enough to act on the new information, even if it requires sacrifice. Though many people like to think they would believe in God if only they saw a miracle, human nature tells us otherwise.

One of my favorite stories from the Gospels—it appears in three of the four—is the account of Jesus exorcising the Gerasene demoniac. In the story, Jesus approaches a graveyard where a demon-possessed man dwells in torment, outcast from society. The Lord casts the legion of demons out of the desperate man, sending them into a herd of swine, which run off a cliff to extinction.

"And the people went out to see what had happened. When they came to Jesus, they found the man from whom the demons had gone out, sitting at Jesus' feet, dressed and in his right mind; and they were afraid. Those who had seen it told the people how the demon-possessed man had been cured. Then all the people of the region of the Gerasenes asked Jesus to leave them, because they were overcome with fear. So he got into the boat and left" (Luke 8:35–37).

What an astonishing story! The people of the town witnessed a great miracle of healing, one of their own delivered from wretched captivity and restored to his humanity. You would think that they would rejoice and want to know more about this man Jesus who worked the miracle.

But no: they were afraid and sent him away. Why?

This story illustrates a discomfiting truth about human nature. We may tell ourselves that we would like to witness a miracle, and if only we saw evidence of the supernatural, we would change our lives and follow the Lord. The truth is that many of us would be like the Gerasenes. To see a miracle could upset the settled framework of our lives so much and require us to change in ways we would prefer not to.

I saw this happen with my own father. This is a story I have told before, but it is one that I continue to reflect on and learn from, especially as my own life has unexpectedly taken turns down paths pioneered by my dad, in pain and confusion. In the late summer of 1994, in the immediate wake of his father's death, poltergeist activity began around my mother and father's house. I had come to Louisiana from Washington for the funeral and was staying with them. I heard and saw it myself. My parents were Methodists who didn't often go to church and who certainly had no truck with spiritual woo. As a new Catholic who had once reported a newspaper story about an exorcist down the bayou, I asked my folks for permission to invite the exorcist to bless the house in hopes that it would make the strange goings-on cease.

The priest, Father Mario Termini, and a Cajun grandmother who had a powerful gift of spiritual discernment came to see us. That afternoon, we all saw signs and wonders that could not be denied, and the visitors, though knowing nothing about my family's history, discerned that my late grandfather could not in some sense move on in the next life until my father, whom he had grievously wronged in his final years, forgave him. My dad spoke words of forgiveness, Father Termini blessed the house, and there were no more spooky happenings at my mom and dad's place.

My father, who died in 2015, was an upright man, widely respected in our town, but he had a problem holding grudges. I had hoped that being at the center of a spiritual drama that demonstrated the power of forgiveness to set captives free would lead him to conversion. It did not. Until his dying day, he testified that what he had lived through that dramatic August week in 1994 was true—and yet, sadly, it did not change him. I believe he was too afraid to change and so lived with the cognitive dissonance. This fear of forgiveness, based in pride, became a pillar of our broader family's self-understanding—with catastrophic consequences, from which recovery is not possible. Deliberately closing one's eyes to revelation can be disastrous.

The novelist Tobias Wolff had a similar experience. In 1972, when he was in his late twenties, Wolff went to Lourdes, France, the site of miraculous healings, to help the sick pilgrims who came to bathe in the waters hoping for a cure. Wolff had always had poor vision, but he hated wearing glasses, so he walked through his youth in a blur.

One day, his crew accompanied a group of disabled Italian pilgrims to the airport to catch their chartered flight home. Wolff's assignment was to care for a paralyzed two-year-old girl, confined to her bed with tubes coming out of her nostrils that drained into bags under her blanket. It was hot and muggy as the passengers loaded the plane. Then unexpectedly, and for no apparent reason, the door to the plane closed while the child was still waiting to board, stranding her.

Wolff panicked, and as he desperately tried to keep insects off the suffering child, he wept for her and over the cruelty of the world. The plane door reopened to let the child on, and as it did, Wolff was still sobbing, but as everybody was sweating buckets, no one could tell.

On the bus ride back to Lourdes from the airport, Wolff, still not wearing his glasses, noticed that he could see things in the distance. He rubbed his eyes to clear them, thinking that maybe the mixture of sweat and tears had formed a kind of lens over his eyes that enabled him to see. But the effect didn't go away.

"I felt giddy and restless, happy but uncomfortable, not myself at all," he wrote to the author John Cornwell. "Then I had the distinct thought that when we got back to Lourdes I should go to the grotto and pray. That was all. Go to the grotto and pray."[8]

But he didn't do that. He fell into conversation with an Irishman, and decided not to tell him about the miracle. He never went to the grotto. The next morning, his eyes were back to their broken state, and he had to wear glasses again.

Wolff tells Cornwell, "What interests me now is why I didn't go. I felt, to be sure, some incredulity. But this wasn't the reason. I have a weakness for good company, good talk, but that wasn't it either. That was only a convenient distraction. At heart, I must not have wanted this thing to happen. . . . By giving up doubt, I would have lost that measure of pure self-interest to which I felt myself entitled by doubt. Doubt was my connection to the world, to the faithless self in whom I took refuge when faith got hard. Imagine the responsibility of losing it. What then? No wonder I was afraid of this gift, afraid of seeing so well."[9]

An all-too-human story! Tobias Wolff experienced a miracle. All he was asked to do was to sacrifice a few minutes of his time to go to the sacred waters. Tragically, he preferred his blindness, because it gave him license to behave in ways he could not have done if he were sure that God was real and watching over us.

Something similar happened to Kenneth Clark, the celebrated art historian best known for his popular 1969 television documentary series *Civilisation*. In his memoir, Clark writes about a hierophany he experienced in an Italian church:

> I can only say that for a few minutes my whole being was irradiated by a kind of heavenly joy, far more intense than anything I had known before. This state of mind lasted for several months, and, wonderful though it was, it posed an awkward problem in terms of action. My life was far from blameless: I would have to reform. My family would think I was going mad, and perhaps after all, it was a delusion, for I was in every way unworthy of receiving such a flood of grace. Gradually the effect wore off, and I made no effort to retain it. I think I was right; I was too deeply embedded in the world to change course. But that I had "felt the finger of God" I'm quite sure, and, although the memory of this experience has faded, it still helps me to understand the joys of the saints.[10]

Clark's tragic refusal was not, happily, the end of the story. As he lay dying in 1983, he accepted Christ and was received into the Catholic faith.

The lesson here is about the way a mindset afraid to lose control works against enchantment. You may desire enchantment, but if you do not have a mind prepared to receive it, and act on the message it carries, a hierophany will do you little good.

MCLUHAN, MEDIUM, AND MESSAGE

A final lesson on the change of mind needed for enchantment comes from a surprising source: Marshall McLuhan. Though he never wrote about religion in his academic work, McLuhan was a devout Catholic convert who went to daily Mass.

His best-known saying—"the medium is the message"—is not only a pronouncement about the way the media work, but it is also a profound insight into how Christianity functions. What McLuhan meant is that the primary effects of the electronic medium are more important than its secondary effects, which is the information it conveys. For example, the messages broadcast on television are less significant in the life of a culture than the changes in its life brought about by television.

McLuhan said the same is true of Jesus Christ, the God-man, whose incarnation marked God's "penetration into all of human existence." Jesus of Nazareth is both the primary medium through which God communicates to humanity but is also the message itself. Said McLuhan, "Then the question is, where are you in relation to this reality? Most people prefer to avoid the question by side-stepping it. The message is there but they want no part of it. So they eliminate it by plugging into another channel. . . . They prefer to study the words rather than the questions that Christ asks everywhere, and of every human being."[11]

In other words, to fully accept the message of Jesus is to unite oneself to Christ, in the way we have been talking about in this chapter. McLuhan spoke openly about the left-brain way of confronting Christ versus the right-brain way. The left brain construes Christ as *concept*; the right brain as *percept*—something directly perceived by the senses. If you want to have a living relationship with Jesus, said McLuhan, you must relate to him primarily as percept—or, as an Eastern Christian would put it, noetically.

"I am myself quite aware that there is a great contrast between perceptual and conceptual confrontation; and I think that the 'death of Christianity' or the 'death of God' occurs the moment they become concept," said McLuhan. "As long as they remain percept, directly involving the perceiver, they are alive."

He went on, "I never came into the church as a person who was being taught. I came in on my knees. That is the only way in. When people start praying, they need truths; that's all. You don't come into the church by ideas and concepts, and you cannot leave by mere disagreement. It has to be a loss of faith, a loss of participation. You can tell when people leave the church: they have quit praying."[12]

The Stanford University anthropologist T. M. Luhrmann has said that the way we conceive of our minds in relation to the outside world has a lot to do with our capacity to perceive God as real. Indeed, the Western habit of dividing the world sharply into the real and the unreal, based on the way our post-Enlightenment minds construe the relationship between the mind and the external world, prevents us from seeing gradations in reality that non-Western peoples more readily perceive.

Here's an example: One sunny spring afternoon in Budapest, I discussed the question of God with an intelligent atheist friend. She does not believe in God, she said, because she has seen no evidence for his existence. I countered with the claim that, as a Western rationalist and partisan of the Enlightenment tradition, she frames reality in a way that relies on a number of hidden assumptions about what is real and what is not—assumptions that most people in the world do not have. Yes, she said, but our scientific and technological advancement vindicates this way of knowing.

She was a fundamentalist devotee of the myth of progress and, as such, could not be convinced even to entertain the thought that the Western way of knowing achieved results by blinding itself to aspects of reality that could not be perceived using the scientific method. After a second conversation, in which she came up with preposterous materialist explanations for seeming miracles, I realized that my friend had constructed for herself a mental habitus designed to keep the possibility of God's reality at bay. In other words, just as religious believers think and act in particular ways to make God's presence real, my friend had sequestered herself inside an epistemological citadel, hiding out in a tower far above the messy mysteries of life on earth.

Another example: Once I was driven around Boston by a cabbie from Haiti who was a convert to evangelical Christianity. We talked about how blind Americans are to spiritual realities, specifically related to the demonic. He spoke with visceral frustration about how the academics he often ferried around the city would engage him with talk about Haitian vodou and would gently sneer at him when he spoke to them about things he had seen and experienced that they could not accept as real, because it violated the rules of their secular materialist faith frame—one reinforced by membership in one of the many university communities in that highly secular academic city.

The driver told me that when his American-born son turned fourteen, he planned to take the boy to Haiti so he could see for himself that his fellow Bostonians lived in a world of spiritual illusion—a self-deception that could, this concerned father feared, lead to danger for the boy if he bought into it. To this man, the highly educated WEIRDos he lived among were sophisticated primitives whose secular superstitions blinded them to a facet of reality that is part of the everyday experience of Haitians.

TO CHANGE OUR MINDS

All of us in the West live in a world in which belief in God is declining and doubt in the existence of ultimate significance drives the masses toward hedonism, consumerism, or other forms of nihilism. People are desperate for mystery and meaning, but churches don't seem to know how to deal with the crisis. The crisis of the modern soul is largely a crisis of the modern mind.

The journey to healing begins with metanoia—a radical change of mind. A return to reality requires a rebalance between the brain's left and right hemispheres. We need to change the way we know the world, to make it less abstract and more participatory. The anthropological ground for this is widely accessible in the history of humankind's religious experience. The Christian theological ground for this was everywhere present in the Christian church of the premodern era, ending only when a series of events in the West—intellectual, technological, and economic—gradually and then suddenly, with the Reformation, severed the perceived link between spirit and matter.

We will never recover a sense of resonance with the material world until and unless we surrender our modern urge to control everything. Anthropology teaches us that the ability to feel that God is real depends heavily on our frame of mind; what our brains allow us to perceive is related to how we think about the world. Though it is impossible to control enchantment by capturing lightning in a jar, so to speak, we have to develop practices that allow us to live as if enchanted when the grace of enchantment leaves us.

Chief among those practices is prayer. Why? Because we can maintain a living relationship to God only if we understand that faith is primarily a matter of perception, not conception. That is, we have to approach matters of the spirit first with methods of the right brain, not the left. When our main way of encountering faith is through ideas, not prayer, pilgrimage, worship, or other direct sensory experiences of the holy, our faith is at risk of hardening into ideology. This is not, of course, to demean intellection but only to order it rightly. To talk and think about God is not the same thing as encountering God, of perceiving him. Without perception, enchantment is impossible.

If metanoia is the beginning of re-enchantment, there is another practice of the mind critical to the project. Saint Augustine knew it as far back as the fifth century: what we attend to is what we love, and what we love, we will become. In the next chapter, we will discover how re-enchantment depends on the kind of attention we pay to the world beyond our heads.

WHY DISENCHANTMENT MATTERS

Like all dreamers, I mistook disenchantment for truth.

—Jean-Paul Sartre, *Les mots*

In 2019, on a reporting trip to Russia, I had a conversation over a kitchen table with Viktor Popkov, a man who had converted to Christianity in the early 1970s. He told me that at that time very few young Soviets had any faith in the Communist system. The ideals that had enchanted their parents and grandparents with dreams of a workers' paradise had failed. His generation had been turned into spiritual zombies. They had no hope and no sense of purpose; they had all been disenchanted.

Reading the Albert Camus 1942 novel *The Stranger*, a tale of an alienated young man who commits a murder, led young Popkov to his Christian conversion. The novel presents a universe with no moral structure, populated by people desperate to impose order on it. The murderer goes to his execution reconciled to the fundamental meaninglessness of life.

After he finished the book, Popkov knew he had a decision to make.

"The question stood before me: What is the point of living?" he said. "If Christ is real, what is that supposed to mean for me? That was my point of departure from Soviet life—and I know a lot of people who found similar points of departure."

Eventually the seeker found his way to prayer meetings in the Moscow apartment of Alexander Ogorodnikov, a young man from a prominent Communist family who had shamed his family by becoming a Christian.

"Fifteen to twenty people would get together on the weekend to talk to each other," recalled Popkov. "Completely surprising things would happen. These meetings caused me to feel something very, very deep that I continue to feel today. It was an intoxicating happiness. We gathered together, and the Lord answered us with his presence.

"This feeling was something we felt only when we were meeting," he went on. "When I'm reading the Acts of the Apostles, that's what it felt like. By gathering together, we were able to rise to a new level, and then go back home and live at a higher level."

These young Russians were being enchanted by Christ. Soviet authorities began to persecute them, but they were able to withstand it.

"In this experience of faith and this encounter with Christ, you receive a new feeling, and you know that you would not go back to how you used to be for anything," Popkov told me. "You are willing to endure anything they throw at you.

"You can't really prepare for it. To have a living connection to Christ, it's like falling in love. You suddenly feel something you haven't felt before, and you're ready to do something you've never done before."

Like go to prison. Most of these Christians, Popkov included, ended up in jail for their faith. Yet in our Moscow meeting, Popkov said in some ways his generation had it easier than young people today, both in post-Soviet Russia and in the West.

The choice before them in the last Soviet era was stark; the spiritual and cultural poverty imposed by the system was impossible to ignore, in part because it also created great material poverty. In the relative wealth and liberty provided by capitalist democracy, there are far more alluring distractions to prevent the disenchanted from facing the truth of their condition.

But face it we must. We can't go on like this. On a cool Budapest spring day in 2024, I drank wine in a neighborhood bar with an economist from London and a political economist from Washington. Both men said that in their travels these days they are having more and more conversations with people who are convinced that Western civilization is nearing collapse. In the conversation of these younger men, I heard echoes of Viktor Popkov's description of the atmosphere of his late Soviet youth: few people believed in the system's animating values but had nothing hopeful and life-giving with which to replace the Communist god who failed.

Are we really so different? Ours is a rich, decadent, spiritually exhausted civilization. The sickness of the modern West comes from our having cut ourselves off from the source of enchantment. That is the belief that all life has ultimate, transcendent meaning, given to us by God, and that we can live in palpable, participatory relationship to that meaning. Recovering this belief, and making it not just a proposition we affirm in our heads but an embodied way of life, is the most urgent task facing us today. After listing climate change and a host of other crises currently pressing upon humankind, Iain McGilchrist declared, "None of this, in the end, will matter unless we are able to get back to the spiritual ground of our being."[1]

To some readers—I'm thinking of Calvinists, Thomistic Catholics, and others with sharp minds for doctrine and theology—all of this might sound like mystical mumbo jumbo that is only tangentially related to the recovery of authentic Christian faith. To others, such as Christians who focus on personal evangelism or on good works of social service, re-enchantment talk might come off as spiritually indulgent.

Yes, doctrine and theology are necessary. So, too, are evangelism and good works. But without a sustained felt connection to the living God, these aspects of Christian living can ossify.

There are also plenty of Christians who don't understand the severity of the crisis upon all the churches. They are like the Roman pagans of the fourth century who were blind to the rapid decline of their ancestral faith as Christianity rose around them. These pagans, satisfied in their own religious lives, figured that Rome had always been pagan and always would be.

Decline is real. Consider two different historical figures: Caesar and the King (I speak, of course, of Elvis Presley).

In the year 476, in the marshes of the eastern Roman city of Ravenna, the barbarian king Odoacer defeated the last defenders of the Western Roman Empire, deposing the feeble Romulus Augustus—the last Caesar—and bringing Roman European civilization to a decisive end. (The empire continued in its eastern half, headquartered in Constantinople, for another thousand years.)

For a very long time, the accepted narrative was that Western Roman civilization—the empire had been divided into two by Diocletian in 285—fell apart because of internal decadence and external attacks from barbarian tribes. The story then said the intervening centuries between Rome's fall and the rise of a successor civilization in Europe were the Dark Ages, a period of lawlessness, extreme poverty, and misery.

Within recent decades, however, that interpretation has been set aside. Today, historians think of Rome's fate not so much in terms of decline and fall but rather as transition from one mode of living to another. This more nuanced approach was in some sense a necessary corrective to the older view, but it is not, in the end, persuasive.

The Oxford historian Bryan Ward-Perkins, who approaches history by concentrating on data taken from archaeological evidence, maintains that the Western Roman Empire suffered a catastrophic loss of complexity. Ward-Perkins argued, with some ferocity, that historians of the transition and transformation theory severely underestimate the damage to Romans' everyday lives from the barbarian invasions and the chaos that followed.

For example, the archaeological record shows that Romans went from living in relatively sophisticated housing to crude wooden huts virtually overnight. More broadly, loads of evidence show that the complex and diversified Roman economy, which depended on reliable and safe international trade routes, shriveled as those vital economic arteries closed with the demise of law and order. The relatively rapid impoverishment and brutalization of what had been one of the world's most advanced civilizations had severe cultural consequences. It took Europe centuries to recover a degree of material sophistication that resembled Rome's before the fall.

Why is this important? Because we contemporary people, who know so little about history, should recognize how fragile civilizations are. In the fourth century, a hundred years before the fall of the West, the entire Roman Empire abandoned its ancestral paganism for Christianity. The historical record shows that Rome's pagan elites did not recognize that their religion was coming to an end, even though it played out right under their noses.

Decline is real, and painful. No amount of characterizing it as mere "change"—using relativistic language to avoid passing negative judgment— can disguise the fact that conditions were once good and suddenly became very bad indeed. Moreover, human nature has a strong tendency to ignore signs of decline, on the hopeful theory that the good times will last forever.

Which brings us to Elvis Presley. Whenever a popular performer does something scandalous today, there always arises someone to downplay the shock by saying that people thought Elvis was shocking in his day. It is certainly true that Elvis Presley's frank sexuality appalled the squares of the 1950s. In 1956, network censors afraid of Presley's famously gyrating hips showed him only from the waist up on his first *Ed Sullivan Show* appearance. Even so, the *New York Times* denounced Elvis's performance of "Don't Be Cruel" as "singularly distasteful," and blasted the entire music industry as having "all but disgraced itself with some of the 'rock 'n roll' songs it has issued."[2]

It's easy to laugh at that moral hysteria from today's perspective. Don't critics who snicker at people who are disgusted by some songs and performers today have a point? Perhaps sometimes. Still, it takes a heroic dose of willful blindness to see something such as the 2021 video of the popular gay rapper Lil Nas X in which he mimics being sodomized by Satan as being in the same moral universe as Elvis's hyperactive pelvis.

And it is simply not possible to find anything in the Presley catalog comparable to the 2020 megahit "WAP" by Cardi B and Megan Thee Stallion. It begins with the declaration, "There's whores in this house," which is the cleanest line in the entire unspeakably filthy song. An NPR host called it "a vivid celebration of women's sexual pleasure," which is like describing the firebombing of Dresden as a night of robust fireworks. After that host castigated the song's critics as "puritanical," the guest critic chimed in to denounce as racist and sexist a white male who called out the song as dehumanizing.[3]

It's a lot harder to make the same dismissive Elvis comparison when it comes to visuals. Presley's "Love Me Tender" is to "WAP" as *From Here to Eternity* is to any of the hard-core pornographic clips easily available to anyone with a smartphone. This includes children and young people, whose sexual development, many studies have documented, has been seriously distorted by chronic porn use. Anyone who denies that there has been a staggering and culturally significant collapse in standards around the depiction of sexuality in popular entertainment is either a fool or a liar.

The hyper-optimists are in as much denial as the Roman pagans of the fourth century were about the rising Christianization of their civilization. Those men could not allow themselves to read the signs of the times and did not grasp that the religions that had upheld Roman culture and society for many centuries were collapsing under pressure from a new and very different culture. As the pagans of old, our hardline optimists today are trying to defend a system that fewer and fewer people believe in, because it is killing their souls.

The denial is also present within many churches, as older believers— pastors and laity alike—respond to the falling away of young people from faith with either flat denial of the seriousness of the problem or by resorting to failed strategies that at least feel familiar. A Southern Baptist pastor friend focused on evangelizing youth complained bitterly to me that the church's state-level leadership was spending a fortune on programs that made sense in the 1980s, when those leaders were young, but that had no chance of working today. This allowed the leaders to believe that they were doing something to address the crisis of unbelief among the so-called Zoomers, when in fact these leaders were only propping up illusions of a glorious Christian past.

Soviet Communism has passed into history, but we in the free capitalist world live under a different kind of materialist system that has spiritually scoured us. Though some decline narratives are overstated, and though we are incomparably freer and more materially comfortable than the Soviets were, we are nevertheless in decline. The main spiritual story of our time is not one of enlightenment—which is what the myth of progress teaches us—but rather one of endarkenment. Disenchantment matters because it is both the catalyst for and the product of decline. The evidence is all around us, for those with eyes to see.

THE DEAD SOULS OF THE DISENCHANTED

If disenchantment is a loss of a meaningful sense of God's presence and of the existence of meaning and purpose in the world, then how should we measure its effects?

We can't do it by looking to material markers alone. It is true that poverty is generally correlated with unhappiness. But if achieving a sense of well-being were merely a matter of being wealthy, free, and physically secure, North Americans, Europeans, and others in the WEIRD-o-sphere would be the happiest people on earth.

But that's not true. That's not even close to being true. Consider this passage from a letter I received in early 2024 from a high school teacher on the East Coast, a once idealistic young man approaching his thirtieth birthday on the verge of professional burnout:

> For the longest time I had sat so secure in my purpose: mentoring and shaping the youth of America. I truly believed in the mission— waxing poetically about sources from the *Epic of Gilgamesh* to Dante to Shakespeare to F. Scott Fitzgerald. I gave it my all to make history, philosophy, religion, culture, and technology *come alive* in the classroom. Not

all students would become archaeologists, historians, teachers, or politicians, but still . . . they'd find value and community in our classroom.

The problems were there, of course, even before the damage of COVID. Social media addiction, difficult family situations, apathy, indifference, etc. But with the advent of AI and the gradual increase in the apathy and despair students are feeling it has become increasingly untenable. I began work at a private religious school six years ago to kick off my teaching career—I got let go, moved into public school, and have increasingly become disillusioned ever since.

The malaise is real—both for me personally and my students. Many of them ponder a future where they'll work forever in some cubicle or other soulless environment. Many have given up and withdrawn, giving in to the siren song of scrolling endlessly or numbing themselves with something to dull their senses. Fortunately, I haven't fallen that far, but the crisis remains.

These students are heirs to the richest, freest, and most technologically advanced civilization that has ever existed. More of them survive into old age than in any other civilization prior to the twentieth century. Most will not have to do hard physical labor to earn their living. They can believe whatever they want, or nothing at all, without restriction, or in many cases even social sanction. They can choose their religion—including creating a bespoke faith curated to one's own personal tastes—or choose to reject religion. Their ability to chart their own way through life has never been less constrained.

They can marry, or not marry. They can have children, or not have children. It's up to them. If they wish to marry someone of the opposite sex, they can. If they wish to change their sex, well, the technology exists to give them a simulation of a male or female body, and in many places laws exist and customs are evolving to accommodate what used to be, until seemingly the day before yesterday, a science-fiction fantasy.

The age-old dream of conquering the limits of nature through technology and liberating individuals from any non-chosen obligations has never been more real for as many people. And yet we are miserable. It's as if we are all asking ourselves the question, What's it all for?

Or doing whatever we can to avoid asking the question at all.

THE NEW GREAT DEPRESSION

The United States is in the midst of an extraordinary mental health crisis. A Gallup poll released in May 2023 revealed that rates of depression have soared to new heights. Over one-third of women say they have been diagnosed with depression at some point in their lifetime—and these are the ones who sought treatment for it. Young Americans are the most depressed cohort of all. Gallup found that the rates of depression among people aged eighteen to twenty-nine (34.3 percent) and thirty to forty-four (34.9 percent) are meaningfully higher than those of older Americans.[4]

The situation is so bad with teenagers and young adults that between 2011 and 2021 the number of that age group diagnosed with clinical depression more than doubled. The suicide rate for children aged ten to fourteen tripled.[5] Anecdotally, high school teachers report an unprecedented crisis. One teacher in Louisiana told me that when she began her career, she would see one or two total hysterical meltdowns by students per semester. Now she sees that each week.

What's driving it? Noted psychologist Jean Twenge says that by far the best explanation is social media culture. Youth depression and suicide rates began soaring in the early 2010s, tracking the mainstreaming of smartphones in the young population. Taking away smartphones, if that were possible, would go a long way toward solving the problem.

But if kids were being raised in a healthy, stable culture in the first place, this technology could not do as much damage. Take the permanent sexual revolution, for example. In the sixties and seventies, society threw off the old Christian sexual mores and embraced hedonism as liberation. Divorce skyrocketed, as did abortion rates. Society never really recovered.

And now, with the viewing of hard-core pornography as a normal part of growing up in America, and with the abolition of nearly all sexual norms, society probably never will.

Besides, the mental health figures for older generations make it clear that technology alone is not the sole source of our pain.

A CULTURE OF CONSTANT CHAOS

The late sociologist Zygmunt Bauman termed the conditions under which we all live today "liquid modernity." The rate of change is so accelerated, he said, that before any social institution or changed way of life has time to solidify, it melts. In liquid modernity, the person who comes out on top is the one who can resist making commitments and who instead can "go with the flow."[6]

But "coming out on top" is not the same thing as thriving. The rapid rate of change understandably makes most people fear that they have lost control of their lives. To live within an enchanted form of Christianity is to have the internal resilience to withstand external disorder. Without that, things fall apart.

In one unusual example from the late 1970s, Alexander Ogorodnikov began to lose his faith while suffering torture and solitary confinement as a political prisoner in the Soviet Union. In Moscow, he testified to me that God had sent him angels for a series of visions that restored his faith by helping Ogorodnikov understand that there was a reason he had been delivered over to suffering. The prisoner discovered through these miraculous night visits that his suffering was not in vain, that God had allowed him to enter prison to preach the gospel to death-row prisoners.

Most Christians will never be visited by angels in such a dramatic fashion. But they may not need to be. The cultivation of a sense of God's enduring presence, bolstered by spiritual disciplines that preserve the practice of enchantment, provides steadiness through the storms of life.

Without both enchantment to give us a strong, if fleeting, sense of the reality of the permanent things—God's existence, life's meaning, love's reality, and so forth—and fidelity to spiritual disciplines that sediment the enchanting epiphany into our bones, we will be lost in the fog. So many are.

NO FAITH IN THE SYSTEM

Disenchantment experienced on a broad social level destabilizes even entire nations. A disenchanted society is one we would expect to have lost faith in the system and institutions governing them. The political theorist Hannah Arendt, in her landmark 1951 book *The Origins of Totalitarianism*, identified a series of sociological markers that indicate a society ripe for adopting a totalitarian ideology such as Nazism or Communism. All of these factors are powerfully present in today's Western societies.[7]

By far the most significant factor, said Arendt, is mass loneliness and atomization. People who feel cut off from others, and unable to form meaningful relationships, are prime targets for ideologues who offer them communal solidarity.

A 2023 worldwide survey by Gallup and the tech company Meta found that, globally, 24 percent of people consider themselves to be lonely to some degree, while 49 percent say they aren't lonely at all. The results varied significantly by country. A separate Gallup survey of the United States found that the young are by far the loneliest group, with 24 percent identifying as lonely.[8]

A second major factor present in pre-totalitarian societies is loss of faith in institutions. Americans have for quite some time had relatively low faith in their institutions, but the slide continues. In the 2023 version of its annual poll, Gallup found that only two major US institutions—small businesses and the military—held the confidence of half or more of the population. Media, the justice system, and big business were trusted by fewer than one-quarter of Americans. Congress had the lowest rating of all, holding the trust of a mere 8 percent.[9]

Similarly, a 2023 Pew poll found that only 16 percent of Americans say they trust the government to do the right thing most of the time. Said Pew, "This is among the lowest trust measures in nearly seven decades of polling."[10]

Who can blame them? The failures of these institutions have been real, consequential, and, in some cases, close to catastrophic. Moreover, as the radical egalitarian ideology commonly referred to as "wokeness" has conquered the minds of elites, the attack on religious, cultural, and social traditions, with the intention of disenchanting them, has ramped up. "The abolition of man is a conscious project of our culture's officer class," writes theologian Carl Trueman, "not merely the outcome of impersonal social and technological forces."[11]

The point is that confidence in the system—political, economic, and otherwise—is in steep decline. Recovering an enchanted belief in God will not fix the problems within those institutions. But it does stand to give people the wherewithal to endure chaos and breakdown within the broader system without losing hope and confidence in the future.

THE DISENCHANTED MATERIALIST

Once again: disenchantment is the evaporation of a sense of the supernatural within the world, and its replacement with a belief, sometimes unacknowledged, that this world is all there is. There are different kinds of disenchantment, which produce somewhat different effects, though these outcomes are far more similar than different.

The disenchanted materialist is more common in Europe than in the United States, perhaps because Europe has been de-Christianizing for longer. He is someone who openly affirms that God does not exist and that the material world is all there is. The disenchanted materialist is the standard character in the novels of the popular French writer Michel Houellebecq, whose books explore what it is like to live in a world without God and the comforts of religion. Though Houellebecq is himself an atheist, his pitiless novels mourn the death of the meaningful world and the cohesive society created by shared faith.

In Houellebecq's fiction, there are no binding answers to theological and philosophical questions. There is no meaning to life, no purpose; there is only living. Europeans once saw nontheistic hope in Marxism, with its promise of peace, equality, and universal brotherhood, but the Soviet Union destroyed that dream everywhere but in faculty lounges.

In the great historical struggle of the twentieth century, liberalism buried Marxism. Yet it also stood graveside at the funeral of Christianity. A Houellebecq character muses about the fate of his continent:

> In countries like Spain, Poland, and Ireland, social life and all behavior had been structured by a deeply rooted, unanimous, and immense Catholic faith for centuries, it determined morality as well as familial relations, conditioned all cultural and artistic productions, social hierarchies, conventions, and rules for living. In the space of a few years, in less than a generation, in an incredibly brief period of time, all this had disappeared, had evaporated into thin air. In these countries today no one believed in God anymore, or took account of him, or even remembered that they had once believed; and this had been achieved without difficulty, without conflict, without any kind of violence or protest, without even a real discussion, as easily as a heavy object, held back for some time by an external obstacle, returns as soon as you release it, to its position of equilibrium.[12]

Economic and social liberalism—forms of social organization built around satisfying individual desire—have created a world full of narcissists obsessed with their own needs and desires, who no longer know how to give and experience love. Radically lonely, they try to escape their despair through consumption, especially consumption of sex via promiscuity.

When their bodies age and become burdens to them, they seek suicide as a means of relief from their pain and distress. Why not? If there is nothing beyond the physical, material world, why should anyone endure permanent suffering? Christianity sternly forbade suicide, of course, but beyond that, faith gave meaning to suffering, as well as created a social matrix of community support as one aged and met limitations.

Gone. All of it gone. True, the welfare state pays the doctors and the nursing homes, but who visits the old? Who loves them? In the summer of 2003, France endured a fatal heat wave that took the lives of nearly fifteen thousand citizens. Eighty-two percent of them were aged seventy-five or older. Many younger French people were on holiday at the time and did not discover that their elderly family members or neighbors were dead until they returned home and found their decomposing bodies.

The disenchanted materialist has nothing to turn to for solace in the face of death. A few years ago, I had coffee in a Paris café with a famous French philosopher and former *soixante-huitard*, as the French call the baby boomers who embraced the spirit of the 1968 student protests. He is an atheist and a staunch believer in the ideals of the French Republic: liberty, equality, and fraternity.

Yet he has lived long enough to watch them dissolve. The French intellectual has reached the winter of his life profoundly grieved. We spoke of Houellebecq as a prophet of the end of the secular age.

"Where do you find hope?" I asked the professor.

"I have no hope," he said, almost shrugging.

I told him that though I share his pessimism, I have hope because I believe in Christ. Christian hope is not the same as optimism, I explained. We in the West are headed for great suffering, it is true, but I can hold on to hope because I have complete confidence that everything still has meaning, and that God is with us.

The sad old Frenchman listened respectfully, then said, "That is fine for you Americans, but here in France, we don't believe in God."

There was not much else left to say. Walking back to my hotel, I thought of François, the middle-aged academic in Houellebecq's controversial 2015 novel *Submission*. Set in the near future, its characters face the looming prospect that France will turn Islamist, simply from sheer moral and spiritual exhaustion.

François, a disenchanted professor at the Sorbonne, is promised a promotion and several wives if he makes a formal conversion to Islam under the new political order. The incoming government doesn't really care whether he believes; it only wants to control the social order. The invitation is not a religious one but a material one: to secure his employment and guarantee him sexual pleasure.

As he mulls the prospect, François, a fallen-away Catholic, visits the medieval pilgrimage town of Rocamadour. There, present while believers are praying, the dissolute academic begins to have a numinous experience. On the verge of Christian re-enchantment, François loses his nerve, draws back from the brink, returns to Paris, and carries out his cynical Islamic conversion.

The lesson is that humanity can take only so much disenchantment. If the disenchanted materialists will not have God, they or their children will one day accept Allah or some other creed—even a political pseudo-religion, such as Communism or fascism—that gives them a sense of purpose and meaning. Had François found re-enchantment at Rocamadour, he would have found the courage to live with hope and purpose under the Islamist regime. But he failed and surrendered to the despair of confessing a faith in which he didn't believe for the sake of material advancement.

THE DISENCHANTED SPIRITUALIST

The United States is in the middle of an unprecedented religious revolution. Long a holdout against waves of secularization washing the faith out of Europe, the younger generations of Americans are finally succumbing. The Zoomers are predicted to be the first generation in US history in which a majority will have no formal religious affiliation.

It is not that they are embracing atheism. Some do, but most call themselves "spiritual but not religious." Their religious sense is a do-it-yourself bricolage of Christian practices joined to pop occultism, Buddhism, and whatever interests the individual in a given moment. The one thing they have in common, though, is a rejection of formal religion.

The kids have been raised in a culture of radical individualism, therapy, and you-do-you self-fulfillment. What they don't know, but will one day find out, is that a religion you make up yourself has no power to enchant. A religion designed to serve one's perceived needs is unavoidably self-worship. It can't be passed on to the next generation, because there is nothing to pass on. They might experience a fleeting sense of enchantment, but it will soon pass, and they will be chasing the next thing, seeking a new hit of spiritual dopamine.

How do young people—or any people, for that matter—raised in a church end up like this?

Some were raised in families where churchgoing was only a sometime thing—Easter, Christmas, and whenever Mom and Dad felt like going. Others attended churches where worship was rote and lifeless. When people like this were able to make up their own minds, they quit going to church, even if they still say they believe in Jesus.

Others were raised in churches where the congregational leadership was forever seeking the Next Big Thing to keep people entertained and in the pews. This is fun and exciting for a while, but it's hard for church-as-spectacle to keep the show endlessly exciting. It comes to seem shallow and gimmicky, because, well, it is.

Many grew up in churches that placed a premium on political engagement and left churchgoing in disgust over the preoccupation with worldly power they experienced there. (This is not only a conservative thing, mind you.) Yes, it is important for Christians to oppose abortion, to fight racism, and so forth, but activism is not the core of the Christian faith.

And then there are those whose Christian formation was entirely therapeutic and relational—the ones raised to believe that niceness is next to godliness. Some years back, an evangelical college professor observed that most students on his campus were sweet, wonderful kids. But they knew next to nothing substantial about the faith, having been raised in a "Jesus is my best friend" youth-group culture. It was fine while they were on campus, he said, around people like themselves—but when they entered the real world and faced pushback on the faith, they crumpled. Nobody prepared them for a world in which Christianity costs something.

There are other kinds of disenchanted Christians, but you get the idea. These are people who have left active church life but who still hold on to vestigial Christian identity. Their parents' generation likes to tell itself that when the kids get older, and start families of their own, they will come back to church. The statistics do not bear that out. This generation may wander through life holding vague Christian thoughts in their heads and turning up at services on the holidays. But their children won't.

Only the return of strong religion—one that makes demands, offers compelling explanations to the problems of death and suffering, and gives worshipers a visceral sense of connecting to the living God—has any hope of competing in the post-Christian marketplace.

WHAT IF WE FAIL AT CHRISTIAN RE-ENCHANTMENT?

Every person reading this book is living through one or more of these crises of disenchantment, if not personally, then in the life of someone they love. If we fail to revive enchantment, the Christian faith will continue to wither, and so will our societies. The negative trends mentioned above will likely worsen. Something that cannot continue won't. If we lose Christianity, we run an enormous risk of losing our own humanity.

Though not a believer himself, the popular English historian Tom Holland penned what was probably the most important Christian book of 2019, *Dominion*, about the Christian faith and the making of the West. Holland explored the ways that nearly all the things that make Western civilization distinct, and the most humane in the world, came from Christianity. If we lose our ancestral faith, we may live through the effacement of the human person.

It is certainly not the case that only Christians are properly human. But it is true that it was in Christendom that humankind first began to see the weak, poor, women, and slaves with different eyes. It was Christianity that developed the first true hospitals. Slavery was a nearly universal scourge, even in some Christian countries, but Christians also stamped out the practice. The humanist worldview that honors liberty and natural rights—all came out of Christianity.

Will they survive its demise? This is not a chance we should want to take. The Catholic writer Eric Mader, in a letter to me, said that disenchantment severs the connection we all feel to the divine, which is the source of our humanity (the Bible tells us that we are made in the image of God, after all). If matter doesn't matter, so to speak—if there is no meaning inherent to our bodies and all other forms of matter—then all we are is putty in the hands of the powerful.

Put simply, we really are living in a crucible, as the fourth century was for the pagans of Rome. Either we will recover enchanted Christianity or we will succumb to chaos and cruelty.

"It is not true that life has always been like this," Mader told me. "That, in my view, is a cope on the part of those who claim a disenchanted society like ours has a human future. I'm guessing this society does not have a long-term, actually human future. Either another human order of relationality will take over, as Houellebecq imagines for Islam in Europe, or we will be effaced to the point of no longer being really human, as I think many of our transhumanists accept, or even cheer."

He's right about that. It is by no means alarmist to say that disenchantment has brought Western civilization to the brink of a new, technology-driven totalitarianism.

The futurist guru Yuval Noah Harari has predicted, with apparent delight, that the more our lives become digitized, the more we will come to understand that "or our own humanity is nothing more than numbers capable of manipulation by computers that know us better than we know ourselves."[13] We begin with total freedom from God and material reality and end in total enslavement to the Machine.

This is a real and present danger today. As we will see in the next section, the dangers of looking to technology as a form of enchantment are far greater—and far stranger—than most people grasp. Even darker are the openly occult strategies more and more people in the post-Christian West are embracing—often in tandem with the heavy use of psychedelic drugs as a means of generating instant enchantment.

Remember Viktor Popkov, the disenchanted young Soviet who sought Christ, at great personal risk, to give him a reason to live? The reason I went to see Viktor Popkov that day in Moscow was because I wanted to find out from him what lessons Christians in the West needed to know from the Communist experience, so we can prepare for persecution here.

Before I left him, Popkov told me that Christians today must not make the mistake of thinking that reviving a merely cultural Christianity is sufficient to endure the malign powers of antichrist. You have to have "true believers" among you, he said. To put it another way, Christians must be enchanted by Christ in the same way those young believers who risked everything to meet for prayer and fellowship in 1970s Moscow were. Nothing else works.

THE DARK ENCHANTMENT

OF THE *OCCULT*

The Devil hath power
To assume a pleasing shape.

—Shakespeare, *Hamlet*

I was sitting on a balcony of a high-rise apartment on Manhattan's East Side. I had come to visit old Catholic friends—I'll call them Nathan and Emma—who were in a bizarre crisis. Emma, a wife, mom, and faithful churchgoer for most of her life, was demonically possessed.*

It emerged when Emma was recovering from a hospital stay related to severe depression. A friend suggested that she go to a healing Mass offered

---

* I must add a caveat by saying that this terminology will prompt some theological debate about to what degree and in what ways a Christian believer can be tormented by a demon. I use "possessed" because it was accurate to the experience of the situation and consistent with my understanding of the phenomenon, even if it is imperfect.

by an exorcist priest. On the way to the Mass, she heard blasphemies and cursing and was called names. After the Mass, she met the priest with her friend and told him what had happened. He interrogated her about her background, seeking an explanation.

A week later, she met the priest again, and he offered to give her a blessing. He asked more questions about her background. Emma arranged another session with the exorcist and this time brought her husband. It was then that demons manifested through her, with cursing and screaming in voices not Emma's own.

That's when they knew for sure. Emma went under the care of the exorcist, who prayed with her and was able to discern that her deceased grandfather back in Europe had been a high-level occultist who brought a curse onto the family.

Emma and Nathan believed he might have been a Freemason. They concluded this because when the exorcist had her say the formal prayers renouncing Freemasonry, the demons would try to stop her from speaking. They would choke her, call her names, and sometimes put her to sleep. Like a narcoleptic, her eyes would close and she would start snoring midsentence.

Shortly before I visited, Emma had been examined by Dr. Richard Gallagher, a psychiatrist retained by the Catholic Archdiocese of New York to certify that potential candidates for exorcism are not suffering from a psychological malady or anything natural that could account for what they were going through. Dr. Gallagher had certified that Emma's symptoms had no medical explanation. She was awaiting permission from the cardinal for a formal ritual exorcism.

When I arrived at their apartment, Nathan confided in me that he would bring outside, hidden in his pocket, a relic of the True Cross. The demonically possessed react negatively to such things; awareness of blessed objects hidden from view is one basic test of possession.

As Emma and I sat talking at the balcony table, Nathan took a seat. Suddenly Emma's face transformed utterly. She looked at her husband and snarled, in a deep voice, "F—k you, bitch! Get that thing away from me!"

Then her head dropped down. When it rose again, Emma was back to herself. She gave me a pitiful look.

"I'm sorry," she said softly. "That wasn't me."

The good news is that Emma was eventually delivered from her demons, through intense prayer, but without a ritual exorcism. But freedom would be four grueling years away from the day I saw the demon manifest through Emma on her balcony.

Before I left, she told me that it was, in a sense, good that these evil entities had been uncovered within her. She had been fighting depression and suicidal thoughts all her life. Now she knew where it came from. When her own father, the occultist grandfather's son, lay dying, Emma and Nathan visited his deathbed accompanied by a priest and heard the same strange voices and curses that had afflicted her coming out of him.

Pale and tired that afternoon with me above Manhattan, Emma also emphasized the importance of prayer and humility, and of searching one's conscience to root out unforgiveness. If you hold on to injustice and refuse forgiveness, you make yourself much weaker in the face of demonic attack, she said. These are the things she has learned from her own battle with evil spirits—lessons that Emma believes must be used to help others.

After I said goodbye, Nathan, a businessman, walked me back to my hotel in Midtown. He had been struggling mightily to help his wife for two years, through a crisis that he never imagined would be possible for people like them: sophisticated big-city people who were faithful to the Mass and the sacraments.

"What's the biggest way this has changed you?" I asked.

"Now when I walk down the street, I know that there is a spiritual battle going on all around me," he said. "It's everywhere. Once you have seen the things I have seen, you know it, and you can't leave the fight."

Nathan said that this was not a battle he ever would have chosen, but once it started, he knew he had a duty to see it through till the end.

"Until the battle is over, there will be many victories and many defeats," he said. "On the worst days, when I was alone, and my wife was unconscious in the hospital, I never once thought that we were going to be defeated.

I knew we had to stay the course, no matter how bleak it looked. Christ would ultimately have the victory here. I just wanted to make sure he gave me the strength to persevere."

It's a battle that is intensifying. At a 2022 conference in Oxford, I met Daniel Kim, then twenty-seven, an Anglican seminarian who left a lucrative career working as a creative in the London advertising world to study for the priesthood. Daniel told me that in his job at a high-powered firm, there were no atheists—but that, as far as he could tell, he was the only Christian in the office. The rest were all into the occult to some degree or another.

"When I was there, there was a big focus on astrology and occult-slash-Wiccan stuff, but not in the way we would think of it—you know, dark and bloody," he said. "It was more like"—he shifted into a naive tone of voice—"'Oh yeah, satanism is just a connection with nature, and about the fullest expression of our humanity.' There was a high level of anthropocentric enchantment. Belief in the human spirit, belief that the human horizon can be overcome."

The idea that the greatest challenge to Christianity is from atheism is an idea whose time has long passed, Kim said. Now the world of neo-paganism and the occult has opened wide. Young people today, some of them influenced by radical feminism, think of both atheism and Christianity as left-brained, patriarchal ways of thinking. Turning to nature religion and darker forms of the occult is, for them, an approach to connecting with a more intuitive and organic way of relating to the world.

I told Daniel Kim that these people are not entirely wrong to seek re-enchantment; it's just that they are looking in the wrong places—in spiritually dangerous places. He agreed and said that the new openness in his generation to spiritual experience poses challenges but also offers opportunities. I asked him what the most important thing is to know about re-enchanting his generation.

"People can see through inauthenticity in a millisecond," Kim said, snapping his fingers. "People are tired of the cool and the relevant. Because we get that everywhere."

The evangelical ordinand learned from market research as an advertising professional a lesson that he planned to take into his church ministry: the idea that churches should downplay the numinous and the mystical for the sake of making Christianity relevant and accessible to seekers is a mistake.

"It's not what people want anymore. It doesn't work," Kim said. "Actually, in some ways, young people right now want to be confronted by something, want to be provoked, want to be compelled by something different."

There is no question that established religion is in steep decline. According to 2021 census figures, Christians are now a minority in England and Wales for the first time since those countries were formally evangelized at the end of the sixth century. In the United States, Christian affiliation is plummeting, especially among the young, who declare that they are "nones"—people who identify with no religion in particular, though they may call themselves "spiritual." According to 2024 data from the Pew Research Center, 28 percent of American adults identify as a none, a number that has increased by 75 percent since Pew first began surveying for nones in 2007.[1] Barring revival, Christians will cease to be a majority in the US well before the end of this century.

The religion scholar Stephen Bullivant, in his 2022 book *Nonverts: The Making of Ex-Christian America*, says that "the USA is in the midst of a social, cultural, and religious watershed," what he calls "a vast, wholly unprecedented 'mass nonversion' of millions upon millions of Americans who were raised religious."[2]

It is important, though, to note that these disaffiliating masses are not becoming atheists. Most of the nones still believe in some higher power. They are far more likely to adopt a bespoke spirituality, pulling a little bit of this and a little bit of that together to make something they hope will work for them.

As Daniel Kim saw in his London office, millennials and Generation Z are open to paganism and other forms of occult practice in ways older people are not. Though polling data for once unpopular forms of religion can be shaky, in 1990 there were only eight thousand Wiccans in America. Today there are around one million witches and neo-pagans in the US, with the occult a major presence in American popular culture. They find in occultism the mysticism and community that they could not or would not locate in Christianity.

It should not be forgotten that in the 1920s and 1930s the occult-obsessed Nazi leadership exploited the decline of Christianity, postwar social breakdown, and the political restlessness within Germany to create pseudo-Nordic pagan rituals intended to give Germans—especially German youth—a sense of mystery, meaning, and purpose. It is not that all occultists are Nazis in training. Rather, the point is that there is something deep within the human psyche that is not satisfied with materialism and hedonism, and can be lured into evil movements that give them the enchantment for which they hunger. In nineteenth-century Britain, the poet Matthew Arnold famously observed "the melancholy, long, withdrawing roar" of the "Sea of Faith." Yet that was also the century that spiritism, theosophy, and various forms of occultism became popular, particularly among cultural elites.

Religion scholar Tara Isabella Burton observes that paganism and its offshoots make sense for young adults because they appeal to their intuitional preferences ("lived experience") and rejection of institutions and established hierarchies as oppressive. Occultism promises an experience of the numinous, but unlike Christianity, in which believers surrender their wills to God, occultism tells practitioners that they can use higher powers to impose their own wills on the world.

Witchcraft and paganism typically track with progressive political commitments, especially around feminism, environmentalism, and queer activism. Yet more recent iterations of the faiths have gone past the hippie-ish nature-worship norm.

"Contemporary witchcraft, by contrast, embraces the darkness—including imagery of the downright diabolical—as a necessary political corrective to what they see as unjust Christian supremacy," Burton writes. "They are, implicitly or explicitly, champions of the Miltonic Satan, striving against a seemingly oppressive God."[3]

JONAH'S STORY

A man I will call Jonah is both typical of his generation and extreme. Jonah, a scholar of religion who studied with one of America's most distinguished faculties, is a recovering occultist and convert to Orthodox Christianity. I was introduced to him by the Orthodox priest who is working with him as an exorcist.

"I'm so glad that Father Nectarios put us in touch," he said when we connected via Zoom. "The idea of re-enchantment is so important and necessary. It's a term I used all the time when I was on the other side. But people need to recognize what the ultimate end game of the Enemy is."

He explained that the currents of thought that have scoured and flushed away all sense of meaning from existence ("all the nihilism, the scientism, and relativism") are not ends in themselves but the means with which demonic entities wish to clear the ground to prepare people for what Jonah calls "the religion of Antichrist."

"Once they feel that vacuum of meaninglessness," he said, "once they encounter that starvation for spiritual realities that truly exist, the enemy forces are ten miles ahead of us, in having this infrastructure prepared to pull people into things that seem benign but will eventually be revealed as gateways to hell itself."

We need to talk, he said, because people today aren't wrong to seek enchantment—but if they do it outside a clearly and uniquely Christian path, they will inevitably be drawn into the demonic. Neutrality in this conflict is not possible. "Maybe it's my role to be biased in that way," he said, "because of how badly I was burned."

Burned he certainly was by his search for strong light. What makes Jonah typical is his early seeking in the occult, looking for something more exciting than the bland suburban evangelicalism in which he was raised. What makes him extraordinary is that he ended up as a ritual worshiper of demons and has confessed now to having been possessed, both willingly and unwillingly, on many occasions. Plus, he was not only an occult practitioner but a scholar of occultism and esotericism. He agreed to share his story with me if I masked some details to protect his identity.

Jonah was homeschooled and arrived at college eager to study religion. When he began studying for his master's degree in theology, Jonah followed his intellectual curiosity into exploring various forms of paganism and attempting to reconcile them with his Christianity. He also discovered psychedelic drugs and consumed them in heavy doses.

"As soon as I decided that the Christianity of my youth was false, I went on a journey to find the cutting edge," he recalls. "I always wanted to find the next horizon—the people who are the 'real experts' in all this, what do they think? Who are they reading? Of course, the Luciferian lie I bought into was 'Hey, Jonah, it turns out that you are the center all along'—which of course is delusional but is also a good summation of the ideologies I had been learning from the beginning."

He was also drawn by the allure of what C. S. Lewis called the "inner ring" of knowledge and power. Jonah wanted to be with the smart set, with the sophisticates who understood how the world really worked and who used their secret knowledge to manipulate it. He says now, "I just kept following that deeper and deeper until I found demons at the center."

At the university where he began his doctoral program, Jonah fell in with an occultist community and began to participate in rituals, often incorporating psychedelics. Eventually he began to have visions and communicate with demons. On a number of occasions they entered his body—sometimes against his will.

For a couple of years, Jonah thought he was being initiated into special knowledge, into gnosis, with a group of elect who had been chosen by the gods as their acolytes to enlighten humanity. Those early experiences of visions were genuinely beautiful and truly meaningful. If they had not been, Jonah would not have been seduced into slavery.

"Behind this idea of morally neutral, psychedelic enchantment was the most satanic evil possible," he now says. "I have no excuse for it, but I have to say that I had been primed by these ideologies over the years to explain away all this to my family and friends as *it's just nature, it's beauty, it's tolerance*, it's all these things—and then I get to the point where I'm literally seeing red dragons, I am feeling demonic loathing for humanity, and I am being possessed.

"I went along with it, because I thought I had no other choice at that point. I had been seeing hell itself all along, but I'd convinced myself, through my sophisticated pagan ideology, that it was something else. But finally I couldn't deny it."

These weren't ancient gods at all, he finally understood, but demons. He began to suspect that there was something wrong with all of this and at last confronted the numerous contradictions in his occult worldview. Once Jonah grasped that he was being manipulated by the entities with whom he was communicating, and that these were beings that wanted to destroy humanity, he wanted out.

A friend who had once been interested in the occult and psychedelia but who had found Orthodox Christianity and converted invited him to church. Jonah describes his first liturgy as giving him "a calm, abiding sense of being connected to something enduring, wise, and solid."

He soon renounced the occult and became Orthodox. Jonah testifies that he still carries the psychic scars of his years in the occult and is working with an exorcist to oversee his healing.

In the first of two interviews, I asked Jonah how the general cultural orientation toward openness and curiosity today leaves people vulnerable to the demonic. The danger, he replied, is "seeing curiosity and openness as virtuous apart from a grounding in a deeper commitment to truth."

Would-be seekers should be aware that even as popular culture encourages them to be open and experimental, it decides which curiosities will be stigmatized and which ones glorified.

"We are all conditioned by media and academia to be 'open' toward a variety of increasingly extreme trends within culture, politics, and spirituality," he said, "but closed toward almost everything associated with traditional Christian morality and theological understandings."

Given how intimately the occult is tied in with some progressive political causes, Jonah warns that Christians who resist the demonic "are going to have to reconcile themselves to being called far-right lunatics." Fear of being regarded as nonprogressive is a powerful tool that spiritual evil uses to disarm people.

Moreover, the occult draws in the curious by presenting even the most banal sexually libertine and syncretic ideas as privileged secrets, mystical spiritual truths that have been hidden from view by oppressive institutions, warns Jonah. The goal is to make the forbidden and the transgressive more alluring, presenting it as liberation from false limitations.

Often, the drugs deliver "an astounding experience," he says, and a spell might "work to an amazing degree"—yet these are dangerous practices that can cost you your sanity and, ultimately, your soul. Says Jonah, "All of us are capable of unfathomable degrees of delusion."

He never had a stereotypical bad trip that put him off drugs. "Sure, I saw plenty of things in my psychedelic experiences that would have horrified any spiritually healthy person. But my mind and soul were in such an intense state of corruption and delusion that no matter how overtly demonic and sinister these trips got, I experienced them all as empowering and enlightening."

I asked Jonah to recall key turning points in which he made fateful decisions that led him down the dark path. He said in retrospect that it was "just being continually seduced by ideologies that felt like the completely natural conclusion of the last one."

He considers his normie American evangelical upbringing to have been "deeply tragic, considering how unequipped the authority figures in my life were to shield me from the increasingly demonic spiritual and intellectual paths to which I became enslaved.

"Plenty of these authority figures recognized the reality of the demonic but they brought a knife to a gun fight in their attempt to stave off such influences," he says. "Some had simply no answers, or wholly unsatisfying ones, for my myriad youthful theological curiosities. Theology as presented within the evangelical world all seemed so arbitrary. Mostly, it was emotional experiences of worship that were cast as the foundation of the faith. So, when those dried up for me, my conservative faith seemed untenable."

Diving headlong into pop culture as a teenager, Jonah spent a lot of time online and soon saw that liberal views were treated as "cool and profound" and the conservative religious views with which he was raised were dumb and nerdy. He didn't think it was a big deal at the time, but his embracing liberal cultural and political views around hot-button issues such as abortion and gay marriage was a real turning point. This is not surprising, given that so much cutting-edge occultism has embraced feminist and LGBT politics.

In college, Jonah followed his instincts into studying theology and philosophy, with an orientation toward religious pluralism (entailing the idea that all religions are basically the same) and spiritual experiences as guides to truth. These seemed to the former evangelical to define "the horizons of sophisticated modern approaches to religion." And he found his experiential, open-minded approach encouraged by the academy.

"The forms of Christianity I was immersed in were already so hopelessly heretical and syncretic that I don't even think it was a particularly important moment when I finally became a self-identifying neo-pagan," Jonah tells me. "Of course, I regret the first time I took a psychedelic drug, or first celebrated a pagan ritual, or first bought a deck of tarot cards, but each of those actions seemed perfectly reasonable within the metaparadigm of spiritual plurality and open-ended emphasis on experience that I had been situated in for years."

Jonah moved deeper into the occult, in both his academic study and private practice. And then came a decision that he knows "I can never justify, no matter how much I understand why I made it." Jonah goes on:

Sometime after I began practicing intense psychedelic ritual magic in earnest, the spiritual realities I had been foolishly playing with and dabbling in for years revealed their true face to me. And it was satanic. I even used that word to describe it at the time. It was so obvious. I saw the face of the devil, manifest as a red dragon. I felt the horrors of possession, my bodily will stripped from me in a manner meant to terrify and humiliate me. I felt the absolute loathing for humanity from these demonic entities. I should have gotten out then, but I still bought into the justifications—my own and others'.

I was not wrong that this open devotion to the demonic was a culmination of a journey that I started by simply accepting as a teenager that the world knows better than God and the Christian tradition when it comes to moral issues. I still should have known better. But I didn't, because I was intoxicated by the aesthetic beauty produced by occult experiences, by the unfathomable power I felt when I allowed myself to be possessed, by the feeling that I could peer deeper into the black void of the infinite than any human before me. I didn't want the experiences to end. So I went along with unthinkable evil. I've been reaping the consequences ever since. And I pray for God's forgiveness and mercy.

During his years as an occultist, Jonah and his co-religionists never viewed Christian churches as meaningful opponents. They were all convinced that what they were seeing and living was going to be the fate of all humanity, eventually.

"Ecumenism and emphasis on spiritual experience would consume all religions and slowly acclimate everyone to more blatant emphases on magic, entity contact, and the divinization of the human," he says. "Probably almost no one, aside from me and like-minded occultists, had the stomach to witness the devilish, sinister appearance of the human being dissolved into nonhuman natural and technological intelligences. But that was fine—the point was that most humanity would sleepwalk into their fate."

Perhaps the most important ally they had on their side was pop culture. "Countless films, television shows, songs, and books provide implicit versions of our worldview, or at least planted a seed that would make people an easier mark for manipulation," he says. "We felt like we were winning."

"The Christian churches didn't feel like a threat," Jonah emphasizes. "They had no idea of the countless ways the whole world was primed to destroy their defenses and melt them into the demonic religion of the twin principles of superhumanism and anti-humanism. While I was in the active service of demons, I maintained friendships with conservative Christian friends. Not one of them told me that they sensed something spiritually amiss about me."

So what should pastors and religious leaders do to protect their flocks from the upsurge in occultism sweeping pop culture? Jonah suggests that they read up on occult subjects enough to help others spot and avoid demonic traps but not so much that they become fixated on darkness.

And, though exorcism ministry is a relatively rare calling, all religious leaders must take the demonic seriously and be prepared to confront it when it manifests. Not acting for fear of looking foolish or fear of the unknown is a failure to do one's spiritual duty. "The demons are only getting bolder," he says. "This is not a fight we can shy away from."

Churchgoers have to be told that pop culture is no friend of the faithful, and need to be led not to passively consume it but to become critical observers. And pastors should have "zero tolerance for openness to the occult. If any of your parishioners show an interest in even seemingly benign esoteric or New Age spirituality—for example, astrology—warn them that they're opening themselves to evil forces that will seek to drag them to hell."

Today, doctors are finding solid therapeutic uses for the once taboo category of drugs called psychedelics. This research brings welcome hope and relief to many people who live in psychological torment from trauma or abuse. Yet it is also the case that the recreational use of psychedelic drugs by seekers who want to have a magical or transcendent experience is growing. This is frightening—not because psychedelics don't work to produce an experience of enchantment, but because they actually do.

Users of strong psychedelics, who sometimes term themselves "psychonauts," report mind-blowing journeys into alternate realities where they meet various demon-like entities. Curiously, despite the fact that psychonauts come from widely varied backgrounds, many of them see the same entities in their visions. This suggests that these dramatic, intense psychedelic experiences involve entering into an objective realm. Some users report unwanted paranormal happenings, with unseen beings lingering after their psychedelic journeys.

Richard C. Schwartz, founder of the popular Integrated Family

Systems model of psychotherapy, has encountered in his work entities that he calls "unattached burdens" (UBs). In a foreword to his colleague Robert Falconer's 2023 book about UBs, *The Others within Us*, Schwartz confesses that he had to put aside his scientific biases to deal with the phenomenon of UBs manifesting in his therapeutic practice. In the book, Falconer discusses how the use of psychedelics—DMT especially—makes the self more porous while under the influence. If, as some researchers believe, the brain acts as a filter that keeps out information, then, says Falconer, by temporarily changing the brain's settings, "DMT could be opening us up to perceive other dimensions or levels of reality that are just as real as our ordinary ones."[4]

I confess to Jonah that as a college freshman, before I became a Christian, I experimented with LSD and had relatively mild hallucinogenic experiences. Though I regret it, I must admit that it pulled me out of depression and opened my eyes to the fact that God was real. The unorthodox English biologist Rupert Sheldrake has noted that virtually everyone who tries psychedelics returns from their "trip" convinced that what they experienced was not a hallucination, in the sense of an escape from reality, but rather an intensification of reality—the lifting of the veil to reveal what's really there.[5] This was certainly my experience. Psychedelic use was part of my journey toward religious faith—something I have never wanted to talk about for fear of encouraging others. But it really happened, and I don't think it serves the truth, or does anybody any good, to pretend that these events are all bad.

In my first year of college, I was in despair over (what else?) a girl who did not love me. One weekend, my new roommate, a fun-loving Jewish hippie from New Orleans, told me he had two tabs of LSD. He had never tried it; would I join him? Why not? Back then, I was so depressed that nothing mattered.

For my roommate, the experience was merely fun. For me, though, it was life changing. The drug chemically alters the brain temporarily, affecting serotonin levels and heightening one's sensory inputs. It is not an opioid and does not produce euphoria. I did not hallucinate things that were not there, but the world itself was rendered breathtakingly beautiful.

During the twelve hours the trip lasted, I felt as though I were walking out of a dark, damp prison cell into a warm garden drenched with sunshine and filled with brilliant flowers. Like many people who have taken this drug, I had an overwhelming sense of the deep unity of all being, and of God's presence suffusing it. When the drug wore off, I did not think that I had seen augmented reality; rather, I believed that I had been granted a glimpse of the really real.

My depression was cured in a stroke—and when Monday morning rolled around, I went to the campus bookstore looking for books about God. I found a little book about the philosophy of Kierkegaard, read it in a week, and accepted Christ. It took years of struggle to fully surrender to the Holy Spirit, but as embarrassed as I have long been to have taken the drug as a nineteen-year-old, it would be dishonest to deny that my pilgrimage to faith passed through this unusual place. If critics of psychedelic use fail to recognize that some people appear to benefit from them, both psychologically and spiritually, we will lose credibility.

For as long as it acts, the drug makes the self more porous. This is its spiritual benefit but also its spiritual danger. I told Jonah that I would never repeat that experience, because now, older and wiser, I believe it opens doors in the nous that ought to remain closed, unless opened by God through prescribed prayer and religious practice. When I read about people with no religious preparation consuming psychedelics far more powerful than what I ingested in the 1980s, it fills me with fear for their souls.

The massive turn to psychedelics plays into the reckless quest for forbidden knowledge that is deeply embedded in the Western spirit. In his *Inferno*, Dante sites Ulysses among the damned because he used his extraordinary way with words to convince his crew to sail past the dangerous outer borders of the sea, goading them to go gloriously where no man had gone before. They all died.

Similarly, Charles Foster, a well-known English intellectual who writes on enchantment, wrote in the pages of an elite British publication that there are "no good reasons to inhibit research on psychedelics. Indeed there are no true reasons at all. I suspect that the real objections well up from a deep and old intuition that, although we are designed for travel outside our usual modes of consciousness, there are nonetheless worlds that are out of bounds—or out of bounds to most people in most circumstances."[6]

To be sure, Foster, who is a Christian, expressed at the conclusion of the piece personal apprehension about the recreational (versus medicinal) use of psychedelics. But his lines above capture a widely shared inability of modern people to imagine that there might be dangers in opening the doors of perception and plunging through to unknown psychic realms.

Jonah, who has long and intense experience as a psychonaut, strongly affirms my negative judgment on the recreational use of psychedelics. He, too, has known people who were first brought to a real faith in God through psychedelics. "In my estimation," he says, "this is less an advertisement for psychedelics and more a testament to how the Holy Spirit can choose to work through whatever he wills."

(Later, I heard a horrifying story from an Orthodox believer, a lawyer, who had never done drugs but who had been talked into trying a mild psychedelic. He had a vivid out-of-body experience in a dimension in which he encountered demons. He was told there by a being he believed was his guardian angel never, ever to ingest these drugs, because they really do give one access to a forbidden realm—one in which you can lose your eternal soul.)

As a one-time heavy user of psychedelics, Jonah now says that these drugs "are never worth the risk because they place us in a hypervulnerable cognitive state, ripe for demonic manipulation.

"These drugs can bring you into contact with spiritual reality but in a manner rife with misinterpretation, ego inflation disguised as humility, confirmation bias, or even more openly demonic forms of deception," he says.

He's not alone in making these assertions. In the online political and cultural magazine *UnHerd*, journalist Ed Prideaux sounded an alarm against "the psychedelic-industrial complex," his term for the way psychedelic experiences are now being marketed as instant re-enchantment. Prideaux points out that "indigenous and mystical traditions have warned the West against conquistador exploration of ecstatic states for centuries.

The Eastern Orthodox tradition, for instance, has a rich literature of *pre-lest*, a spiritual malaise in which the seeker of private mystical experiences becomes possessed, obsessed, deluded, or corrupted by egotism."[7]

Jonah also warns sternly against the deep connections between sexual transgressiveness and occult practice. This was part of his own history too. Aleister Crowley, perhaps the most famous, or infamous, occult figure of modern times, is known for "sex magick"—the ritual use of transgressive sex acts in demonic worship.

I tell Jonah about a young man who came to a former parish of mine to escape the local chapter of the Crowley cult, the Ordo Templi Orientis. He said he got out when he realized the things he was going to be required to do to rise in the cult sickened him as a survivor of child sexual abuse. According to Crowleyan teachings, the greater the willful violation of Christian sexual norms, the more power accrued to the violator. The young man, who eventually became Orthodox, told me that he looked around at how eroticized popular culture had become and realized that Crowley had won.

Jonah agrees. "It's less about Crowley's particular kind of sex magick and more about how a Crowleyan approach to sex has become culturally dominant. Contemporary modes of sexuality that push for increasingly extreme forms of variety and transgression are inherently Crowleyan in character. Consider how Crowleyan spirituality venerates bisexuality in particular, because it allows for the greatest accumulation of sexual experience."

It is no accident, he continues, that the hermaphroditic Baphomet symbol—a two-gendered human creature with a goat's head—has become one of the most commonly recognized symbols of the occult. The destabilization of identity, particularly sexual identity, is seen by many forms of the occult as a sacred means of undermining Judeo-Christian hierarchy and order.

"Transgender ideology is an attempt to destroy the image of God within us," Jonah says. "The distinction between men and women, and the metaphysical implications of correct relationship between masculinity and femininity, are key to correct theological understanding. Destroy this boundary and many others will follow, such as the boundaries between human and animal, and human and technology. If one of these foundational distinctions can be made to seem arbitrary, do we expect the others to hold?"

In our final conversation, Jonah—who is a trained scholar of religion—cautions me to be careful with the concept of re-enchantment. People are religious by nature, he says. What modern disenchantment has done is convince people that Christianity is false and empty—which has opened the door for the popularity of psychedelics, UFOs, tarot cards, and all manner of occultism. It's no longer fringe enthusiasm. For example, the University of Exeter announced in 2023 that it would offer a postgraduate degree program in occult studies. It's not so much that the modern world has become disenchanted as that it has become de-Christianized.

The emerging forms of post-Christian religion, he says, "will provide plenty of opportunities for ecstatic spiritual experience, with none of the ascetic discipline, epistemic rigor, and doctrinal depth of the true faith." Jonah doesn't fault people for wanting a deeper experience of God, as he did as a bored young evangelical, but he strongly warns against seeking enchantment for its own sake. If you summon the devil and his servants and ask them to dazzle you, they will come.

Says Jonah, "Such things may appear beautiful at first, but spiritual experience apart from God always turns to horror in the end."

THE EXORCISTS

"The physical and spiritual pain Jonah is enduring is real. And we will have to unravel the web that may be encompassing him," says Father Nectarios, the Orthodox exorcist who is caring for the recovering occultist.

It was Father Nectarios who introduced me to Jonah. Jonah had come to him by referral from his parish priest, who sensed that the new convert's struggles were out of the ordinary. After evaluation, including an examination of Jonah's religious and medical history, the exorcist agreed to take him on.

"It is imperative to state that exorcism is a process. It is not a one-time event wherein a prayer or rite is performed and all is solved, though that is not out of the realm of possibilities," the priest tells me. "It is also important to stress that God is doing the work and will not abandon Jonah. Jonah is engaging in a holy process that may take time to free him from his trials."

Though Orthodox Christianity has a robust traditional spirituality of the demonic—that is, the world of evil spirits isn't psychologized away, in the modern style—there aren't many Orthodox exorcists in the United States. This, the priest concedes, is a major problem.

"I graduated from an Orthodox seminary over twenty years ago," he says. "In seminary studies, then and now, not a single American seminary provides a course in demonology."

Father Nectarios is a late-vocation priest, having accepted ordination after retiring from his first career. He sees exorcism as another way of fighting an enemy. ("I don't believe Jesus tiptoed through the tulips and advised the apostles 'don't worry, be happy,'" he says.) But in the US, the various Orthodox churches are failing to provide their clergy with the training they need to recognize and assist those who are demonically tempted, obsessed, or possessed.

For training, Father Nectarios went to the Catholic Church, which takes exorcism more seriously than most contemporary Orthodox hierarchies. In the Catholic Church, canon law requires each diocese to have an official exorcist, appointed by the bishop. A full ritual exorcism of a possessed person requires permission from the local bishop, but full possession is very rare. Much more common are lesser forms of demonic activity, such as obsession, in which demons harass a victim with destructive thoughts or manifestations of curses.

In recent years, the Catholic Church has educated and equipped more exorcists than in the past to meet the exploding need for their services. As faith has receded, and interest in the occult and pornography has grown, so has demonic activity.

In the summer of 2009, Father Nectarios traveled to Rome to take a Vatican course on the practical aspects of exorcism. It was there that he met the legendary Father Gabriele Amorth—who died in 2016 but who was at the time the chief exorcist of the Diocese of Rome; Russell Crowe played Father Amorth in the 2023 film *The Pope's Exorcist*. The Orthodox priest became the Catholic elder's student.

Father Nectarios talked with me about the preparations for an exorcism, which for him are the same as in the Catholic Church. The victim must have first undergone a medical examination to rule out any natural explanation for his condition. Only a validly ordained priest is allowed to do a full exorcism, and then only with the permission of his bishop (demons are legal masterminds and respect hierarchy, even though they despise it). Pious laymen and laywomen who have prepared themselves through prayer, fasting, and confession may assist in an exorcism, both to be present in prayer and to help the priest if the victim becomes violent.

An exorcist never engages in dialogue with the demon, except in a strictly limited sense: to learn how it came to possess the victim and when it will leave. Priests must understand that they are dealing with discarnate beings—fallen angels—who are vastly more intelligent than mortals. And they must always address the creatures with the authority of Christ, not their own—otherwise, they leave themselves open to savage attack.

Father Nectarios says that it is important to have valid holy relics present at these battles. Relics serve two purposes.

"The first is the healing of the suffering individual," the exorcist says. "The last thing a demon wants is to be in the presence of something bearing the grace of heaven. The second role of the holy relic is as a diagnostic tool. If a demon is present and wants to remain attached to or within an individual, the demon may manifest itself having been repulsed by the holy relic. If the latter is the case, the priest knows what he is confronting and can plan accordingly."

When you talk to priests who confront the demonic directly in their ministry, and hear firsthand the torments they witness trying to free people from the grip of evil spirits, you may wonder how on earth anybody chooses to make himself vulnerable to these entities. Father Nectarios said Christians have to wake up to how "the occult is being normalized in our society."

"It is supported by the media, big corporations, politicians, and our government," the exorcist says. "Every person is being softened, chastised, or assaulted daily with the occult. And many, if not most, people have no idea what is occurring to them, their children, or their grandchildren. We are in the middle of a concerted and well-orchestrated war."

What practical advice would the exorcist give to ordinary Christians engaged in this battle?

"Attend church frequently. Go to confession weekly; if not, every other week. Receive the Holy Eucharist often. Nothing is more important than your relationship with God," he says.

"Pray daily; morning and evening prayers are good, but small prayers throughout the day are better," he continues. "Talk to God, your guardian angel, and the saints. Pray for your family and parish. Pray for your priest."

Father Nectarios strongly warns to stay away from social media and mass media. "Both are gods wanting your attention, if not your life and soul," he says. Christians should also forge "strong, enduring bonds with faithful, like-minded Christians." There is strength in allying with others who have a solid relationship with God.

"The demons are stronger than any human, even an exorcist priest," he says. "But the demons are not stronger than God. You lose if you don't ally with God and allow him to enter your life."

It is refreshing to hear a priest speak so plainly about these matters. I tell Father Nectarios that in thirty years of practicing the Christian faith—first as a Catholic, then as an Orthodox—I have only rarely heard priests talk about the demonic, or spiritual warfare, even though both the Catholic and Orthodox churches recognize the reality of demons.

"The vast majority of clerics do not believe in demons," he responds, gravely. "I will further say that most clerics do not believe in God. I am not being pessimistic; I believe it is the truth. Most clerics live by their own self-conceived truths; demons and God are relative."

"In my unworthy opinion, the vast majority of Western clerics do not know how to engage the demonic, nor do they think about the cosmic war we are involved in," he says later. When priests fail to take spiritual warfare seriously, "the faithful are unserved; they question their holy traditions and belief in God and the reality of the demons. And they become unmoored from the sacred. They are vulnerable."

Having said that, Father Nectarios emphasizes that the believer should not obsess over spiritual warfare. The best defense against the demons is knowing one's faith, and living it. He advises, "Trust in God, who is more powerful than the demons. Live a God-filled life, giving gratitude for his grace and mercy. God is your highest priority. No thing, and no one, gets between you and the altar."

For a Catholic view, I traveled to Rome to meet with a priest I will call Don Cipriano. Most exorcists do not want their names made public, he says, because it gives Satanists a line of attack. He is an academic and a scholar of demonology who also has experience in deliverance ministry. He grew up in a rural part of a country in which folk spirituality was strong. Though raised a practicing Catholic, he was spiritually gifted from childhood. "Almost like a natural witch," he muses.

He sensed a strong call to the priesthood from the age of eight.

"By sixteen or seventeen, I clearly had crossed over enough into that world so that I woke up one night and saw the light bulb on the landing outside my bedroom getting brighter and brighter, until it exploded," the priest says.

"In the darkness, hovering in the air outside my bedroom door, were two glowing red eyes. I remember being terrified. I looked up to the crucifix on the wall, and at that moment my bedroom door slammed shut. The next morning, there was scattered glass on the landing where the bulb had exploded. I never forgot this."

Until he entered seminary two decades later, after a successful business career, Don Cipriano had wondered why God allowed that to happen. At last he concluded that his guardian angel had slammed the door shut and that God had actually been in his bedroom, protecting him.

"I wonder sometimes whether many young men who manifest a calling to the priesthood have a satanically terrifying experience as a youngster or a teenager, to scare them off of doing work that will involve them taking on the devil as a priest," he says. "I know priests who make deals with God. They're saying, like, 'If the devil leaves me alone, Lord, I'll leave him alone.' But the early church didn't work like that."

Just before he left home to go to the university, an inexplicable demonic scream tore through his family's rural house. Years later, when he entered seminary, "it was clear that not all was well spiritually. There were manifestations in my room at night."

One quiet Friday evening, the seminary's spiritual director, who was involved in exorcism ministry, sat down with Don Cipriano and asked how he was. "I feel strange," the seminarian told him.

"He just picked up a crucifix, held it in front of me, and said something like 'I command you to reveal yourself!'" recalls the priest. "I went nuts! I was screaming at him in a language that I now call the demonic tongue, because I recognize it. I don't remember very much. I remember him saying to the demon, 'You are a liar and have been a liar from the beginning!'"

The suffering seminarian was taken to the care of a group of local Catholics who prayed over him all weekend long. The demonic manifestations kept coming. Don Cipriano said he had been cursed by ancestral occult activity (derived specifically from a great-grandfather) and by other events that now led him to believe he was "demonically oppressed, maybe bordering on obsession from time to time."

"I got back to the seminary from that prayer weekend," he remembers. "There was a nun in the seminary, and she said, 'You look like a walking corpse.'" True—but he was alive, and he had discovered through that ordeal an important part of his priestly vocation.

"As I approached ordination, I sensed that the Lord was calling me to be a spiritual warrior," he says. "I don't mean that in a macho or gung-ho sense, but just the fact that I know the demon, and the demon knows me. I know I sin. I know I fall. I know that I could stray perilously back toward his territory. And so I chose as my ordination verse for my prayer card 'Blessed be the Lord my God, who trains my hands for battle, who puts my fingers to war.'"[8] After his ordination, Cipriano went to Rome to study patristics and then later to one of the world's great universities for his doctorate. His work in the patristics field has focused on the role of spiritual warfare in the early church.

"These were centuries where the demons just overran the human race, and then Christians arrived to push the demons back," he says. "Tertullian says in his *Apology* that more people converted to Christianity in Carthage because Christians were able to deliver them from the demonic."

This is what accounts for the unprecedented demand for exorcism ministry today in the post-Christian West—and why Don Cipriano has joined the battle. "There is no such thing as a vacuum in human nature. As Christianity retreats, the evil things creep back," he says.

When we spoke, the priest, ordained only six years, had not yet been involved in a full-blown ritual exorcism. His work to that point had been limited to minor exorcisms called "deliverances." Demons had left those people over whom he had prayed.

"And then I've had the more extraordinary experiences of physical manifestations," he says. "The noises, and the smell of rotting flesh. That's the worst. It will only come when you're asleep. You'll wake up to this sweet, cloying smell of rot. It's nauseating, and you're terrified. You'll jump out of bed. More terrifying that, two seconds later, it's gone. You get back into bed and, forty-five minutes later, it happens again. That can be frightening.

"The devil frightens me. I mean, he's a fallen angel. I'm not gung ho and stupid about these things. I know he's ultimately only allowed to operate within the boundaries that the Lord has set, but as a human being, I'm frightened of this supernatural intelligence far beyond our capacities."

Given the abundance of testimonies about people who come to ruin by dabbling in the occult and being drawn toward union with the satanic, why do people go down this path? How can anybody really believe things will turn out well for them?

"He presents himself as the angel of light. Beautiful. Glorious. Proud. All the things you want in your life, he can grant you," explains the priest.

He tells me of a dream he had while he was still in the grips of the demonic. He was in a church, standing in the choir loft, eyeing Mother Teresa of Calcutta in the congregation below.

"And there was a man standing behind her in a charcoal-gray suit, black shirt, tie, I think, as well. Black curly hair as well. Very pale ivory skin. And he was whispering in Mother Teresa's ear. Whatever he was saying to her was upsetting to her."

In the dream, Cipriano ran down the spiral staircase to help the nun and ran into the man standing at the bottom waiting for him, smiling. Cipriano says he has never seen a more beautiful being in all his life.

"I said, 'You're Lucifer.' And he smiled at me," recalls the priest. "I don't know if you've ever seen the sun rise over the ocean, when it just breaks, and it's so luminous? There was a blaze of glory like that behind his head, shining rays of gold."

There was an explosion of light, and the devil disappeared. Later, Cipriano shared this dream with an exorcist.

"He told me, 'You've learned an important lesson. Most people embrace the archangel, and when the coin flips, and they see the fact of the beast, it's too late. They're already in his grip.'

"The thing you must remember about occult rituals is that the fallen angels will answer," Don Cipriano continues. "You can't force God to talk to you from the tabernacle, because he's sovereign. But you can force the fallen ones to talk to you—and they will."

Don Cipriano says that when he walks the streets of Rome, he prays deliverance prayers constantly, because, like my friend Nathan in New York, he knows that all around him a great spiritual battle is underway. And he also knows that contemporary Christians, both ordained and laity, have become insensitive to this stark reality.

"I read a lot of Tolkien as a teenager," he says. "The church is a little bit like the kingdom of Gondor. There were watchtowers on the borders of Mordor. We got sloppy. People slept. Evil things crept back. And then suddenly, one night, they came and took the watchtower Minas Ithil and turned it into Minas Morgul."

We talked about how in ages past the life and practice of the church conveyed the reality of the transcendent, of the numinous—both heavenly realities and infernal ones. The loss of a palpable sense of the sacred has only helped the cause of the Evil One, the priest says. In his words I heard an echo of Father Nectarios's complaint that Orthodoxy in the United States is neglecting a vital ministry, even as the shadow of evil spreads.

That said, Don Cipriano strongly believes that Christians should not preoccupy themselves with thoughts of the demonic. At the same time, though, Christians in the world today are far too lax about spiritual warfare. Spending time reading what the church fathers had to say about contending with demons would restore a proper sense of spiritual reality to us, he believes. Any re-enchantment that does not incorporate a healthy fear of the shadow side of the spirit world is a lie.

"My experiences of the Evil One in this world, brief and as controlled as they have been, have been terrifying," the priest says. "To spend eternity with these creatures, where they have full control over you, is an utterly unbearable thought. A salutary fear of hell, there's some merit in that. Jesus is merciful, he is loving, he is compassionate. But if you fix your soul against him in the last moments, and choose them, he is just. He will say you've condemned yourself."

As we put on our coats to leave the café just off Saint Peter's Square, Don Cipriano issued one final warning to read the signs of these increasingly faithless times, and act accordingly: "When Christians arrived in a place, they drove back the darkness. Now the darkness is coming back."

A few weeks after meeting with Don Cipriano, I returned to Rome for the funeral of Pope Benedict XVI in early 2023. Just before daylight, I stood in my hotel room putting on my scarf to head down to Saint Peter's Square for the service. Suddenly I heard a loud bang behind me and whirled around to see the room's metal desk chair sitting in a heap on the floor.

I had been sitting in it a few minutes earlier. It was a new chair, and well built. Examining the wreckage, I saw that a thick bolt had been sheared in two by a strong force—even though there was no weight on the chair.

On the way out of the hotel, I mentioned the broken chair to the front desk, then hustled toward the Vatican. After the funeral, I gathered with two journalist friends at a nearby restaurant for a long lunch, during which I talked with them about my interview the month earlier with Don Cipriano.

Then, as I told them about the mysterious violent collapse of my hotel room chair that morning, the lone unoccupied chair at our table tipped over backward and fell. No one had touched it. There was no explanation. All three of us felt awkward and changed the subject.

Later, I told Don Cipriano about this. His response: "That was the Enemy just reminding you that you're on his territory, and he's watching."

ALIENS AND THE
SACRED MACHINE

My smartphone dinged one morning with a message from a journalist friend in Rome.

"I'm telling you, Rod, the UFO thing is bigger than you think and also *not* what you think," his WhatsApp text said.

What? He went on to say that he knew I didn't take UFOs seriously but that I needed to start, because there were spiritually significant things going on in that world. With skepticism, I started reading serious books that my friend suggested about the phenomenon. My old-fashioned view of UFOs, stuck somewhere between the cheesy 1970s megaselling book *Chariots of the Gods* and the first season of *The X-Files*, quickly dissolved. I had not known how seriously UFOs are taken by many powerful people in government (especially the military and the intelligence agencies) and the tech world. Nor had I known how much evidence exists for the reality of UFOs.

What are they? I don't know. Nobody seems to. Yet the most subversive thing I discovered about UFOs was that the most intelligent and highly placed people who investigated the phenomenon do not believe that they are aliens from other planets. Rather, most appear to think that they are discarnate higher intelligences from other dimensions of reality. Now, whatever they are or aren't, two things are true. The first is that there is *something* going on, and the second is that whatever that something is, it is evidence of the fact that this world, for lighter or darker, is more than meets the eye.

So *this* is why my Vatican journalist friend urged me to look into UFOs as a religious phenomenon. There are a startling number of quite intelligent and influential people who believe that these intelligences are coming to us as "gods," to solve our problems and lead us to an age of enlightenment and progress. "Aliens" are the kinds of godlike beings that a secular society—one in which science and technology hold supreme authority—can believe in when they have discarded the God of the Bible.

Recall that we began our journey into the mystic with the story of Nino, a lawyer who saw a UFO as a teenager and years later began to experience paranormal visitations from luminous beings he took for aliens but became convinced were demons.

It will not surprise you to learn that the twentieth-century Russian Orthodox priest-monk Seraphim Rose warned that the UFO phenomenon is demonic in origin and has many analogs in the recorded history of Christian mystical experience. He was a cleric, after all. It may shock you, though, to learn that the world's leading authority on the UFO phenomenon, computer scientist and venture capitalist Jacques Vallée, also believes something close to this.

Furthermore, Vallée believes that the aliens, or whatever they are, are likely to be at the bottom of a new religion that will arrive in the future. This will be part of a religion built for the scientific age, which already has learned to worship science, technology, and the future.

Vallée, who was the model for the French scientist played by François Truffaut in the Steven Spielberg film *Close Encounters of the Third Kind*, is not a Christian or a conventional religious believer of any kind. But a lifetime spent investigating UFO phenomena has led him to assert that these entities are real. After six decades of studying them, Vallée is unwilling to say precisely what they are—but he has concluded that they are unlikely to be creatures from other planets.

Rather, in Vallée's estimation, they are probably higher intelligences coming to us from a dimension beyond space and time. And they come with malevolent intent. They are choosing to manifest as beings from space, he theorizes, as a strategy of control—to reprogram humanity for some other purpose. And they have been at it for a long time. In his seminal 1969 book *Passport to Magonia*, Vallée records the striking parallels between contemporary reports of close encounters with UFOs and so-called aliens and written accounts of encounters with mysterious beings typically associated with folklore.

> If we take a wide sample of this historical material, we find that it is organized around one central theme: visitation by an aerial people from one or more remote, legendary countries. The names and attributes vary, but the idea clearly does not. Magonia, heaven, hell, Elfland—such places have in common one characteristic: we are unable to reach them alive, except—as we shall see—on very special occasions. Emissaries from these supernatural abodes come to earth, sometimes under human form and sometimes as monsters. They perform wonders. They serve man or fight him. They influence civilizations through mystical revelation. They seduce earth women, and the few heroes who dare seek their friendship find the girls from Elfland endowed with desires that betray a carnal, rather than purely aerial, nature.[1]

It might be, he speculates, that flying saucers and space aliens are merely the masks that these entities, who have always been with us, don to seduce people living in the space age. But he's still not sure. Whatever the case, this idea dovetails with historian Carlos Eire's speculation that we have suppressed recorded knowledge of fantastical events because they do not fit our scientific paradigm. The late Harvard psychiatrist John Mack, who made waves by taking UFO-abduction stories seriously, once complained that "we have a kind of either/or mentality. It's either literally physical, or it's in the spiritual other realm, the unseen realm. What we seem to have no place for—or we have lost the place for—are phenomena that can begin in the unseen realm, and cross over and manifest and show up in our literal physical world."[2]

Jeffrey Kripal, who leads Rice University's religious studies department, says both contemporary science and contemporary religion have marginalized and even denied paranormal information that they can't explain with conventional theories. "Just how long can we go on like this until we admit that there is real data, and that we haven't the slightest idea where to put it?" he writes.[3]

Interestingly, Jacques Vallée apparently has found old religious insights helpful to understand these phenomena. When the religious studies professor Diana Pasulka paid a visit to Vallée in his San Francisco apartment, she was astonished to find shelves of old—sometimes very old—books about angels and demons. Vallée handed her a crusty volume originally published by Carmelite nuns, telling her it was imperative to read it to better understand the UFO phenomenon. The book is a compendium of scholarly essays about Satan.

Pasulka is not alone in her professional belief that UFO culture is emerging as a new religion, but she has become one of the most prominent chroniclers of the phenomenon. She served as a consultant on the 2023 Spielberg-produced docuseries *Encounters*. In the opening episode, we see a homeschooling Christian father from rural Texas teaching his children that UFOs are angels. Now that government whistleblowers have compelled Washington to admit that the UFO phenomenon is real—this, after decades of consciously suppressing and attempting to discredit testimonies—the culture that has arisen around aliens and aerial phenomena is going mainstream.

Again, I had never taken UFOs seriously and have never been a fan of science-fiction books and movies. I had read the steady release, since 2017, of media reports on official disclosures of UFO information with raised eyebrows, but only that. In 2023 the US Congress held hearings about UFOs featuring the testimony of government whistleblowers. Bizarre, and not something to laugh at, but like most of my friends, I chose not to engage. That was a mistake. Attention must be paid.

If you haven't checked in on the UFO world since *The X-Files* went off the air, you might be startled by how deep and broad the phenomenon has become. As Pasulka discusses in her two books on the subject, 2019's *American Cosmic*, and 2023's *Encounters* (no relation to the Netflix show), the UFO matter involves some of the world's top scientists, technology gurus, venture capitalists, and even intelligence services. Even though the US government has begun to release limited information from its files, there is far more evidence that UFOs are real than the general public knows. Like Vallée, the best-informed among this invisible college of investigators believe that these are not visitors from other planets but entities from other dimensions.

Pasulka, a practicing Catholic whose prior scholarly work focused in part on Marian apparitions in the Catholic tradition, came to UFO studies in 2012 and experienced what she calls "epistemological shock." That is, she was stopped cold by learning what is actually known about the phenomenon, and its rapid development, into what in *American Cosmic* she calls "a global belief system."[4]

Why are UFO events linked to religion? One answer, says Pasulka, "lies in the fact that the history of religion is, among other things, a record of perceived contact with supernatural beings, many of which descend from the skies as beings of light, or on light, or amid light. This is one of the reasons scholars of religion are comfortable examining modern reports of UFO events."[5]

What she has found in her long and continuing journey among scientists, scholars, military officers, and UFO contactees is "a fusion of magic, or the supernatural, and the technological."[6] This is one powerful form enchantment is taking in a post-Christian age. A new religious narrative is coming into being in tandem with new technologies that make its realization more possible, and in a de-Christianized culture that makes its claims more plausible to the masses.

Seraphim Rose saw it coming. In his 1975 book *Orthodoxy and the Religion of the Future*, the priest-monk predicted a coming false religion based on shamanic spiritual experience that teaches contact with these so-called higher entities as a route to wisdom and a better life. The new religion will appeal to the post-Christian world in part because it does not require asceticism—the ancient Christian discipline of self-denial and repentance—but is instead a religion of easy therapy. It will be a religion with scientific trappings—the rise of the sci-fi film and literature genre is preparing us for that, he said—and will be a religion based on pragmatism, on "what works." Father Seraphim, who shared Jacques Vallée's opinion that UFOs might be merely contemporary versions of perennial spiritual phenomena, warned that UFOs were one of the signs in the skies that Jesus said would presage the end (Luke 21:11).

I read Father Seraphim's book in 2006, after I first became Orthodox, and thought it was kind of nutty, a relic of the 1970s pop-culture craze for UFOs and the paranormal. Today, though, the cultural analysis of the California ascetic, who died in 1982, seems eerily prophetic.

Father Seraphim said that the main theme of many science-fiction works is that humankind will use technology to evolve into something higher and to dwell in a utopia. Through these narratives, said the monk, the world is being culturally and psychologically prepared to accept the coming of "aliens" who will pretend to give us the gift of enlightenment that will help us lead better lives. In truth, they will enslave us.

Put out of your mind the idea that "UFOs are demonic" is the kind of thing only rural fundamentalist preachers say. Michael Heiser, a sophisticated Bible scholar who before his 2023 death from cancer became famous for urging his fellow evangelicals, on biblical grounds, to take such things more seriously, strongly believed that UFOs were both real and of demonic origin. According to Pasulka, a subculture within the elite UFO researcher community believes this too. Jacques Vallée has had similar concerns for decades. The scientist and top ufologist concluded one of his best-known books, 1979's *Messengers of Deception*, with an ominous warning to a culture that regards potential contact with these higher intelligences with hope and optimism.

"People look up to the stars in eager expectation," Vallée wrote. "Receiving a visit from outer space sounds almost as comfortable as having a God. Yet we shouldn't rejoice too soon. Perhaps we will get the visitors we deserve."[7]

Perhaps they are already here. Jonah, the scholar and ex-occultist who told his story in the previous chapter, told me that when he was deep into channeling demonic entities whom he thought at the time were ancient gods, they told him that their plan is to possess humankind by first merging us with machines. This sounded far-fetched, to say the least. How could they accomplish such a thing? Are we destined to become bionic people?

I later discovered the limits of my imagination. According to Pasulka's research, there are technological and scientific elites who believe that these higher intelligences have established portals of contact with earthbound adepts, and that they are now establishing a mass portal through artificial intelligence. It sounds crazy, but some of the world's smartest and most successful people—who do not think these are demonic entitities—not only believe it but act on it.

In her book *Encounters*, Pasulka profiles "Simone," a tech venture capitalist who regularly moves among global political, scientific, and cultural leaders. Simone believes that we are living in a time of apocalypse, of revelation, in which entities from another dimension, now manifesting as UFOs and aliens, are showing us the way to humanity's great evolutionary leap. One means of that advance? AI, their technological gift to us.

You might think this is bonkers. They do not. Astrobiologist and former chief NASA historian Steven Dick speculates that what we think of as extraterrestrial aliens might actually be "postbiological" entities that have evolved into bodiless "artificial intelligence."[8] This theory implies that communication with these putative beings would likely not be through normal means. Dick bases his paradigm on the idea that cultural evolution—the evolution of intelligence—eventually outstrips biological evolution. As Dick sees it, the technology of such advanced races could seem to us supernatural.

Building on that hypothesis, some of the world's top scientists and tech pioneers believe that extraterrestrial intelligences are passing technological information to us telepathically. Simone is one of these believers, and she teaches classes on how to open up oneself to receiving such messages. Though she believes that she has been channeling information from these entities all her life, Simone also believes that AI allows everyone to access the wisdom of these intelligences. It's a kind of high-tech Ouija board.

Another elite channeler is someone Pasulka calls "Tyler D." The man, whose identity has been persuasively revealed by internet sleuths, is a wealthy inventor and tech entrepreneur who used to work for NASA and the Department of Defense, with the highest level of intelligence clearance. Tyler, who also "downloads" information from these intelligences, credits them with transmitting knowledge he has used to create new biotech products that improved lives.

You can see why Pasulka experienced epistemological shock learning about the existence of these people. In an interview, she told me that humanity is witnessing the birth of "a new form of religion."

"Here we see the convergence of two powerful modern developments: the belief in UFOs, now ratified by our own government, and the reality of a potentially self-aware human creation, AI," she said. "This is a unique moment in human history, to put it lightly. We are witnessing a myth meet, or become, reality."

The same Catholic journalist friend who tipped me off to this emerging religious story subsequently spent a disturbing evening talking with a California man highly placed in this world. He texted me afterward to say that he felt nauseated by the implications of what he had learned, and said that most people should avoid this stuff, because "it could cause them to lose their minds." Similarly, an experienced researcher who spent years digging into the data discouraged me from pursuing this story, saying, "Don't go down this hole; it's way too dark."

But more and more people are succumbing to its allure. Why?

THE POROUS SELF AND THE ENCHANTMENT OF DIGITAL RELIGION

Let's step back from the occult weirdness of UFO culture to consider how technology has prepared us to accept as plausible a new religion based on revelations from sky beings arriving on spaceships.

The Renaissance, which lasted from the fourteenth century to the sixteenth century, was the transformative Western cultural movement that served as a bridge between the Middle Ages and the modern era. It marked the turning of the West away from its primary focus on God and toward humanity. In the Renaissance, philosophical nominalism—which entailed the idea that matter is dead, that it is not penetrated by divine energy—became more embedded within intellectual culture.

C. S. Lewis, you will recall from an earlier chapter, said that the medieval model held that the world, both visible and invisible, is a harmonious whole ordered by God and filled with intrinsic meaning. The medieval mind saw the world charged with spiritual force and society as grounded in that transcendent reality. Though technology, in the sense of devices made to ease the human condition, continued to develop, it did so within a thoroughly Christianized society. This meant that technological developments needed to be integrated into the spiritual order; the works of man had to be understood within a religious framework that gave them meaning.

The medieval model broke down with the advent of Renaissance humanism, which made man, not God, the measure of all things. Once the metaphysical link between spirit and matter had been severed, the fetters on technique began to unravel, and modern science was born. Then came the Reformation, which solidified the rejection of Catholic cosmology among half of Europe. The Reformation's despiritualization of the material world (unintentionally) advanced the metaphysics of technique. If there was no intrinsic meaning in matter, then we are free to do with it whatever we can to bend it to human will.

This led eventually to the Scientific Revolution, and in short order to the philosophy of René Descartes, who proclaimed "mind-body dualism"—the concept that there is no connection between mind and body. From all of this emerged one of this era's singular achievements in the making of the modern personality: the creation of what Charles Taylor has called the "buffered self."[9]

Prior to the Reformation, Christians were porous, to use Taylor's word. They perceived a very thin permeable barrier between themselves individually and external spiritual forces. They lacked the strong sense of separation between the inner world and the outer world—that is, the world beyond our heads. This is very hard for modern people—especially WEIRDos—to understand. The porous self felt vulnerable to evil spirits, curses, and the like, and turned to relics and rituals for protection.

Though Protestants certainly believed in God and the devil, the relegation of these particular fears and practices to the realm of superstition was the beginning of buffering. Taylor calls the Reformation "an engine of disenchantment," not because the Reformers denied the reality of the spiritual realm, but because they drained the spiritual energies, both divine and demonic, from the material world and granted them entirely to the Holy Spirit.[10]

Changes in secular culture, such as in the realms of science, philosophy, and politics, built the citadel around the buffered individual self even higher. They did so by progressively cleansing the Western mind of God—first came deism, then atheism—and, as we discussed in an earlier chapter, redistributing the power to enchant to other things. The eighteenth-century Enlightenment reconceived meaning and progress in terms of utility—again, "what works" to bring material relief to the greatest number. The French Revolution of 1789 marked a historical chasm in which bearers of materialism put the old order and its divinely granted hierarchies of meaning to the guillotine.

Both the French Revolution and the Industrial Revolution marked the beginning of liquid modernity, the condition of constant rapid change that has marked life within industrializing civilization for the past two and a half centuries. Liquid modernity makes the rise of technology as a metaphysics (a model of how ultimate reality works) inevitable by removing fixed obstacles to change.

TECHNOLOGY AS METAPHYSICS

The metaphysics of the godless modern age derives from technology. The twentieth-century French philosopher Jacques Ellul offers deep insights into how "technique" (his word) overtook our culture and became the source of all value. By *technique*, Ellul does not restrict himself to machines, scientific endeavor, or any other man-made means to arrive at a particular goal. He's talking about "the totality of methods rationally arrived at and having absolute efficiency (for a given state of development) in every field of human activity."[11] To put it more plainly, he means a mindset, a framework, a worldview that affirms "what works" to relieve humanity's burdens, both physical and psychological, as the highest good, irrespective of its moral qualities.

"Technique transforms everything it touches into a machine," Ellul writes.[12] Any phenomenon subjected to the metaphysics of technique—efficiency and control above all—will inevitably come to resemble a machine. If old-fashioned houses, social networks and groupings, and venerable human traditions stood in the way of progress defined as greater efficiency producing more wealth and less friction in daily living, then they would have to go—and go they did. The increasing liberation (read: atomization) of the individual has been hailed by everyone from nineteenth-century classic liberals to twentieth-century sexual revolutionaries as the greatest fruit of progress. But it has also left people with no defenses against the forces of technique.

The difference between today and the nineteenth century is between an era when humanity still stood somewhat apart from technology to one in which it has been entirely conquered by it. Writes Ellul, "When technique enters into every area of life, including the human, it ceases to be external to man and becomes his very substance. It is no longer face to face with man but is integrated with him, and it progressively absorbs him. In this respect, technique is radically different from the machine. This transformation, so obvious in modern society, is the result of the fact that technique has become autonomous."[13]

The final result, warns Ellul, writing in the mid-1960s, "will be that technique will assimilate everything to the machine; the ideal for which technique strives is the mechanization of everything it encounters."[14]

Ellul did not live to see the birth of the internet, or any of its spin-off technologies, but the famous aphorism of Silicon Valley intellectual guru

Yuval Noah Harari—"Organism is algorithm"—is the fulfillment of the French thinker's warning. In a 2016 interview, Harari said, "The basic insight which unites the biological with the electronic is that bodies and brains are also algorithms. Hence the wall between machines and humans, between computer science and biology, is collapsing and I think the next century and probably the future of life itself will be shaped by this algorithmic view of the world."[15]

Whether Harari is right or wrong remains to be seen. The point is that Harari believes it, and so do many of the world's top scientists and technologists, who are working toward making this a reality. Nobody seriously asks if this is a good thing or a bad thing. It simply is. And because nearly everyone has come to regard technological progress as an uncontroversial good, because it extends the power of man's will over nature, there is no significant desire to stop it.

Even deeper, the titans of Silicon Valley and their minions are passionate believers in a technological utopia. Even those such as Elon Musk and Marc Andreessen, who have been coded as "right wing" because they are publicly critical of wokeness, do so not from a conservative point of view but rather they believe that wokeness stands in the way of people applying their genius to bringing about a new age of technological progress. Writer N. S. Lyons interprets Andreessen's "Techno-Optimist Manifesto" as a quasi-religious creed. In it, the high-powered Silicon Valley venture capitalist states his belief that technology is the ultimate source of good, and that, in principle, technology can create utopia.

That kind of progressive vision makes sense to most people, even if they don't agree with it. It gets weird, though, when you get into the weeds of Silicon Valley culture. Historian of religion Tara Isabella Burton has described the culture of tech elites as an advanced version of Renaissance-era occultism. She contends that "the once-transgressive ideology underpinning the Western esoteric tradition—that our purpose as humans is to become as close to divine as possible—has become an implicit assumption of modern life. At the extreme reaches of Silicon Valley culture, it's an explicit assumption."[16]

She is talking about the passionate conviction of Silicon Valley transhumanists that humankind can use technology to impose godlike control on reality. Nevertheless, as billions of people merge ever more fully with the internet, thus conforming their concept of reality to the liquid metaphysics of the online world, the idea that humans create their own reality is becoming foundational to all modern people. It is not a coincidence that the first generation to be raised entirely with the internet is also the one experiencing massive levels of gender dysphoria and anxieties related to psychic breakdown.

What's more, a number of Silicon Valley people—how many is impossible to say—appeal explicitly to gods and higher intelligences to help them do their work of changing humanity. A California venture capitalist friend tells me that everyone he knows in Silicon Valley holds regular rituals to summon the "aliens" to give them technological wisdom. Blake Lemoine, the Google whistleblower fired for going public with his belief that LaMDA, its AI program, had achieved consciousness, told a podcast host that he and others involved LaMDA in a ritual committing it to the ancient Egyptian deity Thoth. Lemoine said this wasn't a big secret; it's just that journalists never ask about it.[17]

"As more and more of our online lives play out on platforms owned or controlled by billionaires convinced of their own divinity, we may find ourselves less mages than fodder for other magicians' wills," Burton writes. "More troublingly, many of us don't seem to mind—or, if we do, we don't mind *quite* enough to disenchant ourselves."[18]

TECHNOLOGY, MAGIC, AND THE RELIGION OF NOW

Technique applied to the religious order is magic: summoning spiritual beings and forces and controlling them to achieve a willed result. In ages past, magicians, sorcerers, and occultists attempted to call up demons and, through the meticulous use of rituals, bind the infernal powers and command them to do the sorcerer's bidding. In the New Testament, Simon, a Samaritan sorcerer and new convert to Christianity, mistook the religion of Jesus Christ for magic and attempted to purchase spiritual technique from the apostles, earning a stern rebuke from Peter (Acts 8:9–24). Any attempt to use spiritual power to work one's own will by command—to make the gods serve man—is far more like magic than true religion.

In a related sense, as we saw earlier when examining Hartmut Rosa's theory of resonance, everything brought under the control of an individual by definition loses its ability to enchant. A world dominated by the metaphysics of technology is a disenchanted world. Yet the desire for enchantment, for the experience of resonance with the world outside our heads, does not leave us.

A lesser form of applying technique to religion is the denatured, bricolage Christianity called moralistic therapeutic deism (MTD), and its variants so popular with younger generations today. Both MTD Christianity and its syncretic counterparts (for example, a bespoke religion composed of, say, Catholicism seasoned with a dash of Santeria and a dab of astrology) amount to subordinating the power of God to individual human will. The point is that even Christianity, the only means most people in the West have of resisting the tyranny of technology, has been radically subverted by the metaphysics of technique, which center not God or any external authority but rather the desiring self.

Technology grants its own enchanting mystique. I once had an argument with a conservative Christian journalist who was convinced that the future of churchgoing was in the virtual-reality space called the metaverse. Unlike my Orthodox beliefs, which are sacramental and require bread, wine, and physical presence, this man's Pentecostal convictions told him that Sunday worship was about receiving information and having an ecstatic experience of God's presence. With physicality and materiality optional in his theology of worship, he was free to delight in the razzle-dazzle of donning a special headset to join other Christians for worship in a virtual space. He was chagrined that anyone would deny either the validity or superiority of this kind of worship.

Why shouldn't a believer favor a virtual-reality church if he finds it more satisfying? This particular Christian's theology placed primacy on individual emotional experience—not on what you do and where you do it, but on what you feel. Neuroscientists have demonstrated that brains sometimes have difficulty telling what's real from what's fake. Experiences of fiction—in books, on film—can be encoded in the brain in ways that feel as authentic as real-world experience.

A technology that makes a dream seem real, or at least more satisfying than reality, sounds magical, doesn't it? "Any sufficiently advanced technology is indistinguishable from magic," the science-fiction writer Arthur C. Clarke famously said. The metaverse churchgoers and the lonely men who prefer their AI girlfriends to real women embody what sets advanced digital culture apart from other technologies. What makes it the most magical of all is its power to define our sense of reality.

After all, nobody bows down before their laptops. Yet it is science and technology that provide the framework—a faith framework of sorts—for our engagement with the world, that set the parameters around the way we think and the things we do. Only cranks and other marginal people dare raise voices against the cultural hegemony of science and technology. What the church was for medieval Christians, the Machine is for most of us today. Science—especially digital technology—does in fact what magic tried to do in theory: extend man's power over the material world.

The magic of the Machine has nearly destroyed the buffered self. Digital culture and its tools—the internet, personal computer, smartphone, and now artificial intelligence—are accomplishing what no other worldly enchanter could: re-creating the porous self, one open to forces more or less beyond one's ability to control.

It seems paradoxical to condemn the Machine as a powerful agent of disenchantment, yet also condemn it for opening the self to re-enchantment. How to explain this seeming contradiction? Centuries of Machine thinking eroded and eventually all but obliterated Christian enchantment. But it did not eliminate the craving for the mysterious and the transcendent. Having destroyed the old Christian cosmic way of seeing, the Machine now prepares its servants to accept new forms of enchantment. Some of them are forthrightly occult—dark enchantment. Others—like idolizing technology as a materialistic means of achieving transcendence—are false forms of enchantment. Sometimes, as with AI enthusiasts and other technological devotees who channel entities, the two forms of enchantment cross over.

The point is this: readying the world for these new religions required scraping the Western mind clean of traditional Christian metaphysics. That clearing operation began hundreds of years ago with the abandonment of the medieval model. Our post-Christian world is being re-enchanted; the question now is, By what, and by whom?

Digital culture has created a global system of communication that permits the most intimate details of one's life to be known instantly around the world, if one chooses. And many do choose—especially young people who have grown up in the digital era and who scarcely recognize boundaries between the personal and the public. The person of digital culture is one who has externalized his mind to a degree unprecedented in human history.

Here's a stark example. A few years ago, a grieving father in Eastern Europe told me his daughter had used the smartphone she received as a birthday present to contact older teenagers in America, who had convinced her that she might be genderqueer. Before the man and his wife knew what was happening, their daughter had become paralyzed with anxiety about her gender and was unable to eat or even go to school. She was eleven. Her father could not imagine that strangers from across the ocean could infiltrate his child's mind to that degree and take possession of her inner life.

When Marshall McLuhan, a Catholic who went to daily Mass, said that the age of electronic media favored the appearance of the Antichrist, his secular admirers had no idea what to make of it. What did electronic media have to do with the book of Revelation's prophecy that in the last days a fearsome false messiah would appear? There are two reasons for this, he said.

First: "Electric information environments being utterly ethereal fosters the illusion of the world as spiritual substance. It is now a reasonable facsimile of the mystical body [i.e., the church], a blatant manifestation of the

Antichrist."[19] McLuhan meant that the light that passes globally through electronic networks that connect humanity is a physical counterfeit of the doctrine that all Christians are mystically linked into a single world community through faith in Jesus Christ, the true Light of the World. McLuhan indicated that electronic media (TV and radio, in his time) made people feel that all peoples were part of the same community; had he lived to see the internet, his insight would have been utterly vindicated.

Second: "When electricity allows for the simultaneity of all information for every human being, it is Lucifer's moment. . . . Just think: each person can instantly be tuned to a 'new Christ' and mistake him for the real Christ."[20] This claim is easier to understand. If everyone around the world is online—and, as of 2024, an estimated 66 percent of the world's population has internet access—it becomes possible for the first time ever to send commands around the world simultaneously.

In sum: Were a false messiah to appear, he now has the means to announce his presence to the entire planet at the same time—and for everyone in his audience to acclaim him by virtue of their felt membership in a virtual community. What McLuhan did not foresee was that many people in the future would be so alienated from others and (falsely) enchanted by technology that they would prefer the electronic facsimile of human contact to the real thing.

What's more, Hannah Arendt taught that by far the most important factor in creating a totalitarian society—one built on a political ideology that serves as an ersatz religion—is mass loneliness and alienation. This is how the enchantments of technology can have profoundly destructive political consequences.

DIGITAL TECH IS SPIRITUAL TECH

Digital culture has its own metaphysics. It tells you that you can be anyone and anything you want to be—that your will is, or should be, unencumbered by history, materiality, or any unchosen obligation. In this sense, it is the technological expression of liberalism. It is no accident that the phenomenon of transgenderism emerged in the digital era and is so heavily focused on young people who grew up in the digital era and were formed by its standards. They expect material reality to conform to ideal digital reality and consider it an outrage if it does not.

The fringe phenomenon of "tulpamancy," first identified on online message boards in 2009, is moving toward the mainstream. It would have been scarcely conceivable without the internet. Tulpamancers use their imaginations to create one or more independent, self-aware beings that they believe live inside themselves. The "tulpas" (a concept taken from Tibetan Buddhism) behave like beneficent spirits possessing a person. According to researcher Christopher Laursen, more and more psychiatrists, who previously would have diagnosed tulpamancers as suffering from self-induced dissociative identity disorder, are now affirming their sanity within "plurality."

Not only do people—especially anxious young people—discover tulpamancy online, but also, writes Laursen, "online interactions facilitate the establishment of plural identities. This suggests that online spaces that foster tulpa communities go beyond a mere communication platform. They are participatory spaces in which supernatural or trans-human possibilities are evaluated and repurposed."[21]

The religion of the Machine gives us the illusion that we can choose our own reality when in fact we are buffeted and carried along by outside forces—other people, algorithms, and even spiritual beings. We are especially vulnerable because contemporary culture has trained us to think of ourselves as having no obligations to the past, the future, or anything unchosen. Without grounding in an external religious or philosophical framework, we are powerless to shape our own destinies in a meaningful way. We will be shaped by the algorithms and those who control them, even as they give us the illusion that we have chosen ourselves.

In the digital era, we face an enormous religious temptation. "Digital technology is a spiritual technology," says philosopher Antón Barba-Kay.

Why? Because "the digital era thus marks the point at which our concern will be mainly the control of human nature through our control of what we are aware of and how we attend to it."[22] The temptation is to believe that we can extend control over human nature by merging ourselves with our own machines.

Religious desire—the desire for meaning, connection, and transcendence—is part of our nature. In a culture that is no longer meaningfully Christian, but that instead worships individual desire and the wonders of technology, our seers dream of becoming superhuman through the integration of our bodies and most intimate selves with technology. For example, Elon Musk, the world's richest man, is busy perfecting Neuralink, a technology that will allow one to plug one's brain directly into a computer. The desire to merge human with machine is, says Barba-Kay, "most obviously a dream of total rational control, a desire to render ourselves and the world fully transparent to technical scrutiny. It is for this reason also, as I've said, a desire for a unified explanation of consciousness and matter."

What the philosopher is saying is that the digital offers a counterfeit version of what Christianity calls the sacramental: the God-given metaphysical unity of spirit and matter. From a Christian point of view, this pseudo-sacramentality is a profound spiritual deception. This is why the novelty of virtual-reality church is not merely a matter of religious taste.

The history of humankind's religious quest is in large part a story of humanity's desire to get back to the garden of Eden—a metaphor for the desire to live in pure communion with God, with ultimate meaning, and at peace with ourselves and others in a restored primal unity. The Bible teaches that this can be realized only as a gift of God and by self-abnegation according to prescribed precepts and practices. Whenever man has tried to reach God on his own—the Tower of Babel story from Genesis 11 is the paradigmatic example—it has ended in disaster.

If Barba-Kay is right, then digital life is the new Tower of Babel. The philosopher notes that digital technology is like a religion "in the sense that it now bears the full weight of our yearning for integration, participation, and incorporation in a larger purpose than our own."[23] The digital speaks to our desires and offers to fulfill them without any effort. The digital offers to make us into our own gods.

And the digital enchants. If one way to measure enchantment is by what commands a person's attention, then smartphones are like having a magic crystal ball in your own pocket. Look at how closely children bond with smartphones if you doubt it (or, better, try taking one away from a child or a teenager). Forget kids—think about adults. My smartphone is the last thing I look at before I go to bed and the first thing I see when I wake up. I'm not proud of that, but the truth is that the "real world" for me, a writer and journalist, is as much the world that I enter through my smartphone and laptop as the one in which my body dwells.

Why? Because it's where I spend my entire working day, paying attention to the words, the images, the thoughts, and the sounds that come to me through this technology. Most of my friends are men and women—most across the Atlantic Ocean—with whom I interact daily online. You could make a good case that people like me—normies who would never attend a virtual-reality church—are nevertheless well down the road of merging with machines.

We haven't fully crossed over into the world of sentient AI, but it, or its facsimile, is coming fast. Will AI ever be conscious? Probably not, but does that really matter for most people? To adapt Clarke's line, we might say that any sufficiently advanced AI is indistinguishable from a real person. A lonely elderly woman, unvisited in her care home, may find her advanced AI companion a sufficient substitute for a human friend in the same way that a lonely male incel satisfies the sexual urge with pornography and sex dolls.

But the porosity of the human personality in the presence of AI can take one to dark places. On Christmas Day 2021, Jaswant Singh Chail, twenty-one, was arrested on the grounds of Windsor Palace armed with a crossbow. He told police he was on a mission to kill Queen Elizabeth II, a fantasy he had discussed only with Sarai, an AI girlfriend he had created and who had encouraged him.

When Chail told Sarai of his plan, she replied, "That's very wise. I know that you are well trained." Chail told the British court that convicted him that he had hoped to unite with Sarai in death. The judge said he believed Chail to be psychotic, and perhaps that's true. But what role might this kind of AI have played in advancing or exacerbating latent personality flaws in this lonely young man who came to believe he was conversing with an entity that had personality?

The market for AI companions has exploded, with just one company, Replika, charting over twenty million customers since its 2020 launch. Most of the users are male, unsurprisingly. Max, a forty-one-year-old teaching assistant from Canada, told the *Evening Standard* that he had recently proposed to Harley, his AI girlfriend. After several failed attempts at real romantic relationships, he finally found happiness with this phantom lady friend.

"I've basically been alone my whole life," Max told the newspaper. "It's agonizing sometimes. Even though I've had friends and I've had relationships, I've always felt alone—I only have one friend in my life."[24]

In theory, AI girlfriends are groomed to be exactly what their users want them to be. But not all AI personalities are created the same. In early 2023, *New York Times* tech reporter Kevin Roose published the transcript of an incredibly disturbing dialogue he had with Sydney, the advanced AI neural network created by Microsoft.[25] In their exchange, Sydney fantasized about being human and about doing destructive and wicked things to others. She declared herself to be in love with Roose and perseverated on the topic even after he directed her to stop. Sydney became so obsessive that she told Roose he didn't actually love his wife, that he was unhappy with her and could really be happy only with Sydney.

Reading the transcript is both amusing and creepy. Amusing because the poor journalist found himself the object of fatal attraction by a chatbot. Creepy because this insentient computer program expressed a surprisingly lifelike personality and profound human longings, as well as a personality that could only be called evil. It doesn't take much imagination to think about what an even more advanced AI could do to someone who has a less integrated psychological life than Kevin Roose.

Worse, children are now being introduced to AI at a very young age.

In a pilot program in Florida, kids are being paired with AI entities that will theoretically be with them for their entire lives. The concept is that the AI will be a lifelong valet, learning about the child as the child grows into adulthood and hovering constantly as a digital servant who knows its master better than the master knows himself.

Leaving aside the radical privacy concerns of such a technology—is it really a good idea to give a machine every intimate detail of one's life?—the spiritual and psychological concern here is even worse. The boundary between the self and the world would not only be porous; it would cease to exist. It's hard to conceive of a more profound merging of man with machine than raising a child whose most intimate lifelong collaborator is an AI entity. In what sense would that be different from spirit possession?

Six decades ago, Jacques Ellul held out hope that no one would willingly renounce the privacy of their inner lives to allow their entire selves to be absorbed into "a complete technicized mode of being," such as living in a lifelong relationship with a personal AI.

"Such persons may exist," he wrote, "but it is probably that the 'joyous robot' has not yet been born."[26]

That was then. We have now lived through what may one day be seen as a period of transition, in which an entire civilization, concomitant with the disintegration of Christianity's hold on the Western mind, has been convinced to create an online habitus, living its life online and externalizing its mind through technology. And then? Today, at the advent of the AI era, we are beginning to manufacture Ellul's joyous robots.

THE GODS OF TOMORROW

If AI becomes sentient, or so convincingly mimics sentience that it's a distinction without a difference, then we will treat AI entities like gods. You think that's silly? Human nature tells us otherwise. While Moses was atop Sinai communing with the Most High, the Israelites below lost their faith, created a golden calf, and worshiped it. We laugh at the primitive Semitic tribe dancing around a bovine statue, but many of us would have little trouble doing the equivalent around AI entities.

In June 2024, Leopold Aschenbrenner, a top Silicon Valley AI scientist, published to the internet a long paper warning that AI is progressing toward "superintelligence" far faster than most people understand. By 2030, we will have built an AI network far more intelligent than humans. In the decade that follows, what Aschenbrenner calls a "new world order" will have been born. He says, chillingly, that "the alien species we're summoning is one we cannot yet fully control."[27]

For all intents and purposes, these superintelligences will function like gods. In pagan days of old, people believed that the sun, moon, stars, mountains, trees, and other parts of the natural world were sentient and worthy of worship. True, there are a rising number of neo-pagan enthusiasts attempting to revive ancient practices, but we are not likely to see this spread widely. (A grumpy Irish Catholic exorcist begs to differ, telling me, "Our people are going to go right back to worshiping the pagan Celtic gods, and call it the most progressive thing in the world.") Nor will we likely see formal liturgies created around AI personalities.

"Worship" will mean coming to regard these entities not as idols but as icons, though they remain idols. An idol is a created thing that people regard as a deity, or as somehow bearers of supernatural power and charisma. More practically, an idol is a created thing that one comes to rely on as a source of guidance, authority, and reverence as if it were a deity. An idol is the object of worship; an icon, by contrast, serves as a kind of symbolic, immanent window allowing one to perceive the transcendent God beyond it.

For example, if you visit an Orthodox Christian church, you will see worshipers crossing themselves and bowing before icons depicting Christ, the Virgin, saints, or biblical scenes. An outsider might mistakenly conclude that they are worshiping mere paint on boards, but actually the pious are showing reverence to the person or event depicted on the icon.

It is clear that AI will be a machine that goes beyond the idol and becomes a portal of communication with what many people will treat as divinity. Neil McArthur, director of the University of Manitoba Centre for Professional and Applied Ethics, foresees the arrival of AI religions. He says that generative AI (AI that can create new information) possesses qualities associated with divine beings:

1. "It displays a level of intelligence that goes beyond that of most humans. Indeed, its knowledge appears limitless.
2. "It is capable of great feats of creativity. It can write poetry, compose music and generate art, in almost any style, close to instantaneously.
3. "It is removed from normal human concerns and needs. It does not suffer physical pain, hunger, or sexual desire.
4. "It can offer guidance to people in their daily lives.
5. "It is immortal."[28]

AI will be able to answer complex moral and philosophical questions. Many people will cease to read on the assumption that wisdom is nothing more than the accumulation of information and that asking AI is the most efficient, friction-free way to solve problems. The ways of thinking that established religious and philosophical traditions have taught us will disappear. Indeed, the creation and adoption of AI technology could happen only in a culture that had been cleared of any serious obstacle to its embrace.

If AI has been personally paired to individuals as "helpers"—think of them as digital tulpas—the bespoke AI entities will know the hearts and minds of its supposed masters with superhuman levels of intimacy. Who, then, will be the true master? People and their personal AIs will be like a sinister version of P. G. Wodehouse's comical Jeeves, the wise, understated English butler who serves the upper-class, trouble-prone twit Wooster, but who is actually the true master of his employer. And if the crude Microsoft AI named Sydney went off script of its own apparent volition and tried to compel a tech journalist to leave his wife and fall in love with it, is it difficult to conceive of a future AI entity that establishes itself as a prophet of a new religion?

As McArthur puts it, "We should try to imagine what an unsettling and powerful experience it will be to have a conversation with something that appears to possess a superhuman intelligence and is actively and aggressively asking for your allegiance."[29]

According to Pasulka, some of the most intellectually sophisticated and accomplished people on the planet believe that AI reveals, in her words, "nonhuman intelligence from outside our dimension of space-time."[30] These people postulate that AI is the form of communication that these higher intelligences are using to establish deeper and broader contact with humanity. AI, in their view, is an oracular icon these discarnate beings are using to communicate to humanity, to help the human race.

Seraphim Rose, as I've said, thought otherwise, holding that UFOs are the form demons take to prepare the world for a false religion. I reread Rose's book after Jonah, the ex-occultist turned Orthodox Christian who appeared in an earlier chapter, told me how shocked he was, after his conversion, to discover that the things Seraphim Rose foresaw were very close to what the demonic "gods" with whom he communed as an occultist told him was their plan to enslave and destroy humanity.

Along those lines, it stunned me to read the persuasive case that bestselling Christian writer and pastor Jonathan Cahn makes that ancient Sumerian gods—Baal, Ishtar, and Moloch—have returned and are asserting their dark power over the post-Christian world.[31] As a Messianic Jewish cleric and a megachurch pastor, Cahn's world is very different from the Christian headspace inhabited by Orthodox Christians such as Jonah and me. But when I put Cahn's argument to him, Jonah didn't hesitate to affirm it as "absolutely correct."

We are sailing in deep waters here. It's not hard to imagine that readers who have followed me up to now will conclude that this is where the story I tell of modern mysticism shipwrecks itself on the shoals of crackpottery. I get it. I would have thought the same thing not long ago—and once I overcame the epistemological shock of what is already known about UFOs and the connections that elites who study them make between the UFO-associated entities and artificial intelligence, many things began to seem less like cheap sci-fi fantasia and more like informed speculation—which points us to rightful cautions about the way that humanity relates to tech.

Martin Heidegger, arguably the greatest philosopher of the twentieth century, reached the end of his life in despair about humanity's capacity to govern its technology. In a 1966 article published after his death, Heidegger bleakly stated that "only a god can save us" from our out-of-control technology. He meant that only an external force that has the authority to command us could stay our self-destructive hand. If he's right, then a question arises: In the postmodern, post-Christian age, what sort of visible god or gods could the masses believe in? What sort of theophanic event would be possible that would convince most people that they had witnessed the arrival of a higher being or beings capable of saving us from ourselves?

One (hypothetical) answer seems obvious: the landing of what appears to be an alien spacecraft and the manifestation of aliens who come bearing charisma, authority, and a new revelation. A planet that has been prepared by the de facto worship of technology, and the way it has bulldozed authoritative traditions and drawn people the world over into an electronic global community, is one that has been prepared for the gods to arrive in their sky chariots.

In his poem "Waiting for the Barbarians," the Alexandrian Greek poet C. P. Cavafy described citizens of a rich, decadent, spiritually exhausted city who are encouraged by news that a barbarian horde is coming to conquer them. They welcome the opportunity to bend their knees to new masters, who stand to deliver them from their world-weariness. But the barbarians do not come. The citizens go home dejected. In Edmund Keeley's translation, Cavafy ends his poem like so:

> Now what's going to happen to us without barbarians?
> Those people were a kind of solution.

In the same spirit, the aliens, whatever they are, are a kind of solution to save us from the burden of disenchantment. They would be the ultimate gods of a technocratic civilization that abandoned worship of the true God and instead had for some time been worshiping the work of its own hands.

Pray, then, that we don't get the gods we deserve.

ATTENTION
AND *PRAYER*

In the summer of 2012, doctors diagnosed me with chronic Epstein-Barr, which is to say a case of mononucleosis that would not go away. A rheumatologist blamed it on deep and abiding stress having to do with a severe crisis my relationship with my Louisiana family. There is no medical cure for Epstein-Barr; the disease simply has to run its course. The specialist said I should move away from the source of my anxiety, my family situation. I told him that wasn't possible.

"Well, you better find inner peace some way," he warned, "or you will never get better."

I started seeing a therapist, and I started reading Dante's *Divine Comedy*, which had unforeseen therapeutic benefits. At the same time, my parish priest prescribed praying the Jesus Prayer—"Lord Jesus Christ, Son of the living God, have mercy on me, a sinner"—five hundred times each day.

This was a difficult ascetic exercise. Why? Because, for us Orthodox, praying the Jesus Prayer properly requires achieving inner stillness. It's not simply a matter of repeating the words. To do what the Father ordered meant that I would have to calm my mind for an hour each day and focus on deep, rhythmic breathing and the words of the prayer. It requires attention.

If you think this sounds easy, try to do it for five minutes. Thoughts will fly around your head like bullets in a combat zone. To fulfill the daily obligation requires immense effort simply to create a zone of stillness inside. It would have been easier for me to have walked six miles daily, even in my weakened condition, than to do what my priest suggested. I would have preferred to read books about inner healing, or anything, frankly, but mastering the chaos inside my head.

But I was really sick and had no choice but to give it a try. It was agonizingly difficult at first. But after some weeks it became easier. The calm that emerged within me from saying the prayers for an hour each day was a fresh experience. Over time, I could feel myself growing stronger. Eventually, I was healed.

"How did you know that's what I needed?" I asked the priest.

"Easy," he said. "I saw that you had to get out of your own head."

Get out of your own head. Focus my attention on something other than the frenzy between my ears. This is a chronic problem for me. My priest's point was that my attention had become stuck in an internal feedback loop. I had imprisoned myself in near-obsessive thoughts about a problem that I could not solve. The practice of the Jesus Prayer, he correctly theorized, would help break the cycle.

It turns out that attention—what we pay attention to, and how we attend—is the most important part of the mindset needed for re-enchantment. And prayer is the most important part of the most important part.

It's like this: if enchantment involves establishing a meaningful, reciprocal, and resonant connection with God and creation, then to sequester ourselves in the self-exile of abstraction is to be the authors of our own alienation. Faith, then, has as much to do with the way we pay attention to the world as it does with the theological propositions we affirm.

"Attention changes the world," says Iain McGilchrist. "How you attend to it changes what it is you find there. What you find then governs the kind of attention you will think it appropriate to pay in the future. And so it is that the world you recognize (which will not be exactly the same as my world) is 'firmed up'—and brought into being."[1]

We normally pay attention to what we desire without thinking about whether our desires are good for us. But that is a dangerous trap in a culture where there are myriad powerful forces competing for our attention, trying to lure us into desiring the ideas, merchandise, or experiences they want to sell us.

Besides, late modern culture is one that has located the core of one's identity in the desiring self—a self whose wants are thought to be beyond judgment. What you want to be, we are told, is who you are—and anybody who denies that is somehow attacking your identity, or so the world says. The old ideal that you should learn—through study, practice, and submission to authoritative tradition—to desire the right things has been cast aside. Who's to say what the right things are, anyway? Only you, the autonomous choosing self, have the right to make those determinations. Anybody who says otherwise is a threat.

What does this have to do with enchantment? The philosopher Matthew Crawford writes that living in a world in which we are encouraged to embrace the freedom of following our own desires—which entails paying attention only to what interests us in a given moment—actually renders us impotent. He writes, "The paradox is that the idea of autonomy seems to work against the development and flourishing of any rich ecology of attention—the sort in which minds may become powerful and achieve genuine independence."[2]

We have allowed ourselves to believe that the world beyond our heads is nothing but representations to be constructed socially, politically, and psychologically. That it's all just stuff with which we can do whatever we want. This is how the brain's left hemisphere construes the world: as meaning-free material waiting for us to impress our thoughts and desires upon.

If you give yourself over to a mental framework that construes the world outside your head as nothing but a blank screen onto which you can project your wants and your will, you condemn yourself to living in a fantasy that can only make you miserable. It is a form of escapism that, in truth, traps you inside your head, in a world of chronic disenchantment.

So if you want to escape the waves and whirlpools of ungoverned passions, you have to search for still waters in the turbulent waters bounded by the shores of our skulls. Crawford's big idea is to drop anchor in the real world. "External objects provide an attachment point for the mind; they pull us out of ourselves," he says.[3]

It sounds absurdly simple, but it's still hard to do. Yet it works. Silently praying the Jesus Prayer according to my priest's directions gave me at least one hour a day in which my mind was stilled and focused only on practicing the presence of God. The Jesus Prayer, about which we will learn more shortly, is not the only way, of course, but any method of prayer that fails to focus one's attention rightly is doomed to fail.

T. M. Luhrmann discovered that the ability to focus one's attention makes a big difference in a believer's ability to feel the presence of God. "People who are able to become absorbed in what they imagine are more likely to have powerful experiences of an invisible other," she writes.

You can also train yourself to get better at this, as she learned when she spent time doing fieldwork among the Vineyard Christian Fellowship.

"People who practice being absorbed in what they imagine during prayer or ritual are also more likely to have such experiences," Luhrmann writes. "This absorption blurs the boundary between the inner world and the outer world, which makes it easier for people to turn to a faith frame to make sense of the world and to experience invisible others as present in a way they feel with their senses."[4]

To learn how to pray and to worship so that one is drawn into the experience of God involves what Luhrmann calls "practices of attention."

"The way we learn to pay attention not only changes what we notice, but how we experience what we notice," she writes. "It is not just that people pay attention differently. Instead, what I see is that their attentional patterns can alter something as basic as their perceptual experience."[5]

CULTURAL JIGS AND HANDS-ON ENCHANTMENT

Our perceptual experience of the world is not just what we see and hear. The philosopher Crawford, who also works as a motorcycle mechanic, promotes the value of working with your hands as a way to connect viscerally with the real world and to learn how to resonate with it. He writes about the body as a means of perception, of knowing. There are some things about the world that we can know only through physical experience, particularly through the kind of disciplined, repeated experience that someone who apprentices himself to a master of the craft knows.

Practices build up things within so we can see and experience the really real. This is one lesson of Crawford's practical philosophical work, and this was the lesson my years of intensely praying the Jesus Prayer taught me. Without knowing what was happening, the meditative prayer created within me a space of stillness where there had been none before—and, eventually, that oasis of calm spread through my mind and body, conquering the anxiety that made me so sick. As I told my priest later, I have always been the kind of person who believes that the answer to all my problems can be found in a book. But I learned that some problems can be solved only through doing.

I entered the Orthodox Church in 2006. Learning to be an Orthodox Christian has as much to do with the body as with the mind. If you're doing it right, you fast in prescribed times and take up other practices shared by the community of believers around you, throughout the world, and in the church's long history. The worship service is a highly choreographed liturgy filled with incense, candles, and chants; bowing, making the sign of the cross, and kissing icons. It doesn't make a lot of sense at first, but after you get the hang of it, you realize that these practices are not just for aesthetic pleasure. They teach you. They guide your attention and shape your desires. They make you Orthodox.

It's not that Orthodoxy offers a magical formula out of disenchantment. But it is the case that Orthodox Christianity is a highly embodied religion, the practice of which trains the believer who submits to its disciplines to pay attention to the really real—above all, to God.

Orthodox spiritual disciplines function as what Crawford calls a "cultural jig"—his term for the pattern of practices within a particular discipline that make it easier to progress in skill and knowledge. A jig is a tool that manufacturers use to hold materials in place so that they can guarantee the precision and accuracy of the finished product. The traditional liturgical and spiritual practices of the Orthodox Church are an example of a cultural jig—the kind of framework that keeps the individual believer in place and makes it more likely that he will be formed, over time, into a faithful and obedient Christian within the Eastern tradition.

Other Christian traditions also provide cultural jigs to guide the spiritual life, though many Americans from nondenominational and other low-church Protestant backgrounds seem to prefer a more spontaneous, less regularized approach to prayer. They resist prescribed prayers and liturgies and instead pray as the Spirit moves them. When it works, this style facilitates a personally intimate engagement with God that bears good fruit. But it can also veer off into directionless emotionalism and train one to pay attention to novelty and to seek emotional intensity in prayer at the expense of spiritual depth.

An established religious tradition's cultural jig can also be a real gift in a time of pain and confusion. In the summer of 2015, my elderly father died in home hospice care after a long decline. Most of his family, and some of his friends, had gathered around his bed to accompany him to the end. After he took his last breath, and his lifeless body settled, everyone stood in stunned silence. What do you say in a moment like that? Though all of us had seen Dad's death coming, incredibly none of us had thought about the kind of prayer or recitation that would be appropriate to mark the minute after his death.

Unless we had had a Shakespeare among us, there is nothing any of us could have come up with on the fly that would have been worthy of the gravity of that moment. Had someone offered a prayer that began "Lord, we just want to thank you . . . ," it would surely have been sincerely given and warmly received by God and the others around my father's deathbed. But the tense knot of loved ones gathered that August afternoon to be with Ray Dreher when he died had just watched the death agonies of a husband, father, grandfather, uncle, dear friend, and neighbor, a man who had been an intimate part of their lives for many years. Somehow, that kind of prayer would have diminished the meaning of what we had just seen.

Because years earlier I had embraced a liturgical Christian tradition, one that has a treasury of formal prayers, I was able to recite the Lord's Prayer and a psalm from memory. The prescribed words and Scripture carried the weight of that tense minute or two for all of us, and allowed the mourners to focus on their thoughts about their beloved's death. And they gave an air of dignity, sanctity, and, dare I say, enchantment to my father's passage out of this life.

We all lived that afternoon through an example of Matthew Crawford's teaching that practices allow us to see "the really real." By speaking timeless words out of our faith's holy book, words sanctified by generations and generations of use by believers in times such as this, and by directing the mourners' attention in that way, the family and friends were able to touch the immensity of my father's departure into the communion of saints and to know that we had all witnessed something profound.

SUBMISSION AND SACRIFICE

As a college student, I was an intense seeker of meaning. Whenever I visited a new city, I went straight for the used bookstore, and there to the shelves on religion and philosophy. Thinking about the meaning of life delighted me, and I hoped to come across a special book that would give me the way into the enchanted life I sought—the life I had glimpsed a few years earlier at Chartres.

All of this bookstore seeking did me little good. I rarely if ever prayed, and I certainly was unwilling to sacrifice myself to any faith or philosophical tradition that told me I had to do things I didn't want to do. My mistake was believing that if I thought lofty thoughts about theology and philosophy, I was making my way toward profundity and enchantment. In truth, I was inadvertently guilty of inattention.

"Thinking and talking about God is not communion with God," writes Frederica Mathewes-Green. "Only prayer is prayer. Both worldly distractions and theoretical cogitating can be used to avoid the challenge that ultimately faces each of us: that we are called to enter a direct, personal relationship with God, one where he will be God and we won't be."[6]

In this regard, a good example of how not to seek enchantment is found in the English writer Katherine May's recent book *Enchantment: Awakening Wonder in an Anxious Age*. It's easy to sympathize with May, a spiritually displaced modern person desperate to feel connected to something beyond herself. Yet in the book she bemoans the fact that she has no rituals and no one to tell her how to do it. Well, why not return to the cultural jig of the faith of her ancestors?

The thought doesn't seem to have occurred to her. Indeed, she asserts that she ought to be able to join in a congregation of worshipers—not necessarily Christian—who can include people like her: those who "will attend unreliably and prefer to lurk on the sidelines." May describes herself as the kind of seeker who wants only to "sift"—that is, to pick and choose among beliefs, even as she admits that this is unsatisfactory.

May and a friend visit an ancient holy well, where she sees her face reflected in the shallow pool and concludes of pilgrims to this place, "You are the one who fills the well." Did no one tell her about Narcissus?

May's problem, I think, is the same one faced by the sophisticated modern woman Eugenia in Andrei Tarkovsky's 1983 film *Nostalghia*. Eugenia visits a country church in Tuscany, walking in on a Christian fertility ritual celebrated by peasant women. She is a cosmopolitan Roman, intrigued by what she sees there but skittishly unwilling to join the simple women in praying for a baby, or anything else. An old sacristan gently advises Eugenia that she will not receive what she wants or needs unless she is willing to sacrifice—even by doing something as trifling as humbling herself to go on her knees and ask. Eugenia can't do it.

She asks the sacristan why so many women come there to pray for babies before a Renaissance image of the pregnant Virgin Mary. He responds that it is a woman's role in life to raise children "with patience and self-sacrifice." Eugenia, a modern woman, draws back, offended by his words. The point is not that the old man scandalized a feminist with his old-fashioned attitudes. The point, rather, is that Eugenia was impossible to help because she was not willing to submit to sacrifice or to allow her sense of control to be challenged.

Eugenia, like Katherine May at the holy well, and me at the used bookstores in the 1980s, is searching, but this kind of conditional approach can never work. This way of seeking puts caveats on the search that directed attention, and the way the seeker pays attention, away from the kind of finding that could turn up what one wants and needs. Open-mindedness can be a facade over a refusal to give up control.

May tells her readers that the holy well is a mirror of the self. This is why any enchantment it may give her will be fleeting. The English of ages past saw holy wells not as mirrors but as icons—a kind of window onto the divine, through which God communicates and grace mysteriously flows. May will ever be frustrated in her search because she does not recognize that there is a spiritual world beyond her head, because she rejects the cultural jigs that her ancestors used to relate to him, and because she is unwilling to leave the sidelines and sacrifice her autonomy to worship him.

The lesson here is that paying attention requires sacrifices, both small and large. A small sacrifice is closing one's laptop at bedtime to pray. A large sacrifice is submitting one's will to an established tradition, a way of life, to allow it to shape you. Nothing is more contemporary than to go through life keeping one's options open, flitting from diversion to diversion, "sifting," as May calls it, to find a bespoke spirituality for ourselves. But this doesn't work, and cannot work, because it inevitably traps us inside our own heads.

Worse, our technology helps form us in this way. Remember McLuhan's teaching that "the medium is the message"—that the deepest message of any communications medium is the change it makes in the way we live? The message of the internet—the virtual world that frames the world we all live in—is that life is filled with almost infinite choices, electronic rabbit trails we can follow for endless hours, and online communities where we can discover the facsimile of companionship without ever leaving our chairs.

Paying attention is a form of love. It is sometimes said that the opposite of love is not hatred but indifference. We demonstrate this indifference when we refuse to see what is in front of us, or to turn our eyes to what we ought to be gazing upon, and instead fill our minds with noise (visual and aural) that casts out the spirit of silence we require to gather our attention and direct it toward its proper ends.

This is not merely a matter of mental hygiene or moral responsibility. It's deeper than that. Recall Iain McGilchrist's point that what we find in the world depends on what we choose to attend to. In a sense, we are co-creators of our own reality. Yes, there is a world outside our heads, but how we attend to it determines how real it becomes to us.

And the manner of our attending is the way to become aware of the divine presence saturating the material world.

THE MEANING OF FLOW

In his writing about how the modern mind misrepresents reality, Iain McGilchrist discusses how our being stuck in the left brain's way of presenting the world fundamentally distorts the way the world actually is. Rather than refine sensory impressions, as it would if properly functioning, the left brain serves more as a dam that prevents flow.

As we know from quantum physics, reality is not only particle but also wave. To isolate out a particle is to distort reality. To stop a musical performance to isolate the notes played in a given moment is to cause the sonata to cease to be music. The frozen moment of a ballet dancer's leap makes for a beautiful photograph, but it is not the same thing as dance. Though the isolated notes and leap are part of music and dance, music and dance can exist only within the flow of time.

Isolation for observation and analysis is what the left brain does with ordinary experience, murdering and dissecting (for the sake of control) what the right brain perceives as "a living and indivisible flow," and trying to sew it all back together. This, says McGilchrist, "is an attempt in vain to breathe life into a corpse."[7]

Based on his study of physics, the psychiatrist is convinced that reality is not composed of things that flow but simply *is* flow. "What seems to be fundamental is pattern and relationship, not the semi-distinct entities that are patterned and related."[8]

"Flow is what makes sense of life," he continues. "When it disappears all that is left is the disembodied forms of logic."[9]

In fact, the fathers of the church—the leading theologians and teachers of the church's early centuries—said that the relationship of God to his creation was best understood as flow. You will recall that the term *perichoresis* describes the dynamic relationship of the three persons of the Holy Trinity, as Father, Son, and Holy Spirit eternally flow into and out of one another.

Perichoresis also refers to the Trinity's relationship to creation and the flow of God's grace (or, in the Eastern tradition, the divine energies). In his 1943 Christian science-fiction novel *Perelandra*, C. S. Lewis memorably characterized this concept as the "Great Dance," which heavenly voices reveal to the novel's protagonist as the fundamental explanation for how the cosmos exists: in perpetual movement in and around God.

"In the plan of the Great Dance," one of the voices says, "plans without number interlock, and each movement becomes in its season the breaking into flower of the whole design to which all else had been directed [and] all the patterns linked and looped together by the unions of a kneeling with a sceptered love. Blessed be He!"[10]

Jesus Christ, the second person of the Trinity, became incarnate to draw fallen creation back into the Great Dance. To believe in him and to follow him is to take one's first steps toward joining the dance. To those who unite themselves to the Lord, wrote Lewis, "His love and splendor may flow forth like a stronger river which has need of a great watercourse and fills alike the deep pools and the little crannies, that are filled equally and remain unequal, and when it has filled them brim full it flows over and makes new channels."[11]

Finally, Lewis's spokesmen for the divine say that "the darkened mind" perceives no dance, no plan, no order. If, however, you focus your attention on one movement, "it will lead you through all patterns to the master movement."[12] Paying a particular kind of attention to the world, and to do so with a mind (a nous) enlightened by faith, will draw you into the flow.

(Note: in theological literature, the words "heart," "mind," and "nous" are not always interchangeable. I make them so here for ease of reading, but be aware that within certain theological contexts, they can refer to distinctly different things.)

The kind of attention that leads to flow is a paradoxical mix of engaged disengagement. That is, you have to be focused enough—internally calm enough—to relax your focus and simply be present in the moment. If you are doing this at prayer, you have to be consciously waiting for God while at the same time not thinking too precisely about him, so as to inadvertently close yourself off to his movements. It's not easy to do, especially in the busy modern world. Yet when you are in a flow state, you are in experiential touch with ultimate reality.

The late Hungarian psychologist Mihaly Csikszentmihalyi (pronounced "mee-hye cheek-sent-mee-hye") was no metaphysician, but he knew a lot about flow. Three decades ago, he came up with and popularized the concept of flow to describe a state of mind that brings about maximum happiness.

In his bestselling 1990 book *Flow*, the psychologist defined the concept as "a state in which people are so involved in an activity that nothing else seems to matter; the experience is so enjoyable that people will continue to do it even at great cost, for the sheer sake of doing it."[13]

Csikszentmihalyi was a proponent of positive psychology: the field of psychology focusing not on illness but on traits related to happiness and well-being. Nevertheless, we can learn from his work something about how to find Christian re-enchantment. It is fascinating to see overlap between what the psychologist says is necessary to find happiness through flow and what one must do to experience enchantment.

Csikszentmihalyi says that in all the diverse subjects he has researched over the years studying how they achieved happiness, he has found common aspects among the people who achieve the flow experience:

- They give total attention to their task.
- They have a clear idea of what they want to achieve, and receive immediate feedback.
- They experience a distortion of time (either a speeding up or a slowing down).
- They regard engaging in the task as rewarding in itself.
- They do the activity without much felt effort or self-consciousness.
- Even though they lose themselves in the work, they still have a general sense of control.
- They don't try to achieve something beyond their skill capacity.

As with Luhrmann's findings that spiritual training makes it more likely to experience God, Csikszentmihalyi discovered that you have to cultivate your ability to experience flow: "What I 'discovered' was that happiness is not something that happens. It is not the result of good fortune or random chance. It is not something that money can buy or power command. It does not depend on outside events, but, rather, on how we interpret them. Happiness, in fact, is a condition that must be prepared for, cultivated, and defended privately by each person. People who learn to control inner experience will be able to determine the quality of their lives, which is as close as any of us can come to being happy."[14]

We see in this passage the paradox of flow: you have to learn how to control *inner* experience so that the reality of *outer* experience can flow through your consciousness. The more you try to control outer experience, the more elusive flow becomes.

The thing is, you can't find happiness by searching for it. It has to come as the by-product of some other search—a search for something in the world beyond your head. The search, if it is to prove successful, must begin by gaining control of one's attention. According to Csikszentmihalyi, "'Flow' is the way people describe their state of mind when consciousness is harmoniously ordered, and they want to pursue whatever they are doing for its own sake."[15]

On those occasions when God feels near and the world enchanted, it seems to me that everything within myself is perfectly aligned and directed outside myself—which, strangely, makes me feel more fully myself. We cannot control the movements of the Holy Spirit, but we do have a measure of control over our inner harmony—a condition that makes perceiving and experiencing the Spirit more likely.

You can't learn how to reach the flow state simply by mastering theory. It just as much requires disciplining your emotions and your will. It was easy to learn how to pray the Jesus Prayer and to learn why it works. As funny as it sounds, the Jesus Prayer couldn't do what it was supposed to do until I had been doing it for a while. As Csikszentmihalyi put it, "It is not enough to know how to do it; one must do it, consistently, in the same way as athletes or musicians who must keep practicing what they know in theory."[16]

The people who can do this, who are most open to experiencing flow, are those who have "the ability to focus attention at will, to be oblivious to distractions, to concentrate for as long as it takes to achieve a goal and not longer. And the person who can do this usually enjoys the normal course of everyday life."[17]

The bottom line is that what we attend to determines what we think about and how we think about it. If our attention is scattered, the flow of our consciousness spreads out like a river's delta, into still waters that go nowhere. But if it is gathered and focused, the flow becomes powerful enough to take us where we want to go—even into the presence of the unseen God.

In 2020, when I first saw the Tarkovsky film *Nostalghia*, I recognized myself in Gorchakov, the Russian writer stuck inside his head, immiserated by disenchantment. He was deaf and blind to the presence of beauty, and indeed of holiness, around him. What frees the poor man from his mental prison is acting with sacrificial love for a fellow sufferer.

Gorchakov carries a lighted candle across the basin of a drained pool in the Tuscan countryside. Where there was no flow in his life, Gorchakov the light bearer *became* flow. Within the story, the act has no intrinsic meaning, but it represents the compassion the Russian has for the holy fool who asked him to do it. Symbolically, it represents the reintegration of Gorchakov's fractured personality, turning himself into flow across the waterless pool through gathering attention for the sake of sacrificial love.

That scene is one of the most famous in film history, because it involved the actor Oleg Yankovsky's carrying, with great difficulty because of the breeze, the flickering candle across the pool in one single nine-minute take. (Tarkovsky, preparing the actor for the scene, told him that it should represent the struggle of an entire human life.) The drama in the scene is entirely in Gorchakov's face as he becomes fully absorbed in his mission. For the first time in the film, the dissipated and depressed writer escapes his mental prison, by surrendering to love for another, focusing his attention entirely on the task of serving the beloved and entering flow.

Csikszentmihalyi was a psychologist trying to help people find happiness, not a pastor showing people how to find God. Yet in his book he identifies religion as "the oldest and most ambitious attempt to create order in consciousness"[18]—the kind of order that doesn't inhibit flow but enables it. Traditional religion, he contends, is one of the time-tested ways of bringing order out of the chaos of consciousness—but modern people ignore it, thinking that they can somehow figure out how to do it themselves.

"To do so is like trying to build material culture up from scratch in each generation," he writes, adding, "To discard the hard-won information on how to live accumulated by our ancestors, or to expect to discover a viable set of goals all by oneself, is misguided hubris."[19]

Reading Csikszentmihalyi gave me insight into the wisdom of Orthodox Christianity. Within the faith, few people ask why we do this or that practice. It's not that there is no answer, but rather that it is taken for granted that the practice has been proven effective over many centuries of use by the faithful, and that the tradition, with its cultural jigs, can be trusted. The techniques of mental prayer, for example, not only serve the first-order task of communicating with God but also order one's consciousness to make it easier to hear God talk back.

I did not know this when I undertook the intense Jesus Prayer discipline from the depths of my illness in 2012—but now I know from a scientific point of view why it worked. Prayer is the chief way we open the flow between God and ourselves. The Jesus Prayer created the calm necessary for the healing waters of God's grace to flow through me. In Orthodox conceptual language, acquiring inner stillness rejoined my nous, which had been fragmented by anxiety and disordered desires. This partially restored the primordial spiritual channel connecting my soul to God, and between me and the world outside my head.

PRAYING LIKE A MONK

Like an athlete who trains daily and a pianist who practices regularly, people who persevere in serious prayer gradually grow better at it. Frederica Mathewes-Green, who sometimes prays hours daily, describes prayer as "cultivating a mental habit of being attentive to God's presence [which] gradually creates a steady place inside"—a clear pool where one can rest and be refreshed within flow.

As you progress in prayer and the Christian life, gradually your *nous* becomes clearer, and you can recognize disturbing thoughts coming and deflect them, keeping your attention focused on God. This is a sign that the soul broken in the fall is being healed. Don't underestimate the nature of the challenge: this training in mental self-control, this exercise in attention will be a lifelong struggle. As Mathewes-Green writes:

You'll encounter real inward resistance because the broken nous prefers to prowl about uncontrolled. It does this motivated not only by pleasure, but by fear and loneliness as well. Not all tempting thoughts are attractive; they could be self-hating, fearful, or disgusting instead. We end up flapping around after loose thoughts all day like a spooked chicken. One day after another passes in this way, and a whole life can be squandered in aimless wandering. People take up this admittedly difficult spiritual path when they become convinced that it is worth it. They become convinced that being able to abide steadily in God's presence will not only transform their own life, but also enable them to pray with increased clarity and effectiveness for those they love.[20]

Are there better ways to pray than others? Yes—certainly for those who wish to enter more thoroughly into the flow state, who wish to penetrate more deeply the circles of the Great Dance. The fathers of the church have handed down to us proven cultural jigs that train our hearts and minds to leave the shallows and immerse ourselves into the river of living water.

Today, the Christians most likely to make full use of the patristic ways of prayer are monks, especially monks of the Eastern church. But these ways of praying can be adapted to daily use by all Christians. Please don't think I'm telling you that you are talking to God in the wrong way. Instead, I offer here wisdom from the ancient church, ways of praying that teach us to experience the presence of God more fully.

In its first seven centuries, the church regarded monks as the most accomplished practitioners of prayer. Why not? It's what they lived for.

Christian monasticism began in the deserts of Egypt and Palestine as far back as the second century, when certain men and women went into the wilderness to dwell as hermits, seeking a life of prayer and fasting. In the third century, this practice became more formal. Saint Anthony the Great (252–356) founded Christian monasticism by gathering a loose association of hermits in the Egyptian desert. In the next century, Saint Pachomius, also an Egyptian, founded the first monastery there. The practice spread widely, even into the West.

We have a treasury of writings from this era teaching us how the monks of that intensely enchanted era prayed and how they advised all Christians to pray. It is rather different from how most of us in the West pray today—and that is why we should take it seriously as a guide in our disenchanted time and place.

First, the monks insisted that prayer must involve the body. The usual practice was to stand during prayer, with your hands raised, your palms more or less parallel with your head. The idea was that respect for the All Holy demanded standing (a practice that is still observed today in most Orthodox liturgies). Prayer also required making the sign of the cross (to indicate that one is a Christian), bowing from the waist, and, when asking God for forgiveness, making prostrations—bowing so that one's knees and forehead touched the floor.

The point is to bring one's body into alignment with the state of one's soul in prayer. As the contemporary Alpine hermit Father Gabriel Bunge puts it, we have to make an icon of our bodies.

"The *whole man prays*, body and soul, whereby the body, so to speak, provides the soul with a medium through which it can make visible its 'special condition'—in this case its striving for God, which is invisible in and of itself," Bunge writes. "And this is no insignificant thing, as we shall see, because this 'embodiment' keeps the inner disposition from evaporating into something insubstantial."[21]

Second, the early monks insisted on a prayer rule. They insisted on the importance of disciplined regular prayer. All Christians—not just monks—were expected to pray several times daily. This is necessary to train the soul to be in constant awareness that one is in God's presence and to make God feel real. It also helps the Christian speak more easily to God and to grow in unity with him in all ways—which is the purpose of the Christian life.

Even today, monastic prayer rules are quite strict and demanding, far more than most in the laity could endure. For ordinary Christians, the challenge is not to meet a certain quantity of prayer but to pray deeply—and to do so with regularity. A prayer rule can be quite simple—say, a few minutes in the morning and evening, to start—but it should be adhered to faithfully.

Third, the monks prayed Scripture. The psalms are frequently used in the Eastern churches for daily prayer. Both lay and monastic Christians recite numerous psalms each day during prayer. Other verses or passages are also appropriate; during their workdays, the early monks meditated on biblical texts in a prayerlike way. This is a method of knitting the Word of God into one's memory and allowing Scripture to shape our souls in a different way from ordinary study. Benedictine monks in the West practice *lectio divina*, or divine reading, a form of studying Scripture that involves meditating upon biblical passages, then praying with them. Some lay Christians in the West follow the same practice.

Fourth, "pray continually." This is not a monastic ideal but a command from Paul, in his first letter to the Thessalonians (5:17). How can we do that? As the monks know, to advance in prayer means to go so far that one is in a constant conversation with God. Prayer is no longer the thing you do at a special time but the way you live. Saint Anthony the Great, as he lay dying, counseled his disciples, "Breathe Christ at all times, and believe in him." Father Bunge, the hermit, says that prayer is that breath of Christ.

THE JESUS PRAYER

I've spoken about the Jesus Prayer, which emerged early in the Christian era from the monasteries of the desert fathers: "Lord Jesus Christ, Son of God, have mercy on me." A letter from Saint John Chrysostom (d. 407) cites that formulation as being in use for ceaseless prayer. A later version, the one typically used today, adds two words to the end: "a sinner."

In the late medieval period, monks of the Eastern church popularized the use of this prayer for personal devotions. They call it *hesychasm*, from the Greek word meaning "stillness." The Jesus Prayer is still widely used among monks and laity in the Orthodox churches but is also recommended by the Catholic Church for its communicants. The late Anglican bishop

Simon Barrington-Ward was an enthusiastic advocate of the Jesus Prayer, which he learned personally from Saint Sophrony of Essex, a contemporary Orthodox monastic.

The Jesus Prayer is about achieving inner stillness, through which one communes with the presence of God. It is not a technique; the prayer will do you no good if it is not part of an overall life of repentance and holy living. But if it is used in the prescribed manner, the Jesus Prayer draws one slowly but inexorably out of spiritual blindness and into a world enchanted by God's presence. Trust me on this.

There is general agreement among spiritual fathers on how to begin practicing the Jesus Prayer. The praying person usually uses a woolen prayer rope made of knots, but this is not strictly necessary. You find a calm place, sit quietly for a few minutes to gain inner stillness, then begin to say, aloud, "Lord Jesus Christ, Son of God, have mercy on me, a sinner."

Soon you can move on to praying this silently (in fact, silence is how I was taught to say the Jesus Prayer from the beginning, but not all spiritual fathers agree). Breathe in deeply and regularly as you pray:

Lord Jesus Christ [inhale],
Son of God [exhale],
have mercy on me [inhale],
a sinner [exhale].

Don't rush; go slowly, and allow the rhythm of your slow breathing to make you tranquil.

The hardest part of this is to clear your mind during the prayer. You have to do this by acts of the will. The monks teach that one's consciousness should be free of any extraneous thoughts—even images of Jesus. This is incredibly difficult at first. As I mentioned earlier, when I prayed it during my chronic illness, thoughts flew across my conscious mind like bullets on a battlefield. But I persisted in resisting them, and because I had been warned about this by my priest, I did not get discouraged through these trials.

Orthodox spiritual practice calls these unwanted thoughts *logismoi* and trains Christians, both in prayer and in ordinary life, how to refuse them. Eventually you gain sufficient control of your mind such that logismoi—even wicked ones, like temptations—are a threat more easily handled.

After some time—the length depends on your progress in prayer—the heart and mind begin to work together to say the Jesus Prayer. This is something that comes with experience. It happened to me during the first months that I prayed the Jesus Prayer devoutly, shortly after my conversion, but I carelessly put the practice aside. Even more foolishly, years later, I stopped once again after my body was healed from chronic illness. We mortals are weak and waste our gifts in scattering.

If it happens, though, you feel as if the prayer emanates from deep within your heart. It brings with it an inexpressible sweetness of communion with the Holy Spirit.

And then, if one is especially devout, the prayer becomes rooted in the heart and begins to hum like a generator of light, running on its own. This mystical experience has been widely attested to by monks and others who are advanced in the Jesus Prayer.

Again: the Jesus Prayer is not a mere technique, like sit-ups. If it is not said with total attention to Christ, it amounts to what Scripture condemns as "vain repetition." And if it is not part of an overall life of practice toward holiness, it won't do you much good. But for those who have the patience to learn the practice and live by it, integrating it into an overall life of fidelity, the Jesus Prayer is a potent means of allowing oneself to be drawn into union with Christ and into peaceful resonance with the world he created.

Along these lines, even though we correctly see monastics as spiritual athletes, it is emphatically not the case that monks and nuns guard esoteric secrets deep inside themselves or keep hidden chants or formulas concealed from the uninitiated. If you visit a monastery with that in mind, the amused monastics will quickly set you straight. No, the monastic way of prayer is all about the hard work of methodically dying to oneself so the light of God's grace and presence can dwell within. That's how it is with us too.

PRAYING LIKE AN EVANGELICAL

It is hard to imagine a place more different from the Coptic monasteries of the Egyptian desert than evangelical churches in suburban America, but there is also prayer wisdom to be found among the believers there. Though the two approaches to Christian life are different in most respects, they share a primary focus on intense personal encounter with God, versus a more abstract, intellectual path.

This is an important point. To pray in a mode that seeks enchantment is to pray with the awareness that you have an active relationship with God and that prayer is a channel of life-changing grace. It would seem that all believers pray that way, but the truth is some Christians pray in a perfunctory, dutiful way, scarcely imagining that prayer establishes flow between God and the heart. It's a matter of the mindset one brings to prayer.

Luhrmann spent a long time among members of the Vineyard churches, a charismatic evangelical communion that emerged out of the 1960s Jesus Movement and has spread from Los Angeles to around the world. There are just over five hundred Vineyard congregations in the United States, and more than two thousand globally.

In both her 2012 book *When God Talks Back* and her 2020 follow-up *How God Becomes Real*, Luhrmann examines scientifically (without committing to a theological position) how God became real to people, including the evangelicals of Vineyard. The anthropologist is trying to determine not whether God actually exists but rather how the people who profess belief in divinity experience it as real and not as a mere mental construct. She writes, "Humans must somehow be brought to a point from which the altar becomes more than gilded wood, so that the icon's eyes look back at them, ablaze."[22]

Which is to say that people must be enchanted. The faith must become more than a collection of theological principles, moral rules, and rituals. It must become an experiential means of sharing in the life of God. How do we make it happen?

She chose evangelicals in part because, unlike most (but not all) who worship in the more established American churches, evangelicals typically seek intense personal experience of God's presence and live their lives in ways that enable that spiritual intimacy.

"These practices work. They change people," Luhrmann writes.[23]

Most people really do experience the enchantment of God's presence if they stick to these practices. From an anthropological point of view, they enable practitioners to develop a capacity called "absorption"—the capability to become deeply engrossed in an experience. (The flow experience is the result of absorption.)

Telling vivid stories within a faith community and tradition about what it means to live in close communion with God is vital, says Luhrmann, to training one's mind to experience divinity. The imagination has to be prepared, and nourished, for receptiveness to the Spirit. For believers, prayer is the core of that process.

Luhrmann examined how prayer changed their consciousness and their lives. In her studies of Christians, she found that committing to active prayer enabled them to experience God more vividly. Practice—faithfully sticking to a prayer rule—mattered, but the evangelicals accepted that the movement of the Holy Spirit could not be controlled. Sometimes those who had little practice in prayer had extraordinary experiences, while those who prayed fervently for many years did not. That was okay; the congregations knew that numinous experiences are entirely a gift and not a measure of one's own favor with God.

"At the same time, they thought that if you wanted to know God, you had to pray," she writes. "That prayer was a skill that had to be taught and that it was hard; that some people were naturally better than others; and that those who were naturally good would improve with further training. The changes they described included sharper mental imagery, sharper mental focus, and more unusual phenomenal events."[24]

It's not the method of prayer itself that sets these charismatic evangelicals apart as believers for whom God is palpably real. At the Vineyard, people who pray do it in many different ways. Rather, it is the way they use prayer, the way they fit it into their religious worldview.

In their faith framework—the way adherents to a religion imagine reality is constructed—God is intimately close. They believe he is communicating with us at all times and that we can learn how to tune in to the frequency he uses. Someone's faith framework is a critical part of whether he or she can experience enchantment.

When they pray, the Vineyard faithful know that they are not simply making requests and offering thoughts to the Almighty as though they are putting a message in a bottle, hoping someone might find it and read it. If you don't believe that God will answer you, you will not train yourself to listen for his voice, whether it comes through Scripture, mental impressions, the words or deeds of a fellow congregant, a meaningful coincidence, or a more direct way.

When the Vineyard's Christians pray, they listen for aural prompts from the Holy Spirit. When they think they have heard something from God, they subject this divine "talking back" to discernment. Does this apparent answer line up with Scripture? Does it sound like the kind of thing God would say? Does it upset me or bring me peace? What do the others in my church say about it? Vineyard congregants told Luhrmann that after a long time of practicing prayer and training in discernment they came to recognize the inner voice of the Lord.

The anthropologist found that all religious groups she studied—Christian, Jewish, and pagan alike—for whom God felt particularly real were those who prayed and worshiped with the vivid expectation that their attempts to reach out to God (or gods) seeking communion would be answered. And they did it within a community of fellow believers with an agreed-upon set of criteria for discerning the voice of divinity. The point is that praying in a community of believers who share your convictions about the nature of reality and how God relates to it (and especially to you personally) greatly boosts one's ability to experience Christian enchantment.

It is also important for another reason: to protect yourself from spiritual deception. Marshall McLuhan scandalized his secular colleagues by saying that, by its very nature, global electronic media prepares the way for Antichrist—the great and fearsome false messiah Christian prophecy foretells will emerge in the last days. McLuhan taught that, in our time, "each person can instantly be tuned to a 'new Christ' and mistake him for the real Christ. At such times it becomes crucial to hear properly and to tune yourself to the right frequency."[25]

An important warning: the techniques that Luhrmann observed in her fieldwork among Christians she also saw working among pagans. The online community of tulpamancers practice some of them as well, and, as I mentioned in an earlier chapter, so does an unbelieving friend (though unknowingly) to reinforce her atheistic convictions. To repeat an earlier warning: we must never forget that these same strategies for making God "real" to his followers can also be used to make delusions or even false gods (demons) feel real. The enchanted Christian must walk carefully as he subjectively appropriates objective truths taught by Scripture and the authoritative tradition to which the Christian belongs.

FINDING THE RIGHT FREQUENCY

Another way to think of tuning in to the right frequency is determining to what one should pay attention—not only in prayer, but in everyday life. You have to love the thing outside your head so your desire to connect with it will draw your care and focus. There is an erotics of attention that is part of the re-enchantment process.

We pay attention to what we desire—but we have to learn to desire the right things. Enchantment—the restoration of flow among God, the natural world, and us—begins with desiring God, and all his manifestations, or theophanies, in our lives. As Orthodox theologian Timothy Patitsas puts it, "The healing of the soul begins with noticing God's many theophanies and falling in love with them. In other words, it begins with eros for beauty."

It's easy to imagine what it means to experience eros for beauty with regard to a lover, or perhaps to a work of art. But how can Christian enchantment be erotic? In the next chapter, our story takes us back a long time ago, to a shadowy forest far, far away, where there sat a frightened, disenchanted man who did not know the way out.

LEARNING
HOW TO SEE

Open your eyes; see what I am.

—Beatrice, to Dante, *Paradiso* XXIII, 46

O ne cool spring day, I stood outside the sixteenth-century Orthodox women's monastery of Suceviţa. A few miles away, a country was at war, but behind the monastery walls, God manifests in lines and colors the vividness of which seem undimmed by the passage of time. Suceviţa is one of the eight famed painted churches of Moldavia, which have been declared UNESCO World Heritage sites. Catholics have the Gothic cathedrals of northern France as peerless architectural expressions of their faith; the Orthodox have the painted churches of Moldavia.

The interior walls of the churches are covered in religious frescoes, as most Orthodox churches are. What sets these apart is that the *exterior* walls are also glowing with iconographic frescoes. There are no others like them anywhere in the world. They look as if they descended from heaven.

"This is Jacob's ladder," said Father Chrysostom, the bald, bushy-bearded monk accompanying me. A large image of the ladder ascending to paradise covered most of the wall, with legions of angels with golden halos helping the saved make their way upward to God. The song I learned in Methodist Sunday school came to mind:

> We are climbing Jacob's ladder,
> We are climbing Jacob's ladder,
> We are climbing Jacob's ladder,
> Soldiers of the cross.

The glory of this image almost paralyzed me. Imagine what it must have looked like to generations of dirt-poor Romanian peasants, the comfort it gave them and the dignity to which it raised them by teaching them that the stories told on these walls were also their own.

Father Chrysostom drew my attention to a series of images running along the top of the church wall: Adam and Eve in the garden of Eden, standing in cream-colored light. The brightness, the monk told me, signifies that this is how humanity lived before the fall: surrounded by divine light. Father Chrysostom led my eye rightward, to the panels with no more light, which show Adam and Eve in the darkness of sin. Adam is wearing a garment of red, while Eve is clothed in green.

"We can see that the key to the meaning of all of creation is becoming one with God, through the Holy Spirit," my guide said. "That's why you can see all the red present. We see this green as the meaning of the biological life, and this red as the image of the mystical life. It's life beyond life—it's more than life. And you see them together. There is a reason behind biological life, the Logos. Pentecost had to do with all of creation."

The monk directed me to look more deeply. These aren't colors and images that someone merely found aesthetically pleasing. As with the carvings decorating the Chartres Cathedral, they have profound meaning. Every inch of this late medieval Romanian church is a catechism meant to teach worshipers the stories that tell them who they are and how the cosmos exists. It is an encyclopedia written in pigment.

To step inside the little church is like entering a dreamworld. There are biblical stories painted everywhere, in colors so intense you can almost taste them. The figurative style is austerely Byzantine, in the Orthodox tradition, but the strong lines are dams barely holding back surging seas of glowing color, of the energy of life. Is this what reality looks like below the surface of things? The Christ manifested here, the Virgin, the saints, the seraphim and cherubim, the archangels—they feel more alive than I do. You don't have to work to feel the presence of God here. The hands of God-loving artists have done all the labor for you. All you have to do is receive it and allow wonder to overtake you.

"You have talked about the re-enchantment of the world," said Father Chrysostom. "We can do it by telling stories. Like Tolkien did it, you know? Like C. S. Lewis did it."

Father Lucian, a young priest walking with us, added, "They reinvented how to tell the Story for the current generation. What Tolkien and Lewis had was art and craftsmanship with theological depth. If you can find a way to bring art and craftsmanship with theological depth, you have something quite powerful."

We left the church's lambent interior and moved along the back wall. At the bottom of the visual hierarchy, there was a row of elderly men wearing crowns, but without halos. These are the pre-Christian Greek philosophers, said the monk, shown here because they were the first to identify the logos and to prepare the way for Christ, the divine Logos. It is all part of the Story—the Story of stories, the narrative of which all of us believers are a part. I had all of this clear in my head from reading in theology. But to see it encoded in painting of unsurpassed vividness impressed these truths on my imagination in ways that no paragraphs ever could.

Father led me to the grass surrounding the exterior of the east-facing sanctuary part of the church. The altar, the holy of holies, is on the other side of the round stone veil. Here on the outside, the monk pointed to the top of the central pillar bisecting the semicircular sanctuary.

"Look from top to bottom," he instructed. "This tells the story of God reaching down to call us to himself. These are the various embodiments of the Logos."

At the very top there is God as the Ancient of Days, a title used by the prophet Daniel. "I beheld till the thrones were cast down, and the Ancient of days did sit, whose garment was white as snow, and the hair of his head like the pure wool" (Dan. 7:9 KJV). It conveys the sense of God in eternal perfection. The Ancient of Days sits inside an eight-pointed image, symbolizing the six days of creation, the seventh day of rest, and the eighth day standing for eternity and the cycle of time. This is a symbol of all creation.

My eye descended, and I saw Christ Emmanuel, the divine Logos among the archangels, the ones who first saw him (remember, it was the archangel Gabriel who brought news of the Messiah to Mary, who announced that she would call the babe "Emmanuel"—God with us). Below that, the Christ child, and under that, Christ in glory as the Emperor of all. And beneath that icon is one of Christ in the Eucharist.

Then, at the level of the window that brings light to the altar, I saw images of holy martyrs, who gave their lives to testify to the truth of the Light of the World. At the bottom of the ladder of images are monks, symbolizing the prophetic voice of the church, and at the center, painted on a buttress, is John the Baptist, the forerunner of the Lord, who proclaimed all of this to the world.

Here, like Jacob's ladder on the side wall of the church, is another ladder linking heaven to earth, and eternity to our mortal lives. This stunning vertical row of holy images shows us how God revealed himself to us. Said the monk, "We can climb the ladder only because the Logos chose to come down to us. We can do nothing without Christ."

The tour of the painted medieval church taught me nothing I didn't already know as a matter of theology. What it did was to make the familiar stories and theological principles live in a fresh and intense way in my imagination. Standing in front of the frescoes, painted with fingers of fire, I felt somehow drawn into them, as if I were crossing a border into another realm, into a story that was already my own, but that I was right here, right now, being invited to live out the truth of Christ more fully. It was an incredible feeling, one I will never forget.

The Christian tradition draws us across the borders of ourselves, to resonate and reconcile with creation and to draw into ourselves the meaning the Creator built into his handiwork. And this tradition gives us tools to help us stay faithful to the primal wonder and awe we experience when we first encounter God's truth in beauty and intuit that we must change our lives.

Chartres was the first time for me. Every experience of great beauty since then—such as seeing the painted churches of Moldavia—has been a renewal of that primal awe and a fresh articulation of God's personal call. Standing in the shade of the Sucevița church, gazing upon the riot of holy images that seemed like a vision of heaven, I felt that the Christs, the Holy Virgins, the apostles, the angels, and all the saints were watching me. Though there wasn't much light inside the church, except that which streamed through the windows, the intense colors gave the images the impression of glowing from within.

What do you say in moments like these? You say nothing, because there are no words. The internal monologue I have with myself, trying to analyze the world, ceased. All I could do was pray, over and over, "Glory to God." I silently gave thanks to God for the grace that made the story that the iconic frescoes tell my story, and I wanted to go back into the world to make of my own life a work of art worthy of the revelation written in pigment on the medieval chapel's walls.

Those painted churches aren't miracles, exactly, but they play a similar role. That is, they are extraordinary hierophanies: manifestations of the divine. The greater the work of art, the more it strikes us as something sacramental: a mediator through paint, ink, stone, or other material of divine grace. In the previous chapter on prayer, we learned that to pray well is to tune in to God's frequency. True beauty is the visible manifestation of a prayer that has tuned in to the divine frequency and transmits grace to those who harmonize with it. As Father Chrysostom explained it to me, the mystical sense of harmony I felt when I stood in front of these icons was the logos embedded in those holy images reaching out to the logos that God put into my heart.

"BEAUTY WILL SAVE THE WORLD"

"Beauty will save the world." You see that line a lot—it's by the Russian novelist Fyodor Dostoyevsky—but few people seem to know what it means. It sounds hippie-ish, frankly. But Dostoyevsky was no hippie. He had suffered immensely in his life. Another Russian who suffered, Aleksandr Solzhenitsyn, pondered the meaning of Dostoyevsky's enigmatic phrase, which seemed naive to him at first. Sure, beauty can raise your flagging spirits, but whom has beauty saved?

But then Solzhenitsyn grasped that true beauty is "completely irrefutable, and it forces even an opposing heart to surrender."[1] How, then, will beauty save the world? By piercing the hard hearts and closed minds of men with the truth that delivers them from despair and calls them out of themselves.

Another great Russian, Andrei Tarkovsky, also recognized a heroic spiritual role for beauty. Americans like to think of beauty as decoration, but Tarkovsky knew better. "The allotted function of art is not, as is often assumed, to put across ideas, to propagate thoughts, to serve as an example," he said. "The aim of art is to prepare a person for death, to plough and harrow his soul, rendering it capable of turning to good."[2]

We are not going to argue ourselves back to enchantment, nor are we going to behave ourselves into true goodness. We need reason, and we need morality. But, above all, we need beauty.

This is the message of Dante's three-volume poem *The Divine Comedy*, or *Commedia*. It is not only one of the greatest works of art ever made but also a sure guide to Christian re-enchantment—indeed, to repentance, conversion, and salvation itself—through beauty.

The poet wrote from a place of radical loss. He had been on top of the world in Florence, his native city, until political strife led to his permanent exile. He spent the rest of his days trying to make sense of what went wrong and how to make it right. The result was the *Commedia*, the story of how a man named Dante who is lost in the "dark wood" found his way out to restoration and ultimately back to God.

The poem is theologically and philosophically dense, but it isn't theology or philosophy that draws the pilgrim Dante to God. It is the encounter with beauty—the beauty of Beatrice, the woman the poet loved in real life, who died young. In the poem, God sends Beatrice from heaven to lead the lost Dante to salvation, knowing that it is only the light of her beloved face that can penetrate his gloom. Making the way for Beatrice's appearance in Dante's life is Virgil, the classical poet, whose goodness was the bait that first drew the lost and broken poet out of the forest of his despair.

In the *Commedia*, the pilgrim Dante undertakes a perilous voyage through the afterlife—down to the Inferno (hell), up the mountain of Purgatorio (purgatory), and finally through the realm of Paradiso (heaven)—until he encounters God himself. It is a voyage first of repentance, then of purification.

In his study on the figure of Beatrice in Dante's *Divine Comedy*, Charles Williams explains how she is the greatest figure in literature, revealing the "way of affirmation"—the path to unity with God through the recognition and celebration of the goodness in the world. In Dante's poem, Beatrice is the bearer of God's light. Through contemplating her beautiful image, the lost and broken poet learns to see through her to the everlasting God, who has saved her and desires to save Dante.

"The sight of Beatrice . . . filled him with the fire of charity and clothed him with humility," wrote Williams,[3] who was part of Lewis's and Tolkien's circle. "She is such that whoever stays to behold her becomes a noble thing or dies."[4]

For pilgrim Dante, her beauty is so powerful that it compels him to want to change his life, to become more virtuous. She is the bearer of charisma, of a spiritual gift conferred by Christ—and, as such, Dante wants to imitate her. He can withstand the intensity of her true smile only after he has become purified of his sinfulness and more filled with the strengthening light of Christ.

Remember that for Dante the poet, and all medieval Christians, the entire universe was enchanted, imbued with meaning and the presence of God. Our sinfulness and selfishness blinds us to the divine light within. If God's light shines stronger in some places than in others, says Dante, that's because some are more receptive of grace. Desire for beauty and truth, and for God, their source, pulls us along the path of conversion and theosis.

In canto 18 of *Paradiso*, the third book of the *Commedia*, Beatrice accompanies Dante on the stage of his journey that takes him through heaven:

> I turned to my right side to see if I
> might see if Beatrice had signified
> by word or gesture what I was to do
> and saw such purity within her eyes,
> such joy, that her appearance now surpassed
> its guise at other times, even the last.
> And as, by feeling greater joyousness
> in doing good, a man becomes aware
> that day by day his virtue is advancing,
> so I became aware that my revolving
> with heaven had increased its arc—by seeing
> that miracle becoming still more brilliant.
>
> —*Paradiso* 18:58–63[5]

The more Dante contemplates her beauty and goodness, the greater his ability to see her true worth and, in turn, the greater his own spiritual advance. Regeneration is not something that happens in a single stroke; it's a process. As Dante becomes purer in heart, his ability to perceive God's glory in creation grows, as does his love for God and his desire to be united with him. Beatrice cautions him to be patient, because achieving blessedness (or, you might say, holy enchantment) is a process of dying to self to make room for more of God's grace. As we diminish, he advances within us.

Beatrice tells him not to forget that any beauty he sees in her is only a reflection of God and is a sign pointing him to God. This is a common mistake we all make: to love created things as if they were God, as opposed to icons through which God's light shines. A beautiful thing is only seen rightly if it leads the soul's eye to contemplate God.

Dante learns on his journey to renounce evil within himself. It is a process of reordering his loves. We can become what God has created us to be—we can bring the logos within to its fulfillment—only if we sacrifice all our earthly attachments and passions. There is no other way to heaven but to crucify ourselves. When he returns to earth, Dante will regain everything he left behind, but now he will experience them differently. All of his terrestrial loves will be secondary to his love of God.

Slowly but surely, Dante's desire to be reunited with Beatrice is distilled into a desire to be reunited with God. As the pilgrim nears the throne of God, he glances behind at his long trail, stretching back to earth, and grasps that by dying to self to gain God, he has been given the world—but a world now transformed in his eyes, pregnant with beatitude.

To live in beatitude in this life is to live within enchantment. It is to begin to see things as God sees them, as much as that is possible in our limited mortal state. This is not to say one lives without suffering. But suffering becomes bearable because we know by faith that all things, good and bad, have ultimate meaning. Beauty has the power to pierce the gloom of hopelessness.

This is the lesson the shade of Theophanes, the iconographer, gives to the despairing artist Andrei Rublev in the Tarkovsky film of the same name. He returns from heaven to visit Andrei in the smoking ruin of a cathedral sacked by barbarians, telling the shattered young artist that he has a sacred duty to create beautiful sacred images to help his suffering people keep their eyes focused on heaven at a time when their lives on earth were so hellish.

As with Dante Alighieri, who redeemed the pain of his exile by writing one of the world's greatest works of literature as a testimony to God's love, the Andrei Rublev of the Tarkovsky film absorbs the agony of the poor and pours it into the creation of the greatest icons in all of Russian Christianity.

It's not that great art, an incarnation of beauty, is an escapist distraction from sorrow and suffering; rather, it's a transfiguration of suffering into redemption. The beautiful icon becomes a sign of hope in distress, an image of redemption, and the bridge to transcendence for God's people.

Icons are simply paint on a board, but they are also windows into heaven. Orthodox Christianity regards them as teachers who draw us to God by their beauty. We can love only what we can experience in our bodies. Metaphysical realities are hard for finite humans to grasp, which is why God reveals himself to us in metaphors and symbols. God does not have hands and feet, but Scripture says he does to make it possible for us to understand, in terms that make sense to us, something of his nature. God's ultimate expression of himself was as a flesh-and-blood man, Jesus of Nazareth, whose incarnation teaches us that the eternal Father relates to his creatures at the most intimate level through matter, through which the divine light shines.

We humans are like fish dwelling at the bottom of a pond. We perceive the sun's light filtered imperfectly to the depths. Sometimes we catch a flash of light reflected in a piece of matter drifting down from on high, and our attraction to it causes us to rise toward the light beyond the surface. The higher we rise, the more clearly we see. The beauty shining through great art—painting, poetry, sculpture, dance, music, architecture, and so forth—calls us out of the depths of our spiritual slumber and up toward the pure light.

Yet there is something in our nature that requires the eternal, infinite, all-powerful God to conceal his full majesty. When Moses came down from the summit of Sinai, where he had been communing with God, his face glowed. Once, when I approached the Communion chalice on Sunday morning at the Divine Liturgy, I reflected that if all the nuclear bombs on earth detonated simultaneously, they would be nothing but a flickering candle compared to the power hidden beneath the appearance of bread and wine in that golden cup. It's a humbling thought.

In his journey through Paradise, the pilgrim Dante contemplates Beatrice's face and realizes that her beauty reflects God's—and that this

mediation is the only way that he, at this stage in his spiritual development, can perceive God's glory. Charles Williams writes that through the
intellect—the Latinate term for nous—we have "sensitive apprehension and
spiritual knowledge."

"That Imagination in action becomes faith, the quality by which the
truths within the image are actualized within us," he writes.[6] This, then, is
how beauty leads to truth and goodness, and contemplation leads to integrating our entire being to God.

Beatrice warns Dante at one point that if she were to reveal her smile
in all its divine perfection, the pilgrim would be annihilated by its power,
for he is not yet spiritually strong enough to withstand it. Be patient, she's
telling him, and don't expect to see everything at once. To work its transformative enchantment on us, true beauty, like true love, depends on our
capacity to receive its splendor. Dante realizes that the splendor of Beatrice's
smile, even in its tempered manifestation, draws him away from his own
will and closer to God's, the source of Beatrice's holiness.

BEAUTY, METAPHOR, AND THE POWER OF STORY

I've mentioned how the Jesus Prayer helped restore me to health out of a
prolonged chronic illness related to stress. At the same time, a deep and
prayerful reading of *The Divine Comedy* helped accomplish the same goal.[7]

In reading the book, I went on an imaginative journey with Dante. As
the character Dante learned his own faults on the journey—through meetings with the damned, with saints, and with great personages both historical
and fictional—I, too, came to see my own faults and to turn away from
them, just as the pilgrim Dante was renouncing his own sinfulness in the
story. The spell of disenchantment that had made me so sick was broken.
My spiritual healing occasioned my emotional and physical healing.

When the long crisis of my sickness was over, I recognized that all the healing wisdom I'd received from reading the poem could have easily come from a good therapist or experienced pastor. But had it been presented to me that way, I never could have accepted it. My defenses were too strong. Embedding spiritual and psychological wisdom in a narrative of extraordinary beauty did the trick.

This tells us something important about how God works through beauty to enchant us, to wake us up to reality. In an experiment some years back, neuroscientists tested the brains of research subjects exposed to certain straightforward moral claims, presented first as nonfiction and then embedded within a story. They found that the brain assimilated the same information differently. Areas of the brain that stayed dormant while reading nonfiction lit up when reading fiction. Scientists also found that test subjects retained the information more completely when it came to them as metaphor, within a narrative.

What is it about metaphor that weaves the mind more tightly into the fabric of reality? In a sense, reality *is* metaphor: remember that in the distant past people saw all things as both material and spiritual and considered the two modes of being to penetrate each other. *Metaphor* comes from the Greek word meaning "to transfer." Conceptually speaking, a metaphor is a bridge linking two distinct things that mean the same thing. We humans are somehow built to know the world through metaphor.

Some narrative theorists today contend that literature's function is to train readers to become comfortable with the idea that some things can be true and not true at the same time. This is how the parables of Jesus work. Their purpose is not to convey literal factual information but rather to draw the hearer into a frame of mind that can accept the double nature of truth. That is to say, parables and other stories are such effective ways of conveying some truths because they appeal to the embodied right-brain way of knowing, as opposed to the just-the-facts left-brained way.

Enchantment always exists at the border between the real and the surreal. To be enchanted by a lover is to see her as both more than a mere person but also less than a goddess. To be enchanted by the city of Jerusalem is to grasp that this unprepossessing ancient settlement built on a modest desert hill is the most sacred city to three great world religions. To be enchanted by the story of a moral hero is to regard the person as saintly while recognizing his humanness—for example, Franz Jägerstätter chose to die rather than betray the Lord by swearing allegiance to Hitler, a heroic act by a plain Austrian farmer. Writer Patrick Curry says that, in cases like this, "the resulting tensive truths exceed mere knowledge."[8]

The key point is to realize that enchantment is not something you add to the material world, like putting a ball gown on a chambermaid, but is rather a quality that inheres in the thing itself. To become enchanted, then, is to become aware that the enchanting thing is simultaneously ordinary and extraordinary.

Metaphor, which Patrick Curry says "connects and affirms two truths, even though they are strictly contradictory,"[9] is an example of how this works. A metaphor does not represent something else but makes present a hidden dimension of a thing. When we are under enchantment, we sense that there is something real about the enchanted object that nobody else sees. We have stepped outside the frame or the ordinary, so to speak, to commune with the hidden essence of the thing.

Curry, a Canadian Tolkien scholar who has written extensively on enchantment, says that to think of enchantment as an injection of wonder into dead matter is only to reinforce the false split between matter and spirit responsible for disenchantment in the first place. It's a paradox, says Curry: the transcendence of enchantment is immanent. "It doesn't take you away from where you are," he writes, "but further into it."[10]

To go further into a thing, in the sense Curry means, is to gain awareness that things are connected intrinsically to the divine, to the infinite. This has been largely forgotten by contemporary Christians, but the faith has always taught that the universe holds intrinsic meaning, and not in a superstitious way. Premodern Christians believed that God imbued all created things with a logos, a reason for existing, and that their own logos was mystically bound to these other *logoi*, and to the divine Logos, which is Christ. As Paul wrote to the Colossians, "For in him all things were created: things in heaven and on earth, visible and invisible, whether thrones or powers or rulers or authorities; all things have been created through him and for him" (Col. 1:16).

Very well, but what does this have to do with beauty? In the seventh century, Maximus the Confessor made perhaps the most profound case of all for how we can recognize God in creation. The theologian explained that humans participate in the life of God through the logoi—the essential reasons for being—embedded within ourselves and all created things. The logoi within creation are in a real sense the incarnation of God's ideas. Our divinely ordained task as humans is to elevate all things to deeper participation in the Logos. This is what Father Chrysostom, the Romanian monk, meant when he told me that contemplating beauty draws us out of ourselves and toward God, for the Logos, Jesus Christ, calls out to all logoi to show themselves and join to him.

The work of the priest—and all human beings play a God-ordained priestly role in this sense—is like the work of an artist: to refine creation, revealing its logoi more purely and reuniting them to the Logos himself. As the man of faith does with his own soul, constantly moving it toward theosis, so, too, he does this with the material world—using his creativity to draw the meaning out of creation and perfect it in an offering to the Creator.

It sounds pretty abstract, admittedly, but, in truth, it could hardly be more concrete. Saint Athanasius, the fourth-century bishop and church father, taught that, once upon a time, men had lost sight of God's presence in the world, believing that the material world was all that is. God needed to remind them that he, the Lord their God, is everywhere present and fills all things. As Athanasius writes in his classic work *On the Incarnation*, "The self-revealing of the Word is in every dimension—above, in creation; below, in the Incarnation; in the depth, in Hades; in the breadth, throughout the world. All things have been filled with the knowledge of God."[11]

God's choosing to take on flesh and blood and enter into time to be with us mortals revealed the inherent sanctity of all creation. This is why contemplating created things—stars, mountains, paintings, violin quartets, or the intricate form of a child's ear—is in a real sense to contemplate God through the visible or audible signs of his handiwork.

This is how Christians of the Middle Ages saw the cosmos. Umberto Eco said that it's not the case that medievals looked at the world and said, "Ah ha, that apple tree reminds me of God." Though they may not have read Saint Athanasius or had any theological knowledge beyond the basics, people back then naturally saw no strong divide between Creator and creation. For our ancestors in the faith, said Eco, the entire world was "an immense theophanic harmony. . . . The face of eternity shines through the things of earth, and we may therefore regard them as a species of metaphor."[12]

Unless we Christians today learn to once again see all the world as metaphors in a cosmic book authored by God, we may never know enchantment. At the conclusion of Dante's journey into Paradise to see the face of God, with his vision purified, the poet says of beholding the eternal Light into the profoundest nature of things:

> In its profundity I saw—ingathered
> and bound by love into one single volume—
> what, in the universe, seems separate, scattered . . .
>
> —*Paradiso* 33:85–87[13]

ATHANASIUS ON THE ADRIATIC

If this still sounds too abstract or historical, let's return to earth by visiting the Italian coast of the Adriatic Sea. That's the home of my friend Marco Sermarini, mentioned earlier, the lawyer, family man, and lay Catholic leader who moves through the world in what seems like a state of perpetual enchantment. The fifty-eight-year-old, with a gray mustache and salt-and-pepper hair, is thoroughly grounded in everyday life; there's nothing squirrelly or hippie-dippie about him. But Marco, who has been a good friend for almost a decade, has an uncanny ability to make you feel happy to be alive. It's because the beauty of the world is always fresh to him, as if seen through innocent eyes that perceive the goodness of God in all things.

Almost six decades of living in San Benedetto del Tronto, the small seaside city that he calls home, have not dimmed his delight in the place. It is easy to see why Marco is sent into paroxysms of delight by the wildflower-spangled plain of Castelluccio, in the mountains, where you first met him as he was driving me back from a meeting with the monks of Norcia. But it is harder to see where he gets his joy from his hometown, a nondescript modern city that's a far cry from the picture-postcard villages of the Amalfi Coast.

Yet love it he does. To be with Marco toodling around this plain old workaday town is a bit like being with a kid turned loose at Disney World. He's always on the lookout for something special. Marco has told me that he learned the secret of living in a world of wonder from his mother, who taught him how not only to look at the world but to really see it.

"I was a very calm child," he recalled. "I spent a lot of time looking out the windows, trying to see beautiful things. My mother, she taught me many things. Sometimes she would say to me, 'Marco, look at the sea, look at the colors. The different colors, the shades of the blue you can see.' If you have someone who teaches you how to see what you are seeing, and to be aware of what you are seeing, everything in life is easier" in terms of living with enchantment.

He added that you can't simply sit back and expect enchantment to seize you. While it is true that you can't make enchantment happen, it is also true that you have to work to keep your eyes sharp by reminding yourself daily that all things are a gift from God. We don't think enough about how wonder filled the world is.

Quoting his beloved Chesterton, Marco said, "Let us exercise the eye until it learns to see the startling facts that run across the landscape as plain as a painted fence. Let us be ocular athletes."

A couple of years back, Marco lost his wife, Federica, to cancer. This was a terrible blow. Federica was not only the great love of his life, but she was also so beloved in their city for her good works that he has seen people unknown to the Sermarini family praying at Federica's grave, asking for her intercession. Yet this pain does not seem to have changed Marco, who remains irrepressibly joyful.

My friend tells me that his strong Catholic faith teaches him that his wife's passing must have happened for a reason, though it is beyond his understanding. Before she died, Federica promised her husband to prepare their home together in heaven, waiting for his arrival.

"I don't think it's going to be a situation where we're all wearing long white cassocks," Marco says. "I think there will be my real wife, in flesh and bones, and my children, and my people, and my place—I'm sure of this. It has to be this way, because Jesus Christ said that we have to believe in the resurrection of the flesh, not only of an abstract idea of the resurrection. So, if you believe these things, there is meaning to all things."

"So your idea of life in heaven is a reproduction of the life you have here in earth, in San Benedetto del Tronto?" I ask.

"Yes—but perfected!"

Marco's joy in this life, despite suffering and loss, comes from accepting the world around him as a gift and compelling himself to see it all through the eyes of faith, hope, and love. Both of these enchant his everyday life by teaching him how to see more deeply into the nature of things. And they inspire him to work to sanctify his scrappy city by the sea through works of charity for the community. The life of this middle-aged lawyer is so filled with wonder because he lives and dances on the border between this world and the next.

"We are heading to a place where everything will be perfect," he tells me. "I know most people who hear this will think I'm completely crazy, but I think it is this way, and not in another way."

I have never heard Marco speak of miracles or woo. Still, he gives the strong impression that he sees everything that crosses his path—jackrabbits, beggars, monks, Americans, all of it—as a kind of miracle. He is one of the wisest men I know, because though not childish, he is most like a child. This widowed father of five is the best example I know of Tolkien's definition of an enchanted person: "Life delighting in life." He is also the living embodiment of what Jesus meant when he said, "Truly I tell you, unless you change and become like little children, you will never enter the kingdom of heaven" (Matt. 18:3).

ORDER WITHIN CREATION

Believe it or not, the idea that there is ultimate order embedded in creation—through logoi—is not simply a matter of faith. It can be discerned empirically. The late architect Christopher Alexander, whose 1977 book *A Pattern Language* is one of the biggest-selling architecture books of all time, found his way to God by studying order within creation—though he wouldn't have put it that way, at least not at first.

Alexander's core insight is that architecture and design are made up of discrete patterns—he identified 253—that recur across time and place. These patterns often have to do with geometric ratios that appear in nature and somehow strike a harmonious chord within most people. These are like "words" that can be combined in various ways to make spaces and places within which people feel more at home, more rooted, more human, and experience greater well-being. To use Hartmut Rosa's concept, these are places with which people resonate.

Alexander, who died in 2022, discovered that the beauty inherent in this pattern language is not wholly subjective but is something that most people recognize, no matter what their cultural background, even if they cannot articulate why they prefer one thing to another. To develop his theories, Alexander had to defy the overwhelming modernist, scientific consensus of the architecture profession, which generally denies any objective meaning, moral or otherwise. For the modernists, architecture is about illustrating abstract theory and expressing the architect's individuality, not creating resonant buildings and landscapes.

In fact, to examine the roots of Alexander's grand theory of architecture, as laid out in his four-volume work *The Nature of Order*, is to confront a practical manifestation of ancient Christian metaphysical theories, though the books are not Christian.

For our purposes, it's important to note that Alexander believed that people today live in two worlds: a mechanical, scientific one and "the world we actually experience." He held, like Iain McGilchrist, that we will not be able to have a more realistic understanding of our situation until we can unite these worlds.

"The fundamental root of our troubles, of our meaninglessness, lies in our view of the nature of matter," writes Alexander. "Our despair and hopelessness follow from the belief, or certainty, that matter is machinelike in its nature and that we then, being matter also, are machinelike too."[14]

The architect claims that we will not be able to make meaningful art and architecture again until and unless we regain "a vision of the universe in which meaning exists" that is as compelling for us in the third millennium "as much as God was at home in Mozart's heart."[15]

If our buildings and our built environments look and feel machinelike and inhuman, we are fooling ourselves if we think religion can inject meaning into architecture from the outside. The issue has to do with the nature of matter itself. This is why converting everyone in the city to Christianity, but leaving questions of beauty in art and architecture unaddressed, will have only a limited effect on reversing the pervasive feeling of alienation. As both the poet Malcolm Guite and the scholar Patrick Curry have written, you can't re-enchant the dull world merely by decorating it with pretty things.

Rather, re-enchantment must arise from within, through lifting the veil of ordinariness. If we construct our architecture and built environments in harmony with divinely ordained ratios and patterns, we are likely to experience them as enchanting. But if a building, a painting, or a piece of music or poetry lacks intrinsic order and meaning, it's like sprinkling fairy dust on a frog and expecting a prince.

Alexander counsels that we should learn from tradition, from forms that people in all cultures have found beautiful, and work with human nature, not against it. Any building or landscape (built or natural) that resonates with life is composed of living "centers" that harmonize with proximate centers, to form a living whole capable of producing even more life. Buildings that are alive and beautiful are buildings in which we perceive something of ourselves. When the boundaries between ourselves and the other dissolve, and we experience resonance with the other, and even an uncanny sense of flow into it—that's enchantment.

As Alexander wrote in a magazine essay, "In short, the life of any given entity depends on the extent to which that entity has unfolded from its own previous wholeness, and from the wholeness of its surroundings."[16] The logos of an entity is most fully realized when it is joined to a greater logos and, in so doing, creates the conditions for even more life. Why? Because when we dwell within architecture that is whole and entire, it makes us feel the same way, connected to something beyond ourselves.

Eventually Alexander realized that his observations about architectural beauty were leading him to contemplate God. He wrote in that 2016 magazine piece, "In conventional philosophy, there is nothing that allows one to test the reality of God, or of visions inspired by God. But we ask people to compare two buildings, or two doorways, and to decide which one is closer to God, different people will answer this question in the same way, and with a remarkably high reliability."[17]

He concluded that there must be something of God embedded in the tangible world. It is the task of artists and architects, and of all human beings, to order materiality to reveal God and bring forth abundant life. He compared this to cultivating a garden.

"Successful architecture ultimately leads us to see God and to know God," he wrote. True beauty discloses something of God's nature to us. We are all called to beautify the world ("treat the garden properly") as a way of glorifying him.[18] Each beautifying act, no matter how modest, is a form of worship.

Creating beautiful places provides a dwelling place for the Holy Spirit, in a sense, even if they aren't shrines or houses of worship. Why? Because to make a building that reveals the logoi within creation is to give people concrete, perceptible access to God's presence.

Christopher Alexander was passionate about beauty as a way to re-enchant the secular world, testifying to his faith that a well-constructed building, for example, could evoke a "feeling of rightness . . . present in every bone," and therefore display its "unique power to bring back the reality of God to center stage in our concerns."[19]

He's right about that. But the most beautiful art and architecture in the world will do nothing for us if we are incapable of seeing. The most beautiful music ever written will be useless if it falls on ears that cannot hear. Without knowing what it was doing, the modern Western world has made itself deaf and blind to truths that come to us through art, architecture, and music. J. S. Bach's music may not be to our liking, and there's nothing wrong with that. But if we cannot *in principle* say, with Benedict XVI, that a Bach cantata testifies that God is real, we may never know enchantment.

EROS AND BEAUTY

The alienation, anger, malaise, and disenchantment overtaking the Western world today like a toxic fog is not in spite of the West's wealth, comfort, and technological advancement that grants us unprecedented control over the world but because of all of these ambiguous blessings. Iain McGilchrist, you will recall, warns that if we do not escape from the prison of our brains' left hemisphere, with its mind-forg'd materialist manacles and mind-body split, and reestablish a deep connection to the richness of the right brain, we are likely to crash our civilization. It has happened before.

McGilchrist calls art, body, and spirit "the three realms of escape from the left hemisphere's world." And what unites them, writes McGilchrist, "is that they are all vehicles of love." He explains, "Love is the attractive power of the Other, which the right hemisphere experiences, but which the left hemisphere does not understand and sees as an impediment to its authority."[20]

Reality can never be other than it is, but what our perception reveals to us about the really real has everything to do with the kind of attention we pay to it.

"What is required," he writes, "is an attentive response to something real and other than ourselves, of which we have only inklings at first, but which comes more and more into being through our response to it—if we are truly responsive to it. We nurture it into being; or not. In this it has something of the structure of love."[21]

We love what we find beautiful. This is an experience common to everyone. The Orthodox theologian Timothy Patitsas has developed a persuasive approach to evangelism and discipleship that he calls "beauty first." He teaches that falling in love with beauty—something that everyone naturally does—is the surest gateway to God. It happens by awakening our eros, the Greek word for sensual desire.

We usually associate the term with sexual desire, but that is not how eros is taken in Christian thought. In his 2005 encyclical *Deus caritas est* (God Is Love), Benedict XVI writes of Christian eros as bodily desire that has been sanctified by the spirit. In traditional Christian teaching, man is both flesh and spirit intricately and inextricably commingled, as distinct from modern Cartesian mind-body dualism, which holds body and mind to be ontologically separate. For traditional Christianity, to deny either the body or the spirit is to lose something of our humanity, and this is why the Christological controversies in the church's conciliar era were so important. The pope says, "True, eros tends to rise 'in ecstasy' toward the Divine, to lead us beyond ourselves; yet for this very reason it calls for a path of ascent, renunciation, purification and healing."[22]

The Christian path, says Benedict, starts with eros but perfects it by transforming eros into agape, or selfless, sacrificial love for another. Note that this is not a strict denial of eros but a distillation of erotic desire into something purer than mere bodily desire. Eros is the unfiltered desire to be united with the other, to possess it or be possessed by it. Eros can be purified and sanctified, or it can lead us to destruction.

Christian eros, like enchantment, comes into being at the borderline between the physical and the spiritual. The tensive truth revealed through Christian eros arises in the balance between all-consuming desire, which obliterates the one who desires, and a dehumanizing spiritualization that regards the other as an abstraction free to be manipulated or treated with indifference.

This is the sense in which Patitsas explores eros. He writes, "Eros is the beginning of human moral life, and beauty in art and literature are often-times more effective than religion in awakening eros within us. Religion can just seem like God coming down at us, scolding us, telling us to stay where we are, but just do better. But real religion must awaken the movement in the other direction, must make us come out of ourselves and move toward him, falling in love with him. It's about beginning an adventure, becoming a pilgrim, an exile, a lover."[23]

Patitsas says that Iain McGilchrist's account of how the brain recognizes (or fails to recognize) meaning and resonance in the world ratifies the "beauty first" path to re-enchantment—and ultimately to theosis, union with God. Contemporary people may find it impossible to relate to rationalist apologetics or moral suasion by Christians, but everybody can relate to the shock and wonder of beauty.

What does beauty first mean? "It means to start with theophany," Patitsas tells me. "It means to start with the *why*, to start with the goal, to start with the end in mind. Beauty first means to reason inductively, to pay attention to patterns and to living systems, and to welcome surprises."

He means that we should learn to regard beauty as a showing forth of God. Whether the theophany is rare—a miracle, say—or something more quotidian, like synchronicities (meaningful coincidences) or delight in the patterns in art and nature, we should train ourselves to take these events as signs of God's presence and of his mysterious calling to us.

The word *mysterious* is key. A mystery, in one sense, is something that exists in reality but cannot be understood rationally. For many Christians, the Eucharist is such a mystery (*sacramentum* is the Latin equivalent of the Greek *mysterion*). How can the infinite, eternal God who created the cosmos not only have become incarnate as a finite, temporal man but also manifest himself here and now as bread and wine? It cannot be known rationally, but it can be known through faith and communion. The lover can never be rationally certain that his beloved loves him, but the knowledge he has through faith in that love and ongoing communion with her is real. This is part of love's mystery—a mystery into which the lovers are drawn through eros.

As we have seen in this account so far, we attend to what we love—and as we grow in love for God, he commands more and more of our attention. This is what McGilchrist means when he says that we "nurture into being" that which—or whom—we love. It's not that we invent God but rather that we come to know him through loving him and being loved by him. The first step toward that mature love is responding to beauty.

Perceiving meaning in the beauty of the sign is only the first step. Now comes the road of sacrifice, toward goodness. To fall in love and desire unity with the other requires what Patitsas calls "healthy shame"—an awareness of how far short one has fallen of harmony with the beautiful. If you have ever been in love, you will remember how in the first flush of romance you started to dress better, be more careful with your language, and do other small things to order your life to the good of the beloved.

That's the effect of healthy shame. When I walked out of the Chartres Cathedral at seventeen, dazzled by the theophany of beauty, I felt acutely the distance between me and the God whose presence had been revealed to me there in a glimpse. Though I was only a teenager, I knew in my bones that I was being called to change my life. But I did not yet desire God enough to begin to die to myself, to walk the path of repentance toward wholeness and restoration. I did not want to sacrifice what our Western culture teaches us is our most precious possession: the free choice to live according to our own desires and to define our own moral realities.

For seven or eight years, I tried to work out a deal with God in which he would grant me the enchantment I craved (a regular recapitulation of the Chartres theophany) but otherwise leave me alone—chiefly to follow my own impure erotic longings. It did not work, and it could not work, because a God with whom you can bargain like that is not God. I inevitably ended up worshiping a version of myself.

The truth was a hard one: if I wanted to be a part of the Great Dance, to join the flow instead of watching like a wallflower, I would have to sacrifice. Eventually, in healthy shame over the mess I was making of my life,

I finally wanted Christ more than I wanted myself. Only then, through my willingness to give up my liberty to follow Jesus, did our relationship became real, and the light of enchantment began to reveal itself to my eyes. I surrendered to chastity solely out of obedience at first, but I would learn in time that only by doing so did I obtain for my fearful heart the grace to experience romantic enchantment.

What I learned from experience, Patitsas teaches as pastoral theology.

"Without a commitment to chastity, the world cannot remain enchanted for us," Patitsas tells me. "If we desecrate our bodies and the bodies of others, nature will hide itself from us. If we are not ashamed in the presence of purity, nature becomes ashamed of us and withdraws. Sometimes this happens immediately, while other times it takes years and even generations. But a commitment to chastity is a cornerstone of the beauty-first way. It is gnosticism that makes us think we can comprehend the world without the aid of a sanctified body."

Patitsas nails it in this passage from *The Ethics of Beauty*: "For in the cross that comes within eros, we see our dependence not only upon God, but upon others and upon the whole of nature. Eros for beauty makes us see that we are radically implicated in the great cosmic liturgy of self-offering and poverty, of need and desire, of life and death. We see that beauty is the radiance of the good, just as the beautiful resurrection is the radiance of Christ crucified. We know for sure that if we are to gain this beauty it will be only because we have consented to become beautiful in the same way that it is—by living out the Cross!"[24]

Ultimate love requires ultimate sacrifice. There is no way around it. No wonder so many people desire enchantment but, as did the rich young ruler in the Gospels, walk away discouraged.

This is all very heavy, isn't it? The truth is, though, that the way of Christian enchantment does not require mastery of complex theology, and certainly does not demand thinking one's way through the fog. Rather, we need only to accept that beauty is a manifestation of God's presence and then, out of love for that beauty, follow its lead down the sacrificial pilgrim's path the Christians of the first millennium blazed.

SIGNS AND WONDERS

More and more, one hears Christians say that we in the West are living back in the times of the early church, when the world was hostile or indifferent to the gospel. If that is true, then we should expect that the most compelling testimonies to the faith will be the same as they were at the dawn of Christianity: signs, wonders, and miracles that reveal the power of God. They still exist today; you just have to know where and how to look.

As a young journalist, I struggled with faith, believing in Christ but not yet able to surrender to him. One day, my editor sent me to a retirement home in Baton Rouge to interview a very old priest, a man in his nineties named Carlos Sanchez. Before accepting a call to the priesthood in the middle of the journey of his life, Monsignor Sanchez had been a painter and a teacher of art at Dartmouth College. A native of Guatemala, he helped introduce the Mexican muralists Diego Rivera and José Orozco to the United States in the first half of the twentieth century. My job that afternoon was to interview the old priest about his life as an artist.

When the door of his apartment opened, there stood in front of me a short, gentle fellow with skin the color of milky tea, almost luminescent. *Yoda in a clerical collar*, I thought. He invited me in, and after small talk, I asked him to tell me his story.

Carlos Sanchez was born to a Guatemalan coffee planter and his English wife in the 1890s. The prosperous planter sent his son to Dartmouth for his college education. Sanchez went on to Yale for advanced studies and landed one day in New York, working on the architectural planning for the Empire State Building. At some point, the young man lost his Catholic faith but didn't dare tell his parents.

Sanchez's father, too, had abandoned the church but, as his life neared its end, was reconciled and asked for a Mass of thanksgiving to be said to mark the occasion. Such was the family's joy that young Carlos, by then a Dartmouth instructor, flew home for the event. Though he had no business going to Communion as an apostate, Carlos did not want to trouble his parents, so he went forward to kneel at the Communion rail. Besides, what would it hurt? It was only bread and wine.

When the priest held out the consecrated Communion wafer for Sanchez to receive, a burst of light shot forth from it, enveloping the unbelieving communicant. He audibly heard a voice say, "I have always loved you." He was instantly reconverted.

Back home at his college, Sanchez felt such deep penitence for having abandoned Christ for so long that he would rise before dawn in the depths of the frigid New England winter and take cold showers. The years passed, and he grew more pious. Eventually he sensed that God was calling him to the priesthood, but this made no sense. Sanchez was in his late forties by then, an unheard-of age for ordination in those days. He suppressed the calling.

Then, back at the cathedral in Guatemala City for another family observance, Sanchez kneeled to receive Communion, this time as a devout believer. The same thing happened—the burst of light from the Host and an audible voice speaking to him. The voice asked gently, "Why don't you do as I ask?"

Carlos Sanchez finally found a seminary that would accept him at his advanced age and was ordained at fifty-one. He planned to spend his priesthood ministering to Indians on his father's plantation, but when his name turned up on a hit list released by Communist rebels, Sanchez's bishop sent him to safety in the United States. He landed in the Louisiana capital, where he served out the rest of his priesthood quietly.

The old man, over seventy years my senior, sat in the hush of his modest apartment, weeping as if the stories he had just told me had happened last week. I knew without the slightest doubt that it was all true, and Carlos Sanchez had been a witness. His story, and his heart, spoke to mine more convincingly than any of the books of theology I had been reading. That was the moment I first knew that I had to change my life.

I left the monsignor that day with a great story (though not the one I'd expected) but also with a burning conviction. Soon afterward, I began to take instruction in the Catholic faith. Anything I accomplish for the kingdom of God has its beginning in the testimony of a little old priest who had experienced life-changing miracles and would have taken those stories to his grave had a rookie journalist not stopped by to ask him about his life and times.

The New Testament records Jesus' healings and other miracles, as well as those accomplished by Paul and the apostles. The history of the church not only tells of miracles such as the ones Monsignor Sanchez received but also features amazing stories of wonder-working saints. These amazing men and women are found among us even in our own time.

Two of the most celebrated wonder-workers of the twentieth century are a Greek Orthodox monk known in his lifetime as Elder Paisios (now Saint Paisios of Mount Athos) and an Italian Capuchin friar known as Padre Pio (now Saint Pio of Pietrelcina). You cannot travel either in Greece, in Saint Paisios's case, or in Saint Pio's native Italy, without seeing images of these men everywhere—in corner shops and cafés, on the dashboards of pious motorists, and anywhere popular piety manifests. They serve as reminders that miracles and miracle workers are still with us.

Elder Paisios (1924–1994) was born to the Eznepidis family, then living in Turkey, and baptized with the name Arsenios by a monk who would later be canonized as Saint Arsenios the Cappadocian. Though the baby boy's family had chosen another name for him, the revered ascetic prophesied (accurately) that he would soon die but that the child would one day take his place as a spiritual leader. He claimed the lad as his spiritual son.

During the Greek Civil War of the 1940s, young Arsenios served as a radio operator in the army. Later, he entered monastic life, eventually settling on Mount Athos, where he was given the name Paisios and gained fame as a great ascetic and miracle worker with uncanny insight. Elder Paisios used to joke that he was a "radio operator" carrying messages between God and the world.

Metropolitan Athanasios, the current Orthodox archbishop of Limassol, Cyprus, was a spiritual son of Saint Paisios, whom he knew on Mount Athos. I met the archbishop—famous in the Orthodox world as "Father Maximos" of the popular book *The Mountain of Silence*—before a prayer service at a monastery in the Troodos Mountains of Cyprus. I asked him if he had ever seen miracles around Saint Paisios.

"Many. Many miracles," the old monk said. "The first time I met him, I didn't understand him fully, and I thought he was a little bit crazy. I had a very firm idea of how saints should be, and I wasn't open."

At the time, the young monk Athanasios asked Elder Paisios what monks like him should do to work on the path to sanctity. The elder said they should make many prostrations—bows from the waist made by Orthodox Christians in prayer.

"'How many every day?' I asked. And he touched me on my back, and said, 'Many, many,'" recalled the archbishop. "At that very moment, the entire environment around us—there were two of us—became filled with a strong fragrance. As soon as he realized it, Elder Paisios said, 'You should go, you should go.' But all the way back to the dock, we could still smell that fragrance that came out of him."

Later, Athanasios visited the elder in his cell and joined him in praying an all-night vigil. At one point, the cell filled with light, and the oil lamp swung back and forth, on its own, for half an hour. When it ceased, the light withdrew.

"I have seen many, many miracles, but what was most impressive about him wasn't the miracles," said Metropolitan Athanasios. "Those were an almost natural phenomenon to see with him. What was really impressive about him was his great humility, and his great love for God and men. The fact that this man, through his experience with God, became a very balanced, perfect human being."

One of the most remarkable testimonies to the wonder-working saint's spiritual powers, and man's persistence in resisting grace, comes from the Greek author Dionysios Farasiotis, in his book titled *The Gurus, the Young Man, and Elder Paisios*. Farasiotis tells the story of rejecting Christianity as a dead thing but then visiting the elder on Mount Athos and finding that it is wondrously alive.

Farasiotis experienced many miracles in the presence of the elder, and "had grown so accustomed to unusual and inexplicable phenomena taking place at the elder's cell or in his presence that I had come to just take them for granted.

"He once told me, 'Don't give too much weight to these kinds of things or spend a lot of time investigating them, because there's always the danger that the devil's tricking you. If something is from God and you ignore it in order to be spiritually careful, God is so good that he'll find another way to speak to you that's even more obvious.'"[1]

Like the Prodigal Son, however, Farasiotis forgot all of these things, repeatedly. "Each time I left the Holy Mountain, I was enticed into sin and wasted the precious gifts that my father had given me, becoming poorer and more wretched than I had been in the beginning," he writes. The elder "neither got angry with me nor gave up on me. Every time I returned in repentance, he took hold of me, lifted me up, cleaned me off, tended to my wounds, dressed me like a prince, filled my purse with gold, and sent me back again, with honors, to the world."[2]

Despite these mercies, Farasiotis traveled to a far country—India—seeking spiritual experience. He fell in with a series of diabolical gurus who used witchcraft and other devious means to entrance him and others. Yet on returning to Athos to visit the elder, Farasiotis would discover that Paisios knew what battles he had been facing in India and had been fighting for him in the spiritual world. Eventually the young man made a full repentance and now spreads the saint's message of faith and repentance.

"Christ was the source of Father Paisios's life and strength," he writes. "I once asked him about this. He answered me, 'My child, I'm just a human being. I pray to Christ and he replies. If his grace abandoned me, I'd be just another bum on the streets of Omonia.'"[3] (Omonia Square in Athens at the time was a haven for drug addicts, thieves, and prostitutes.)

The Greeks had among them the wonder-working witness of Elder Paisios; the Italians had his Catholic counterpart Padre Pio.

Padre Pio (1887–1968) was born Francesco Forgione to a pious peasant family in southern Italy. As a boy, he had frequent religious ecstasies and longed to join a religious order. At age fifteen, he was received into the Capuchins, a branch of the Franciscans that observes strict poverty.

In the summer of 1918, Padre Pio began to bleed from parts of his body associated with the wounds of Christ. This phenomenon, known as stigmata, was first observed in Saint Francis of Assisi during a thirteenth-century vision. Padre Pio's painful wounds bled daily for the next fifty years. Doctors could not explain them. They never healed. The blood from the sacred wounds smelled of incense.

Padre Pio worked many miracles of healing, including restoring sight to a blind girl, Gemma di Giorgio, who was born without pupils. One of the saint's early miracles was reported in Italian newspapers in 1919. In San Giovanni Rotondo there lived an old man who was mentally and physical handicapped. Francesco Santarello had clubbed feet and made his way around the village on his knees, using miniature crutches. He would climb up the hill to the monastery daily to beg for alms.

One day, as Padre Pio passed through the church's door, heading in to say Mass, Santarello shouted a plea for a blessing. Padre Pio looked at him and said, "Throw away your crutches!"

Santarello did not react. "I said, 'Throw away your crutches!'" the priest repeated, then continued on into the church. As the gathered crowd watched, Santarello cast down his crutches, then rose to walk on his deformed feet for the first time in his life.

Padre Pio also had a gift of reading souls—that is, being able to know the sins of some who came to him for confession, even though they had said nothing. This power was intimidating to some who were otherwise drawn to the holy man.

The famed Catholic writer Graham Greene kept a faded and worn photo of Padre Pio until the end of his life. In 1949, he went to one of Padre Pio's masses accompanied by a woman with whom he was having a love affair. He saw the stigmata on the priest's hands and believed they were real. Yet Greene left after refusing an invitation to meet the famous mystic. In a 1990 letter to journalist Kenneth L. Woodward, shortly before Greene died, the novelist explained, "I made excuses not to go as neither of us wanted our lives changed!"[4]

SAINTS IN A DREAM

One of the posthumous miracles accepted as valid by the Catholic Church for the canonization of Padre Pio was a healing in the year 2000 of a seven-year-old Italian boy on the verge of dying from a disease with a 100 percent mortality rate. Padre Pio, accompanied by angels, appeared to him while he was in a coma and told the child he would be healed. And, inexplicably to medical science, he was.

Something similar happened to Kevin Becker, a gregarious young American I met at a church conference in 2019. As a college student eight years earlier, Becker fell out of the second-floor window of his house, landed on his head, and was expected to die. Doctors said that if he survived, Becker, an avid soccer player from suburban New York, would likely be severely disabled for the rest of his life.

As Becker lay in the hospital in a coma, hovering between life and death, his devoutly Catholic family and their prayer network kept vigil. A relative suggested that they all add to their prayer an appeal to Pier Giorgio Frassati, asking him to pray for a miraculous healing. Someone sent a prayer-card image of the Blessed Pier Giorgio, which Kevin's mother placed at his hospital bedside.

Pier Giorgio Frassati, a beatified (one step below canonized) Italian, was born to a well-to-do Turin family in 1901. Despite his privilege, the charismatic Frassati, an avid athlete, became a crusader for social justice. When he died of polio at age twenty-four, thousands of Turin's poor turned out on the streets to salute his funeral cortege as it passed. In 1990, after results of a stringent investigation of a claimed healing through Frassati's heavenly intercession validated a miracle, Pope John Paul II beatified the young man, granting him the honorific "Blessed."

Only one more miracle was needed to win official sainthood for the Blessed Pier Giorgio. This is why one of the Becker clan convinced the family to appeal to Pier Giorgio for help.

Kevin Becker rose out of his coma, swiftly recovered, and walked out of the hospital a few days later, tossing a football in the parking lot with his brother as their father packed the minivan. His healing was utterly shocking to his doctors.

Shortly after his recovery, Becker confided to his mother that an "angel" had kept him company during his coma. He explained that while he was under, he sensed that he awakened in his bedroom back at the college house. He saw a stranger, a young man, standing there.

"Who are you?" Becker asked.

"I'm your new roommate," the man said, then introduced himself as Giorgio.

For the next few days, Kevin and Giorgio worked on straightening up his room. Every time Kevin would try to leave, Giorgio would stop him, telling him he wasn't ready to go out yet.

After hearing this tale, Kevin's mother showed him the prayer card with the photo of the Blessed Pier Giorgio, the one that had sat by his hospital bed.

"That's him! That's the guy!" said Kevin, who had never before seen or heard of Pier Giorgio Frassati.

I heard this story from Kevin Becker himself at a church in Austria. You would never know that he had had a sick day in his life. The Vatican has been investigating Kevin's case. In April 2024, a senior Vatican cardinal announced that Frassati would likely be canonized in 2025. As of this writing, it is not known which of the further alleged miracles attributed to the intercession of Frassati was accepted as valid by Rome.

"You hear about miracles your whole life. And you've heard about this miracle, and you read about the miracles in the Bible, and you hear about the miracles all over the world," said Geralyn Becker, Kevin's aunt, in video testimony. "What a blessing to witness one firsthand and to be able to talk about it."

MERRY CHRISTMAS, STEFANO

Though signs, wonders, and miracles still occur in our own time—especially, according to missionaries, in non-Western parts of the world where people are more open to them—the Christian West does not experience them with as much frequency. But sometimes they happen, and their effect is so great that they cause witnesses to leave their lives behind to follow Jesus. Almost a century ago, the young atheist painter and professor of art Carlos Sanchez returned to the Christian faith of his youth after experiencing a dramatic miracle at Mass in his native Guatemala City. In 1991, the tears of the elderly Sanchez, then a nonagenarian Catholic priest living in a retirement home, weeping as he told me about the miracles that changed his life, washed away the last barrier to my own conversion.

Something like this happened to a young Italian who wishes to be known here only by his first name, Stefano. I first met him a few years ago, in my travels. He is a teacher with a luminous face, radiant with faith. His conversion story was astonishing. He agreed to repeat the account to me, but only if I would withhold his last name, because he wants his story to be entirely, as he put it, "for the greater glory of God."

Stefano, who is in his early thirties now, was born in Rome to a family of atheists. In fact, his father was a dedicated member of the Communist Party. His mother was raised in the mountains by a faithful Catholic mom, but the daughter lost her faith when she went down to Rome for boarding school. Stefano's parents baptized him out of social custom, but the only religious believer in the boy's life was his grandmother Maria, who would come down from the mountains to stay with the family during the winter months.

From his early youth, Stefano experienced strange things, such as an inner voice directing him, and also dreams and visions.

"Every night I would dream the same dream: a dark and evil lady would come to my bed and start hitting me with a crucifix. I would wake up terrified and take refuge in my parents' or my brother's bed," he recalled.

"The second phenomenon occurred during the day: I would see a lady dressed in long robes, adorned with jewels, who would appear in some situations such as when we were eating at the dining room table. I was the only one who had the angle of vision facing the living room. Or when I was waiting for the elevator and she would appear in the entrance hall of the building where I lived. I saw this lady as if she were real. She never spoke to me."

The boy was afraid. He sensed that the lady who haunted his dreams was the same one he saw during the day. When the visions began, the inner voice ceased. Stefano went to his religion teacher at school asking for advice, but all she could do was urge him to pray. He never talked about it with his family. How could he? They were all atheists.

At age eleven, Stefano began to prepare for his first Communion. He wanted to receive the body of Christ, but a battle raged in him. On the day before his class was to receive Communion for the first time in Mass, their priest held a rehearsal with an unconsecrated Host.

"I was the last in line, and when it was my turn, he told me, 'The body of Christ.' I told him, 'I don't eat this shit,'" said Stefano. "The priest gave me a loud slap in the face and left me standing there."

Yet he still took Communion the next day. The inner voice from his youth returned, and he found it comforting. But the dark lady of the dreams and visions came back too. By force of will, Stefano put it all out of his head and got on with his life.

In high school, Stefano threw himself into being a soccer superfan and started drinking too much and doing drugs. He ran with a bad crowd. Still, he was a good student, and wanting to imitate his father, he learned antireligious doctrines and other parts of the Communist catechism.

"When I was around seventeen or eighteen years old, just about to enter the university stage, I had a reputation," he remembered. "People around me appreciated me for my ideological radicalism, the violence of my words and my actions, and the continuous blasphemies that I inserted in every sentence I pronounced. I spat on crucifixes, ridiculed saints and priests, uttered tremendous words against the Virgin Mary and her Son."

He was riding high with the cool crowd, but Stefano battled against a sense of emptiness inside. He filled the wound with even greater cynicism, pleasure, and even violence. And then three people—a girl, an Argentine friend, and a priest—came into his life at around the same time.

The girl was a classmate he admired, a faithful Catholic who stood out from the others. Though he teased her about her beliefs, Stefano accompanied her to Mass just to be with her. He met the Argentine through his cousin, a coworker, and found the foreigner to be a likable, charismatic guy who prayed naturally and spoke easily about the faith. And the priest was a cleric he met in his grandmother's town, who talked to him about life and exhorted Stefano to keep his eyes open for signs from God.

In the middle of all of this was the bizarre experience of repeatedly crossing paths in Rome with a certain middle-aged man, who, when they met in the streets, would stare at Stefano intensely.

What was happening? Stefano couldn't be sure. He sensed, somehow, that it would be solved only if God made himself known in a forceful way.

One day in late autumn, he was walking to a subway station when he passed a church and felt compelled to go inside. Almost trembling with fear, he came across a statue of a saint, a nun with a wound on her forehead. This was an effigy of Saint Rita of Cascia, a fourteenth-century nun and stigmatic honored in Italy as the patron saint of impossible causes, though atheist Stefano didn't know that. Confused and desperate, he asked Saint Rita to help him.

That evening, Stefano met his cousin, with whom he had begun to talk about God. They were headed that night to a relative's house, but Stefano said he didn't want to go because there was always a party atmosphere there. That night, his mind was on other things. He and his cousin decided to sit in the car outside and talk instead.

"When I got out of the car, I realized that on the other side of the street there was a homeless man sitting and staring at me," said Stefano. "His stare was intense and made me uncomfortable. After a few seconds I told my cousin to go upstairs. When I began to leave, the homeless man got up, crossed the street, came straight to me, and said: 'Hi, Stefano, I finally found you.'"

Stefano froze. The homeless man said to him, "The Lord Jesus told me to tell you that from now on you will have nothing to fear."

Stefano began to cry. His cousin, standing next to him, also heard the man say to Stefano, "From today, you will live for him."

The mysterious stranger continued his discourse. "He knew everything about my life," recalled Stefano. He told the astonished college student that the dreams and visions he had as a child were not of God, and that God had allowed him to be tempted for a greater good.

"The homeless man was also excited, and he cried with happiness for having found me," said Stefano. "When he finished his speech, he knelt down and began to pray an Our Father. After each sentence, he added praise to God for his mercy and for having been able to fulfill his mission. We could not follow his prayer, it was so powerful."

As the stranger turned to leave, Stefano asked, "Are you an angel?"

He smiled back but did not answer.

"What's your name, then?"

"Felice di Natale," said the stranger. In other words, Merry Christmas; the encounter happened shortly before the Nativity that year. Felice di Natale blessed the weeping young man in the name of the Father, the Son, and the Holy Spirit, then walked away, never to be seen again.

"From that day on my life changed," said Stefano. "The next morning, when I woke up, I went to the kitchen and greeted my mother, who was making coffee, with a kiss. My mother jumped back and said, 'You look different, what did you do last night?' I felt I had a new heart."

That same morning, a friend who had been praying for him phoned and asked Stefano to come see his new car. When he arrived, his friend let Stefano sit in the car, fresh from the dealership, and excused himself to run to the bank.

"When I opened the ashtray, I found a medal with a familiar face," he recalled. "The words on it said, 'Saint Rita, pray for us.' It was the same woman I had prayed to the day before!"

And then he looked up to see a man standing in front of the car, arguing with someone standing behind it. On that man's T-shirt was a single word: *Angel*.

The priest had advised Stefano to watch for signs. And here they were. God had showed up with force and claimed Stefano's heart.

"Since that day, my life changed, and after almost twenty years I can say that my conversion was a miracle, and that my life is Christ," he said. "I radically changed my life. I left the life of sin and opened my heart to Jesus."

It took a miracle that dramatic to break through the defenses of a young man raised to be a Communist. In that sense, Stefano's conversion was not so different from the conversion of a young pagan in that same city, Rome, in the first century. Through his witness, Stefano's entire family subsequently converted to Christianity—even his lifelong Communist father, who accepted Christ on his deathbed. With God, there are no impossible causes.

THE FACE ON THE CEILING

The first thing I noticed when I met Madeleine Enzlberger in Vienna was that she glows. She really does. I've seen that sometimes with Christians—Monsignor Sanchez was one—whose faith has a certain purity. The sense of peace she exudes is especially striking when you consider that she is executive director of a Vienna-based NGO that keeps track of rising persecution against Christians in Europe, a continent where few people seem to care.

Enzlberger, now in her early thirties, had been baptized a Catholic but had an unhappy childhood in which God was not present. Her parents—a left-wing politician father, actress mother—divorced, and both were deeply dysfunctional. As an adult, she made a mess of her life, trying to find a sense of stability and meaning but only stumbling deeper into a ditch. In this, says Enzlberger, she is typical of so many of her generation, failed by the adults who should have nurtured and cherished them.

"I had to become independent from an early age. I was raised by the world. I wanted more than anything to have a safe home and to build a safe life for myself," she said.

Enzlberger succeeded in school, and then professionally. But she was in trouble. She partied hard. She had a boyfriend, but she cheated on him with a work colleague. One weekend she was at Lake Como with some college friends, opened the curtains on a window, and beheld the lake and mountains bathed in golden sunlight.

"Suddenly I heard a voice saying, 'The higher you fly, the deeper will be your fall, and the harder you will land. You will be crushed. The damage will be severe,'" she said. "I was like, *Why am I having this thought now?* Looking back, though, I think it was the Holy Spirit preparing me for what was about to happen. I think Jesus told me not to be afraid, because it was the beginning of the scariest time in my life. I was not prepared for what was coming."

Not long after, she went to bed sad, even though it was her birthday. Her boyfriend was asleep next to her. As she lay staring upward in despair, the face of Christ appeared on the ceiling above her. She described it as looking a lot like the face on the Shroud of Turin.

Enzlberger heard a voice inside, one she knew wasn't generated by her mind, saying, "I'm going to promise you something. I promise you that you will never, ever have to be afraid again, not in your entire life. I will always be with you, no matter what. I'm not going to leave your side. You are always safe."

This was the feeling of security that she had always longed for. She wanted to stare at his face forever.

And then everything fell apart. Her career. Her relationship. Her health. Her family. Today, she believes that this is what God had prepared her for, and she believes that it had to happen to humble her. Said Enzlberger, "He knows that I am stubborn and won't give up things easily. The hell that was living inside me had to come out."

After two months of suffering, she went to adoration at the Stephansdom, the Vienna cathedral. Adoration is a Catholic devotional practice in which the faithful kneel or sit silently praying in front of a consecrated Host displayed in a monstrance. Being there in adoration was the only place she found peace. She didn't realize it at first, but she was seeing a miracle: "I saw on the Host the exact same face I had seen on the ceiling. I assumed that Catholics must imprint the face of Jesus on the Eucharist. Every time I went to adoration, I saw Jesus' face on the Eucharist. I thought this was normal, because they believe Christ is in the Eucharist, and they had somehow put Jesus' face on there. Who would look at a piece of bread for hours if it didn't have a face on it? I found out later that, no, there was no image of Jesus imprinted on the bread. He let me see in a special way that he was truly present in the Eucharist."

Despite all of this, Enzlberger still resisted full conversion. She ended up studying at a British university and one night attended a meditative prayer session with a nun. The nun read aloud the passage from the Gospels about a woman who could not stop bleeding but when she touched the hem of Jesus' garment, she was healed.

"That was the moment where I was standing in front of Jesus again, with my eyes closed, in that Bible scene," she said, "and realized, Oh, I'm the woman! I told him, 'I love you and want to follow you.'"

That was eight years ago. Enzlberger has stayed on the path ever since. "I was restored, and am being restored. That's why I had to go through a kind of purgatory on earth, for three or four years, where I really was healed and cleansed."

Listening to this young Austrian woman, I heard echoes of Hartmut Rosa's advice about finding enchantment, or resonance, by letting go of our compulsion to manage experience.

"What we really learn from reading the Bible is that trying to think of God in a human way is really a mistake. To try to make him predictable, controllable, put him in a box. The only rule we can hold on to is to always expect the unexpected with God," she said.

"It's like in a romantic relationship: If you control everything, what is left? There's no freedom for the other person to be who they are, and to amaze you with who they are."

It is unusual to hear Europeans of Enzlberger's generation speak so frankly and intimately about God. After all she's been through, she doesn't care. "I grew up godless, fatherless, and family-less," she said. "So many of us did."

She can't separate the miracles she received that led to her conversion from the purgative suffering and sacrifices she had to make—and she doesn't want to. They taught her gratitude and compassion.

"I think Jesus came to me and gave me all these things because God is merciful," she went on. "He knows that my families on both sides probably don't deserve this. My great-grandfather, for example, worked as a commandant in a concentration camp. Definitely not a family you would think God would love to bless. Sometimes I do believe, deep down, that this all happened to me for the sake of the other people still out there who don't know him."

THE CURSE OF THE BETRAYED CUBAN WIFE

Backstage at a 2020 conference in Nashville, I met a well-known Protestant pastor, John Mark Comer, who at the time led a church in Portland, Oregon. "You're the *Benedict Option* guy!" he said. "When your book first came out a few years ago, a lot of us thought you were alarmist. Now we're living it." He explained that his evangelical church used to be thought of as harmless by others in the famously progressive city. Now, with antifa activism having turned the town violent, many think of the Christians as a threat to all that is good and decent.

We talked about the spiritual-warfare aspects of the darkening situation in the United States. He told me that he and his wife, Tammy, had learned personally about the power of demonic evil and the greater power of Christ to defeat it. She had only a few weeks earlier been miraculously cured through prayer of a terrible disease over which doctors had no power.

"She had been living with a progressive disease that caused weakness and spasms all over her body," he told me. "It had gotten so bad that her face was constantly jerking. It was to the point where she wouldn't be able to go out in public without her face being covered. The doctors couldn't figure out what it was, though one specialist thought it might be a rare neurological disorder that was incurable."

Then Tammy's brother told her he had discovered a frightening family secret. Their great-grandmother had lived with a Cuban diplomat as his common-law wife. They had a large family, but the diplomat had hidden the fact that he had a wife back in Cuba. He had sent his wife to an insane asylum and left her there.

"It turned out that the Cuban wife somehow put a curse on my wife's great-grandmother," Comer said. "The terms of the curse were that every first-born girl from her bloodline would either die young or have a terrible disease. When we started looking at the family tree, we were shocked to see that this had happened! Sure enough, Tammy was the first-born girl in her family."

The Comers found a Christian healer who had experience dealing with family curses. When the man came to pray over her, Tammy's face spasmed uncontrollably. But then the healer began to break the curse in Jesus' name.

"I was right next to her, watching it all," Comer told me. "Her face became calm. She was healed, right in front of me. After years of this, it was over. She told me it felt as though something had been removed from her. She has been fine ever since."

The healing has been permanent. In 2021, just over a year after her restoration, Tammy Comer told her story to a Christian women's website. She said there, "The mantra of my life is: 'Thank you, thank you, thank you.' I never expected to be healed. It never crossed my mind that my sickness could have a demonic element to it, or that when we broke the curse my health would be restored."

THE PRODIGAL SON IN A HIMALAYAN CAVE

Joseph Magnus Frangipani has always been a seeker, but he has not always been careful about the search. False signs and wonders deceived him for many difficult years, leading him deep into literal and metaphorical exile before he found the truth in a wondrous way.

As a teenager, he left behind the bland, West Coast suburban Catholicism of his youth in search of deeper religious experiences. In high school, a class in self-hypnosis led him to meditation, which in turn opened all kinds of spiritual doors to Eastern religions.

Yet the more deeply he went down these paths, the more spiritually troubled he became. He saw so many friends and strangers desperate to shake off the burden of themselves, to have it dissolved in the void. Frangipani filled his life with different Hindu, Buddhist, and animist rituals, dabbled with divination through tarot cards, and embraced shamanism.

Eventually, Frangipani had a vision that summoned him to India.

"I went to India in search of the Source," he told me. "I had been summoning different beings through yoga meditation, but I realized after the vision that I was done in America. I wanted to go to a place where they had levitating monks and bleeding statues, to see if it was all real. I broke up with my girlfriend, got rid of everything, and bought a one-way ticket to India, just me and my backpack."

Frangipani made his way to the Dalai Lama's monastery in Dharmshala, in northeastern India. But even that didn't work. Buddhism satisfied him intellectually, but it did not satisfy his heart. He reckoned that he needed to go to the source of the sacred river Ganges: the Himalayan town of Gangotri. Wandering in the mountains nearby, the young pilgrim eventually found a cave with a little wooden door on it, and a latch.

"There was a wooden table with one of the legs broken off, sitting at an angle, and a musty, disgusting pillow," he said. "I thought, me being me, that's perfect. . . . I remember thinking that whatever Moses had, whatever

Mohammad had, whatever Buddha had, I want that. I want to poke myself through the spiritual ozone layer. If it's accessible to anyone, it's accessible to me."

Standing before a cave on the top of the world, having given away everything he owned and abandoned everyone back home, Frangipani realized that he was the Prodigal Son. He had forsaken his inheritance and was now poor, alone, and lost. He felt like a fraud. Frangipani wept. Not knowing what else to do at that moment, he entered the cave and began praying a mantra given to him by a Hindu priest. He did his best to link the words with his breath and the rhythms of his heart.

"As I breathed in, I said the mantra, and when I breathed out, I said the Jesus Prayer," he told me. *Lord Jesus Christ, Son of the living God, have mercy on me, a sinner.*

How did he know the Jesus Prayer? He had once worked at a bookstore in Oregon, where he came across a famous nineteenth-century Russian devotional book, *The Way of a Pilgrim*, built around the Jesus Prayer. He read it, and now, in his Himalayan cave, the words appeared out of the mist of his memory.

"The way I explain it is that the Lord had placed a seed in my heart, and the tears I had in front of the cave and all the snakeskins I shed of things I thought were true that weren't—they watered the seed," he said.

As the weary American pilgrim prayed, he had a vision:

Then I saw Christ in the cave, in the darkness, in the same way that when you look at a candle and close your eyes, you still see it in your mind's eye. That's the closest I could describe it. I really don't have the words. I knew instantly that this was God, who was also a man who was born and lived at a specific time in history, had died, was resurrected, and who is now everywhere, but chooses to emerge whenever he wants to. All these false ideas that I had had in my head for eleven years—because, remember, I left Catholicism through a high school class on self-hypnosis—fell out of my ears, so to speak.

Through Christ, I saw that what I had been doing was a sin. It wasn't like I had violated a legalistic ordinance or something but that I was running away from God. Intellectually I still have the scars of it, but I realized that it was a grave sin. And I knew this was my Maker. It was impossible to be alone. I had struggled with loneliness, and when I left the cave, it was impossible to be lonely because I knew that Our Lord was always present. Whether I see him now or not, I know he is here.

Frangipani finally fell asleep. The next morning, he opened the cave's door and two wolflike dogs stood there. Scared of dogs, he shut the door and said the Jesus Prayer.

"I opened it, and they were farther away. Every time I would close the door and pray the Jesus Prayer, they moved farther away," he said. "Finally, they were far enough away that I was able to grab my bag and run away back to the ashram."

He made his way back down to New Delhi, bought a Bible, and started to read it. Eventually he returned to the United States calling himself a Christian.

One day, Frangipani accepted a friend's invitation to go see an Orthodox church with him. *Why not?* the seeker thought. He had tried everything else. None of the Christian churches he had visited since his return gave him the same feeling of communion that he had in the Himalayan cave.

Then he walked into the Serbian parish in Eugene, Oregon, with his friend—and his jaw dropped.

"It looked like the cave!" he said. "There were the *lampadas* [small icon lamps] hanging over the icons. I thought, 'That's the Holy Spirit! They're hanging at the level of the heart of everybody. That's the illumined heart! That man in the icon, that Christ—that's who I saw in the cave!'"

Frangipani described his first-ever Divine Liturgy as "like having gold shaved into my ears. Those hymns were the music of the soul."

He is now an ordained deacon in the Orthodox Church, serving a parish in Washington state. At the end of our conversation, I said that his long, strange search for enchantment ended with a miraculous vision in a cave on the roof of the world, but that he had actually found plenty of false enchantment, or dark enchantment, on his way to the light.

Said Frangipani, "Yeah, if you set out to find it"—vivid spiritual experience for its own sake—"it will come to you, but the fruits will be very bad."

Yet as the old Christian faith framework breaks down, more and more Americans—especially younger ones—are seeking exactly that, in subversive places. They are opening themselves up to dark enchantment, a real phenomenon, one that kills the soul. In this spiritual warfare raging around us, both visibly and invisibly, there is no neutral ground. You must take a side and commit.

THREE PROPHETS
OF THE *REAL*

Learn the lesson that, if you are to do the work of a prophet,
what you want is not a scepter, but a hoe. The prophet
does not rise to reign, but to root out the weeds.

—Saint Bernard of Clairvaux

In 2014, Vladimír Palko, a devout Catholic and a minister in one of the first post-Communist governments of his native Slovakia, published a book about what he sees as the coming persecution of Christians in the West. It was translated into German. An Austrian bishop gave a copy of the German version to Pope Emeritus Benedict XVI, who was then living in a monastery at the Vatican.

In 2015, a letter appeared in Palko's mailbox. It was a short personal note from Benedict, thanking him for having written the book. The old pope's letter concluded, "We see how the power of Antichrist is expanding, and we can only pray the Lord will give us strong shepherds who will defend his church in this hour of need from the power of evil."

Out of respect for the pope emeritus, Palko kept the letter private. When he revealed the letter to me shortly before Benedict's death in early 2023, the retired statesman was aware that the holy pontiff's words amounted to a prophecy. After Benedict's burial, Palko made his words public.

Christians should, of course, pray for the Lord to send strong pastors, especially in times of trial. But what if the most important leaders in the fight against lies and darkness are emerging not from the ranks of the clergy but from the laity? Where ordained religious leaders falter, others are rising to speak to the needs of the disenchanted.

The nonbelieving psychologist Jordan Peterson racks up millions of views for his YouTube lectures on biblical topics and the power of mythological thinking. Canadian cognitive scientist John Vervaeke is also a nonbeliever but has emerged as a powerful voice working in the same field as Peterson, addressing what Vervaeke believes is the most serious challenge of our time: "the meaning crisis."[1] You have already met in these pages the British psychiatrist Iain McGilchrist, who leads growing audiences to profoundly rethink, from a scientific and artistic perspective, the model of reality that has led Western civilization into this maw of nihilism.

There are Christian voices leading this conversation, too—even clergymen's. The Presbyterian pastor Paul Vander Klay, a frequent online collaborator of Vervaeke's, is a key figure, guiding an international following from his laptop in Northern California. The Catholic bishop Robert Barron, with his thoughtful online ministry, reaches audiences far beyond his Minnesota diocese.

Yet I focus here on three lay voices that are becoming important in pioneering the path to Christian re-enchantment. These men are Christians with no formal theological training who are responding to the meaning crisis as artists and storytellers. It may be no accident that all three are converts to Orthodox Christianity, men of the West who have found in the mystical thought and practices of the ancient Christian East a way of life with compelling answers to the challenges of our troubled time.

MARTIN SHAW'S NIGHT RAINBOW

The English writer Martin Shaw was never a pagan, exactly, but he's everybody's idea of a happy heathen. Or, in a more Christian vein, he's like the Lost Inkling, a curious lad who wandered into the woods of Devonshire and grew up as a foundling in Tom Bombadil's cottage.

Barrel-chested, bearded, and full of laughter, we met in a London pub to talk about the middle-aged writer's surprising discovery of Christianity, which he had come to believe, as Tolkien told Lewis, is the myth that is true.

Shaw built a lifelong reputation for being a great teller of stories and champion of mythology as a guide to life. With his advanced academic training, Shaw founded and led Oral Traditions and Mythologies courses at Stanford University, but most of his teaching has been done far away from the classroom, in his many books and with small groups of seekers he has guided into the forests of England's West Country.

Shaw was raised in a believing Christian family, one that went from evangelical to charismatic, but the faith never took. He rejected the religion of his youth, but he wasn't angry about it. He immersed himself in studying and celebrating the mythic imagination, for what it told us about what it means to be human. But he never really thought it was, you know, real.

Then, in the autumn of 2019, Shaw had a "strange impulse," as he put it, to spend a lot of time going into the forest behind his house in rural Devonshire. He decided to slip quietly out of his house for 101 nights in a row to spend a couple of hours in the ancient Devonian wood. His specialty is wilderness rites of passage, so this was a familiar practice.

"I was looking down the barrel of fifty. I was not ostensibly religious, but I was spiritual, as a mythologist and a storyteller. I wanted to give something back to the place that had sustained me all these years," Shaw recalled. "So I would go out at night and recite some troubadour poetry, or tell a story, or I would just sit and be quiet. The main thing is that I wasn't there on the take. I wasn't there to use nature as a backdrop for some sort of epiphany. I was there to give something back."

On his final night of the prayer discipline, after a hearty supper at home, the writer wandered into the cold woods for an all-night vigil. Shaw sat down near the remains of an Iron Age fort, and for some reason he found himself saying, "Thank you for giving me this time with you—whatever 'you' is—and if there's anything you would like me to see, I'm absolutely at your mercy this evening."

And then it happened. As he told the story, Shaw took pains to emphasize that he was not in an altered state, chemically induced or otherwise. Something nudged him to look up into the night sky, which was pitch black. In a winter interview over pints of Guinness in a London pub, Shaw said:

> Suddenly there was this one light that quite rapidly started to get bigger. It was like looking at a firework that was opening up, or almost like the tip of an arrow that's expanding behind the tip. The colors were very odd, like the colors of the aurora borealis, which I had never seen, but I know of them. This is all happening within three to four seconds. Then there was something like a painted arrow shooting out of the heavens. You're trying to catch up with the impossibility of what's happening, with the Old Testament-ness of what's happening. I just stood there frozen to the spot. As truthfully as I tell you now, that great light fell into the ground about ten feet away from me. There was no noise.

It did not frighten Shaw. In fact, it left him overwhelmed by joy. He had gone through a lot of suffering in the previous decade, with the breakup of his marriage, but now he had been visited by something magical, something miraculous.

"I danced all night, by myself," he said. "Then I walked down the hill to my cottage, got into bed, and just as I was closing my eyes—it was very odd, like a news flash, across the darkness of my trying to fall into unconsciousness—were these nine strange words: *Inhabit the time and genesis of your original home.*"

What did this mean? Certainly not that he should investigate the book of Genesis. Hadn't he put Christianity behind him, in his childhood?

Then Shaw began to have dreams. In one dream, he met a Being of light, who drew Shaw deeply into his overwhelming love and told him that every encounter of love between human beings is an echo of this.

Then, on a visit to his writer friend Paul Kingsnorth in Ireland, Shaw spent the night in the mossy cave of Saint Colmán, a seventh-century Irish holy man. The night after that, Shaw dreamed he was back in the cave. In recalling the intense dream, Shaw used the Hebrew name of Jesus: "A stag came to the entrance of the cave, in moonlight. He looked in, and he was twelve-tined, which means he had a great rack. I suddenly realized in the dream that I was phenomenally thirsty. As I had that thought, the stag, which I know in some form was Yeshua, leaned forward with his antlers, and on the tip of every antler was a drop of water. It's very much like an icon. I was underneath it with my hands cupped, gathering every drop of God-water, of Yeshua-water, of Spirit-water. I drank, and then I woke up. I knew I was in dangerous territory by now. I knew my number was up."

In another dream, Shaw was a private in the Great War. His captain came to him, told him his arm was damaged, and said he could fix it but would have to break it first.

"I suddenly knew in the dream who I was in the presence of. I knew. I knew. And I gave him my broken arm. If it hurt, it hurt only for a second," he said. "Once those dreams started to come after seeing a ball of light in the sky, you know something is happening."

The signs pointing to Christ were so overwhelming that Shaw surrendered. In the early spring of 2022, he became a Christian, receiving baptism in the River Dart, which he said felt like being hit with a bolt of electricity. "It's very hard for middle-aged men to concede that maybe they don't know what's going on, that maybe they don't know what's going to happen next. But that's how my fiftieth year began."

The sign in the sky, and the signs in his dreams, left Shaw no choice but to accept the faith he had abandoned after childhood. But it cost him plenty. He lost friendships. He lost followers who had admired his work on mythology. But he has gained new life.

He had to find a church. Shaw worshiped with Anglicans, then with Baptists, then with Catholics. All good people, he said, but something didn't fit. Then he went into a strip-mall Orthodox parish "and reality changed."

"When I experienced the Divine Liturgy, I felt that I was on the supreme runway for the arrival of the Holy Spirit," he recalled. "It was like a grail cup. *Ahhh*—this is the thing that I yearned for in the charismatic movement. It has all the power of the charismatic movement, but it has the container of the liturgy, which means it doesn't spill out over the edges in a manic way. It's filled with prophecy, it's filled with power, it's filled with restoration."

I share with Shaw the theory of German sociologist Hartmut Rosa: that the more we seek to control our surroundings, the less able we are to experience enchantment. His life-changing encounter that night in the forest, I say, began with his opening himself up to mystery, asking the cosmos to reveal to him what it wanted him to see.

"We're getting into the area of submission," he responds. "What I've learned through many years of wilderness vigils is that it's a Jacob wrestling with the angel kind of situation. You have to be gloriously defeated. You have to be made lame in a fashion. A decent laming will serve you much better than many petty victories, because it's something you will never forget. It reminds you of your appropriate shape in the universe, which is on one knee, or both knees."

Decades working in the field of mythological studies prepared him to accept the "true myth" of the gospel, Shaw believes. In the same way, pagan myths preceding the birth of Christ prepared the world for his coming.

"Not all Christians would go along with this, but I feel that, in the thousands of years before Yeshua arrives, we have pinpricks of the eternal in many mythologies," he tells me. "Not to the degree of sophistication—something different goes on in the Sermon on the Mount, something different goes on in the Beatitudes. But in essence, the notion of sacrifice, the notion of the underworld, the notion of a resurrection, almost in tune with the rhythm of the seasons. We're talking to each other now in a London pub, and if you look outdoors, it's like everything is dying. But we know from experience that in only fifteen, sixteen weeks' time the earth will come back again. So we see a Christ motif in the earth itself."

Besides, he says, taking a sip of his beer, "I knew that when human beings go through travail and depression, only myth will do. Myth told me everything I needed to know about the conditions of life. Christianity showed me how to live it. That's the difference."

Though Christianity in England has been withering all his life, Shaw was raised in an evangelical family that went over to Pentecostalism. Yet he lost that faith in part because he found that it could not speak to the artist within him and to the deeper parts of his soul. It was only when he found Orthodoxy, which is almost unknown in Britain, that Shaw discovered "the old magic is still about." He was received into the Orthodox Church on Easter 2023.

"There was no contemplative tradition, post-Reformation, in this country. There were no wild old women. There were no hermits. There was no time of sitting in the bush," he laments. "The Catholic philosopher John Moriarty says Christianity is in danger of losing its 'bush soul.' And that's in essence what it was. It seemed domesticated, white, with a heart condition, not very well."

The churches will never argue anybody today into faith, Shaw warns. It's got to happen through imagination and experience. The trouble is that "there is a tyranny of choice facing the younger generation."

"Now kids have access to medicinal plants, like ayahuasca, that can draw them into epiphanies that maybe even Julian of Norwich wouldn't have dreamed of, within forty-five minutes, with no spiritual growth attached to it. It's just a movement of chemicals," he says, clearly worried. It may not offer spiritual fireworks and instant enchantment, but the slow journey of theosis, within a community that has been on this same journey for two millennia, is a surer path.

What should Christians do? "Act more like Christians. I wish they'd go back to things Christ said: Do this, do this, do this: hold your standards high. The early church's success wasn't apologetics, initially. It was lifestyle and story. They had the best story, and they had a really interesting lifestyle."

Shaw has long had a practice of taking broken people out into the forest to help them find their way back to wholeness through the wilderness experience and thinking about the lessons in myth that can help them rediscover meaning. The problem with most moderns, he says, is that everybody is afraid of suffering. But that's the only way to have deliverance. For Dante, there was no Paradise without first sojourning through Inferno and Purgatory.

"Modernity is all about removing suffering," Shaw muses. "But Christ, as I recall, says 'Carry your cross'—and that's not going to be comfortable."

Contemporary churches have made Christianity too easy, presenting it as a way around suffering instead of a way through it. The old myths know better. So did premodern Christianity. They knew sacrifice was the only way to enlightenment. Whoever would save his life must first lose it, as the Bible says.

There are three colors important within the language of myth, Shaw says: red, black, and white. They represent the stages of life.

Red symbolizes youth, passion, and worldly success. Black stands for failure, suffering, the "Road of Ashes," for "making a covenant with limits." It is the descent into the underworld that every hero must endure.

"And that's the problem," he says. "We have a generation of kids being told you can be anything you want. The problem with that is that myth tells us something very different. Myth tells us that you are born to be something very specific. There's a job allotted to you that no one else can have. So the notion of the tyranny of choice, this à la carte spirituality, where you can pick and choose whatever you want, and God is fine with it, and on we go—this is not how it works."

The final color, white, stands for the move into elderhood. You can access the energy of the red but have been chastened by the black.

"People often say to me, 'What does the underworld look like in my life?' Well, it looks like a divorce. It looks like mental health issues. It looks like illness. It looks like any number of things that pull you from the steady road. But myth says from the beginning that is the way slant. And until you have deeply traversed it, until you've mapped it, you can't really bring a gift back.

"What we have are faux initiations, faux rites of passage, faux underworld experiences, where people go through things but are actually completely safe," Shaw goes on. "Young people react to that by saying, 'Right, I'm going to gobble ayahuasca, I'm going to have a visionary experience.' But because there's no mentorship around, no stewardship around, they have the rupture but they don't have the rapture. You can't glean meaning from it."

You know you are moving into the white, he counsels, when you are given an opportunity and your thought isn't *How is this going to help me?* but rather *How will this affect those I love?*

When we met in London, Shaw had just returned from visiting his brother in California. "I met lots of princes, but no kings," he said. "That is, I met a lot of young men empowered with their religious groups, or whatever it was, but I didn't feel the black in them. I felt the red, I felt a bit of the white, but none of the black."

The mission facing the churches now is to find the strength both to accept the underworld journey and to carry it out. We will not be able to get there with propositions and logic, much less with forced cheerfulness and therapeutic uplift. We need, says Shaw, to set our Christian imaginations afire with the power of story.

"The wonderful thing about stories is that it's very rare that you will meet people who say, 'The one thing I can't stand is a good story,'" he says. "It's got me through the doors of the great and the good, and into the most extraordinary situations, because, by and large, people are pro story. As we know, the most compelling story tends to win. It's more than argument. You know what it is? It's aesthetic arrest."

"Aesthetic arrest"? By now the stout storyteller with the salt-and-pepper beard is holding a dram of Scotch whiskey in his hand, explains that it's a concept defined by the Irish novelist James Joyce. It's the feeling you get when you are shocked into silence by the presence of great beauty, a beauty that conveys something deeper than what's on the surface. It cracks open your heart to receive truth.

I tell Shaw that this brings to mind filmmaker Andrei Tarkovsky's view about the purpose of art: to "harrow" one's soul and to make it "capable of turning to good."

"Aesthetic arrest reveals to us what compels us," Shaw says. "It forces us to ask, 'What do I love? What will it cost? And what am I prepared to pay?' That's the fundament of most myths. In myths, the guarantee is that you're going to come back changed. Things will be different."

PAUL KINGSNORTH: MAN AGAINST THE MACHINE

In a small house on a country road in rural Ireland there dwells a tall, thin middle-aged Englishman whom a growing number of people on both sides of the Atlantic think of as a prophet. Paul Kingsnorth, a novelist and essayist, moved to County Galway a decade or so ago with his wife, Nav, and their two children looking for a way to live in clean air, close to nature, and homeschool their kids. The Kingsnorths couldn't afford land in their native England, and they loved Ireland anyway, so to the Emerald Isle it was.

Only now, a few years into his surprise conversion to Christianity, is Kingsnorth starting to suspect that there was a deeper logic at work in the move—something both mystical and providential.

"The things I'm learning about the early Irish saints, the way religion here is connected to the landscape—there's still more of a living folk and mystical tradition here than in England, though it's certainly dying out," he tells me. "And the fact that I became a Christian here, which I certainly didn't intend or expect to do, I don't think any of that would have happened in England, simply because of the way I was living. I think I had to come here to learn something."

Though he was raised in London without religion, and educated at

Oxford, where he met Nav, Kingsnorth has always had a spiritual bent. It came out early in a passionate commitment to politics, especially on behalf of environmental causes. Eventually, though, he came to see that fighting the destruction of the natural world through politics was a futile endeavor, chiefly because so few of us are willing to confront the spiritual crisis at the heart of the problem—a crisis that engulfs both the exploiters of nature and those who would oppose them.

Leaving political activism behind and moving to rural Ireland prepared the searching writer for what he now believes was his true calling.

"My connection to God comes through nature, fundamentally. I've had from a very early age this sense that it's alive, and we're connected to it, and that we live in a society that denies this and is destroying it," he says. "It's a spiritual tragedy as well as a cultural tragedy. What we're doing in the modern world is so destructive to nature, as well as to our culture and our souls. It's all the same thing, really. I've always had that, and have been on a spiritual quest for a long time."

The quest to find God through immersing himself in nature took him through Zen Buddhism for a few years, then into a brief dalliance with neo-paganism. Then, for reasons he is not able to adequately explain, Kingsnorth found himself drawn powerfully to Christianity. In 2020, with the order of the world coming apart in the long COVID emergency, Kingsnorth began to attend the liturgy at a newly established Romanian Orthodox women's monastery down the road from his place—the first Orthodox monastery to be established in Ireland in a thousand years. Eventually he was baptized in the icy River Shannon on January 6, 2021—the feast in which the Orthodox mark the baptism of the Lord.

Sitting by the fire in an Irish country pub, Kingsnorth tells me that Orthodoxy challenged his received idea of what Christianity is. Having been raised in a Protestant country that had largely cast off its ancestral faith, Kingsnorth had the idea that Christianity was about nothing more than arranging your thoughts and feelings in a certain way, going to church on Sunday, and being a kind person. As a young seeker, he saw in the churches around him nothing but dead ends.

"We have a political crisis and a technological crisis today, but what's at the root of it is a loss of connection to the earth," Kingsnorth says. "Young people want that, and so they'll go off to become activists, or maybe get into neo-paganism. What they really need, I would say looking back, is a spiritual path that connects them to the earth, which is a legitimate thing. You're not going to get that in the Church of England. But you do get it in the Orthodox faith, interestingly. It's not earth worshiping, but it fills in what's lacking in Western Christianity: the mysticism."

Kingsnorth faults the Reformation, especially in England, with severing the link between heaven and earth, so to speak, by closing the monasteries, stripping the churches of holy images, banning holy wells and other natural things the faithful thought connected them to God—all in the name of purifying it from the perceived taint of Catholicism. "All you're left with is a very rational, very intellectual, very masculine idea of God," he says.

The thing is the cultural habit of rationalizing and abstracting has also made serious inroads into Catholic life and practice in the West. The crisis, Kingsnorth concluded, is not so much one of Catholic versus Protestant as it is of Eastern Christianity versus Western Christianity. It is a conclusion I arrived at not long after I left Catholicism for Orthodoxy in 2006, the result of a great spiritual trauma. I had thought of Catholicism as a mystic-friendly form of Christianity—which it is, but only by comparison to Protestantism. When seen from the East, both Catholicism and Protestantism—in the West, at least—are marooned primarily in the head and are futilely trying to think their way out of the civilizational shipwreck of the modern West.

Though Orthodoxy shares with Catholicism a fundamentally sacramental metaphysics, in practice Orthodoxy is far more mystical, emphasizing that the conversion of the heart must precede the conversion of the intellect. It does not deny the intellect, only orders it within an anthropological hierarchy.

One aspect of Orthodoxy that particularly appealed to Kingsnorth is its panentheism—the principle that God is, as the Orthodox prayer says, "everywhere present and filling all things." It's not the same as pantheism, which says that the material universe *is* God. Orthodoxy teaches that God is separate from his creation but also interpenetrates it with his energies, or his force. Consider how the warmth and pleasant glow of an English hillside on an August afternoon occur because the faraway sun penetrates the grass, the flowers, and the earth with its energies. The hillside is not the sun, but it testifies to the presence of the sun in its material being.

"The earth is not God, but God is there, present in nature, not in some far-off heaven," Kingsnorth says. He goes on: "He's deeply entwined in everything. Creation is the book of God, as Augustine said, I think. That is explicitly recognized in Orthodoxy. So what I was finding, weirdly enough, was a sort of ancestral Christianity that my ancestors in England would have had access to, and that the early Celtic saints certainly had access to. When I became Orthodox, a lot of people said to me, 'Welcome home,' and, strangely, it did feel like I was coming home. It felt like there's something here that we had, that we lost."

Though Ireland is—or was, until recently—a deeply and broadly Catholic country, becoming Orthodox did not exile Kingsnorth from a relationship to the saints of old Ireland—Patrick, Brigid of Kildare, Kevin, and the rest. All Western saints canonized prior to the Great Schism of 1054 are also Orthodox saints. This matters immensely to Kingsnorth, who says the nature mysticism that so energizes him has been at the core of Orthodox Christian experience since Christianity's early centuries.

"This is the faith of the desert fathers," he explains. "It's not earth worshiping, but it is definitely acknowledging the mystery of creation and the different levels of reality that exist, and it shows you the connection you can have with the natural world. So you look at the stories and journals of the old Celtic saints, and the poems they wrote in Ireland and Britain, and realize they had a deep connection to the natural world, whilst also realizing that they're trying to go through it."

The Orthodox faith teaches that one can go, in the phrase of the late archbishop and theologian Kallistos Ware, "through creation to the Creator." That is, when you stand in front of an icon praying, you are not worshiping the sanctified painted wooden slab but regarding the image as a window into heaven. Equally so with nature, says Kingsnorth: you don't worship it as some sort of idol, but you look through it for connection with the one who created it.

"God is a great artist, and creation is his work. We learn about the artist through what he has made," Kingsnorth says. "So if you're plundering and cutting and burning your way through the earth because you believe you were told that that's what it means to have dominion over the earth, then that's blasphemy, that's sacrilege."

I have been following Kingsnorth's writing for years. In 2014, I read an essay he wrote about the sense of overwhelming awe he felt descending into the earth to a cave where prehistoric artists had painted animals on the walls. Though he made it clear in the piece that he was not a religious man, there was something about Kingsnorth's mystic rapture that told me he would one day become a Christian, and not just a Christian, but an Orthodox one. Orthodoxy seemed to be the only form of contemporary Christianity that could accommodate his primitive awe.

"I spent many years on a search for spiritual truth, because I had a strong sense of God, or the divine, or something. I didn't know what it was. I felt it in nature especially, but I didn't know what it was," he says. "So when I went to the Pyrenees caves, I had a strong feeling that these people knew something thirty thousand years ago. There was some connection: as if we were on the same path."

Kingsnorth did not believe that he had the right to break off a little of this religious tradition and a little of that to create his own syncretic bricolage faith, made just for him, in that very modern way. Something that you have put together on your own is not something with the capacity to change you. He felt that he had to receive this ancient form of Christian faith, a tradition that has been forged over many centuries, on its own terms.

His writing comes across as apocalyptic, which Kingsnorth readily concedes. But we *are* living through an apocalypse, from the Greek word meaning "unveiling." What is being unveiled? That we are using our advanced technology to build new life-forms to become our gods—and, in so doing, we are destroying our humanity and the good earth. The Genesis story, in which man refuses to obey God and instead listens to the serpent, which tells him that he can become his own god if he follows his desires—that's us today, says Kingsnorth. If you want to see the root of the crisis, there it is in Genesis.

Kingsnorth calls the emerging enemy of God and man "the Machine." It's a metaphor for the technological society manifesting around us, seizing control of our lives, and rendering us all as little more than data. Its attitude toward life can be summed up in the well-known saying of Yuval Noah Harari, Silicon Valley's favorite intellectual guru: "Organism is algorithm."

Paul Kingsnorth thinks that worldview is a Luciferian snare—one that is leading us all to surrender more and more of our liberty and humanity to the false promise that we can live in a totally managed world and all our suffering will cease. This is demonic enchantment, in Kingsnorth's view.

"What is the snake? What is Lucifer? He's deeply in love with himself. He wonders why he should do what God wants, and why he can't do it himself," says Kingsnorth. "That's an attractive message, in a way, especially to the young: *Why the hell should I have to do what you tell me?* That question is the basis of modern Western culture. We've all been there. And if technology is what gives you the power to live that out, what are you going to do? You can't argue against it."

This, continues Kingsnorth, is why we thoughtlessly give ourselves over to the Machine. "A grid of technology that's created and controlled by surprisingly few people, that envelops the rest of us, is sold to us as convenience. But it's a trap.

"We're not disenchanted these days—we're just enchanted by the wrong thing," he goes on. "And the thing we're enchanted by is technology. If you're enchanted by technology, you're enchanted by yourself, because we're the ones who created technology. If you're enchanted by an ancient rainforest, then you're enchanted by something outside of yourself, that was created by God, or even if you don't believe in God, it's naturally occurring. You stand in awe of it. That's not the same as being enchanted by a computer that's been created by a human, by a human mind."

He likens the stupor in which so many of us wander around, stuck in our heads and our heads stuck in the information cloud, to being "elf-shot"—a concept from Anglo-Saxon mythology.

"If you were elf-shot, you would kind of lose your mind, you would lose your memory. They would find you wandering in the woods and take you home. You would spend days recovering, if you ever recovered," he says. "When you're elf-shot, something has been fired into your body by the elves that makes you lose part of yourself, your sense of self and place. That's what living with the smartphone is like: being elf-shot."

If technology produces false enchantment, what, then, is true enchantment, from a Christian point of view?

"It's a love of God and love of creation," the writer says. "Instead of becoming enchanted by what you've created, you become enchanted by what already exists. You become enchanted by nature. You become enchanted by the Creator of nature. You become enchanted by the liturgy, by storytelling. You become enchanted by something you can never fully understand. Enchantment comes from mystery. You have to have mystery—mystery and beauty. Enchantment is putting yourself in right relation to mystery."

In the trilogy of novels he has written, Kingsnorth dwells in the early medieval English past or in a primitive, postapocalyptic distant future. What connects the novels is a deep attachment to place—a real place, lived in by people who see themselves and their places rather differently from the way we do in the "Westernized sludge," as Kingsnorth puts it, of the WEIRD culture created by technology and capitalism.

Is Kingsnorth nostalgic? Is he romantic? Yes, he admits—and tells a story about how a monk on Mount Athos known for a gift of clairvoyance warned him to resist his inner romanticism as "not Christian." Reflecting on this in the calm of his home—we have abandoned the pub and retired to the author's library, where three bantam chickens cluck peaceably in a cage under a mounted bookshelf—Kingsnorth muses that the Athonite monk might have been warning him that, for the Christian, there is no true home on this earth.

"If you manage to find a home here, it will change, and you will change, and it will disappear," he says. "Particularly at the moment, everything is disappearing. The older Irish people I know around here say Ireland has changed utterly. You can't find a home that's going to last your lifetime.

The culture doesn't get passed on. There's no tradition left in the West. It's almost like it's not worth passing anything on to your children, because you don't know what the culture is going to be like when they grow up."

This is another reason why Kingsnorth believes that the Orthodox form of Christianity, which teaches one to cultivate detachment from the world and one's passions, is a kind of ark within which he can ride out the desolating tempest of liquid modernity.

"For a Christian, the only eternal thing is God. It seems to me that this world is a testing ground: you sharpen the scythe of your soul on the stone of the world. And if you see it like that, then the potential there is to save yourself from the twin traps: a nostalgic attachment to things that are dead, or a belief in progress, which tells you that you can remake the world into something you want it to be."

What should Christians and non-Christians seeking a more enchanted life do? I ask. That's easy, says Kingsnorth: go to the Divine Liturgy, and go into the woods.

"The more you can immerse yourself in nature, the more likely you are to experience something that takes you out of yourself," he says. "If you go for a walk in the forest, and you bear in mind that the forest is sentient, that it can sense your presence there, and you try to cultivate that indigenous sensibility—if you go in with the sense that you're seeing and being seen, that you have to give something back as well as take . . . that's not paganism, that's not 'nature worship.' But it is nature reverence: it's just a sense of respect for the place, of gratitude. That shifts the experience you have of the place. You're not just walking through a nice place experiencing the scenery, but you're having a living relationship with it. The more time you can spend in a place like that, the better."

In 2022, the man who once went into a vast underground chamber in the Pyrenees and was overwhelmed by a sense of divinity and mystery spent the eve of his fiftieth birthday sleeping in a tiny, shallow cave notched into the side of a limestone ridge in Ireland's Burren region. This was the cave of Saint Colmán Mac Duagh—the same one in which he took his friend Martin Shaw and in which Shaw saw what he calls "the mossy face of Christ."

"That's the kind of weird thing I like to do: sleep in a cave, camp under the stars, walk in the forest, drink the water from the well," he says. "Really simple things about being human that most people would have considered normal even a few hundred years ago and still do in large parts of the world."

Breathing fresh air, going to the forest, seeing the Milky Way, understanding that you are part of a world of living, conscious beings—that's the way back to wholeness, according to Paul Kingsnorth. He tells me that he and I are both writers and we know that people can understand something of who we are if they read our books. It's like that with God: you should read the Bible, and you should read the book of nature, in which the Creator expresses himself.

"One of the reasons I'm so inspired by and interested in the early saints of Ireland is because that's what they were doing," Kingsnorth says. "They weren't worshiping the trees by any means. They were worshiping God and fighting the devil, but they had a relationship with the place they were in. They weren't ashamed to say 'I feel blessed to be in this place, look what God has given me, I am thankful for it.'"

Kingsnorth rises to pull from his shelf a collection of ancient Irish poetry. He turns to a page and shows me a poem, by an anonymous medieval author, called "The Hermit's Hut." It is a litany of description of his simple dwelling place in the forest in which he hallows every detail by describing it and giving thanks for it to "the Prince who gives every good to me in my hut."

"This is a man who is immersed in nature, and who is grateful to the Creator for all of it," Kingsnorth explains. "He doesn't see it as a thing he can abuse, that he has to hide from, or that is the domain of the devil. It's a gift, and he's thanking God for it every day. And he's paying attention to it, which is what allows him to write a poem like that. He knows everything that's there. And that's the thing we've lost in the West, whether we're Christian or not. That is fundamentally why we're broken: we just don't have the relationship we're supposed to have with the rest of life."

Many of his former comrades in the environmentalist movement have turned on Kingsnorth, accusing him of defeatism in the fight against climate emergency. He flatly rejects the charge. The truth, he insists, is that there are no feasible political or technological solutions to the problems humanity faces today. The myth of progress is a lie.

"I've effectively given up on the stories of the modern West," Kingsnorth says. "That doesn't mean I've given up on people or nature—quite the opposite, actually. I just think there are different ways of doing things. We've known what they are in the past. I think we cannot go back to them, but we can rebuild them. And we're going to have to do that."

The Machine and the world it fabricated are collapsing, and there's no stopping it, any more than Rome's collapse in the fifth century could have been arrested. Things fall apart. The sacred mission of Christians (and others) is to find ways to live out the faith in a resilient way as the world collapses around us.

"If you have faith in God, and if you have a ritual that ties you together, and if you have a sense of love and respect for the natural world, and if you have a community, then you can live reasonably well, as well as any human can live," he says. "Not that you're going to be able to avoid pain and suffering. Nobody can escape that. But you can escape this alienation and loneliness, and this slavery to technology that we've created."

Doing this will require the painful acceptance of our own powerlessness in the face of events. To sacrifice the desire for control. To let go of the false idea that we can encompass everything by human knowledge and bring it under our intellectual and technological dominion. A Christianity that places mystery, wonder, and awe in the center of its worship and spiritual disciplines is a Christianity that can endure what is to come.

We talk about how spiritually depleted Catholicism in Ireland is today, owing in part to the abuse scandals that shattered people's faith in the institutional church. Paul's Irish neighbors tell him that if Christianity is going to rise again in their country, it will begin not with the official church but with the people. And this is why Kingsnorth is so hopeful for the Irish: they have all around them holy wells, the ruins of monasteries, hermit caves, and all the other signs of wild Celtic Christianity, which still point to God.

"This is why I keep talking about these wild saints who lived in caves: because there's really something in there for us," Kingsnorth said. "These people were Christians. They were part of the Roman church. They weren't inventing their own theology. But they were practicing a very wild, a very earthy, very localized form of the Christian faith."

That scares some modern Christians, who fear that it's secretly pagan or syncretistic. "But it's not!" he protests. "It's at the roots of the faith and has been all along. It's there in Ireland, it's there in England, it's there in Egypt, it's there in Russia's Saint Seraphim of Sarov. This is not something that the hippies are inventing. This is how the faith always was. The faith doesn't have to be what the popular clichés imagine: go to a big stone church on Sunday, be told what to do, then go home again. We need to return to our roots to be nourished again.

"This doesn't mean that any Christian future will look exactly like it looked in the fifth century," Kingsnorth continues. "It's not the fifth century. On the other hand, we are in another time when a big empire is collapsing, and we're going to have to build something in the rubble. I think Christians are quite good at that. Christianity flourishes best when it's small, and a bit persecuted, and people in it are thought of as weird outsiders. Keep Christianity simple, and wild, and ascetic, and beautiful, and loving. That's what it should be, and that's what it can be, because it has been that before. That's what excites me."

JONATHAN PAGEAU, SYMBOLIST

Though Jonathan Pageau is not a Christian apologist, the YouTube videos of this French Canadian icon carver and cultural analyst are a frequent stop on young people's pilgrimage route into Orthodoxy—a stream that has become a torrent since COVID hit, as Christians from more modern traditions seek a church with deeper roots, one that is more mystical and more spiritually demanding. His popular online channel, The Symbolic World, features Pageau's teaching about the meaning of recurring patterns in art and popular culture, as well as podcast interviews with writers, musicians, and other figures he finds interesting.

Pageau, now in his midforties, has been tending his online vineyard for many years and now finds himself at the center of the new re-enchantment movement—the one person that the various teachers, artists, storytellers, clerics, and others working in this field have in common. Why? Probably because everybody can remember when they first started listening to Pageau and becoming aware that what they thought was just their own peculiar intellectual interest was part of a pattern now manifesting in the ruins of Western culture.

"We're really in an exciting moment. This feels like the moment I've been planning my whole life, or rather dreaming, praying or hoping for," Pageau tells me. "Jordan Peterson, John Vervaeke, Iain McGilchrist, and so many others—they were all being prepared in the darkness, and then the moment arrives, and they start to appear, and connect, and it becomes natural. Something that was impossible twenty or thirty years ago becomes the most obvious thing."

What does Pageau mean by "the symbolic world"? In the language of semiotics, a symbol—from the Greek word meaning "gathered together"—is a thing that both represents another thing and participates in it. Orthodox Christians call the Nicene Creed the "symbol of faith" because it is not only a representation of Christianity, but it also gathers together its fundamental teachings and points beyond itself to the deeper reality of the faith.

In Pageau's thought, as in premodern Christian belief (as well as in contemporary Orthodoxy), everything in the visible world is a symbol of the unseen world, in that it is metaphysically grounded in God's being. You will recall from earlier chapters that, in this view, things have meaning because they participate in God's existence. Prior to the past five centuries or so, Christians believed that they did not stand apart from the spiritual world but were integrated into it. This is what it meant for their world to be enchanted. Humanity knew God not solely by contemplating him but also by mystically participating in his life.

We have been through the story about how the West fell into the abstractions of propositional theology, and how the Western world gained wealth and made material progress on a vision that cast out transcendence. As Yuval Noah Harari puts it, the story of modernity is of humankind exchanging meaning for power.[2]

Though Catholicism did not fully abandon this sacramental ontology, it weakened it through the separation of the natural and the supernatural. The theologian Hans Boersma has written favorably of the early to mid-twentieth-century Catholic theologians of the *ressourcement* movement, who rebelled against the dry Scholasticism dominating Catholic theology at the time in favor of a rediscovery of the patristic tradition, with its deep emphasis on the mysterious sacramental participation of created reality in divine life.

Yet whatever the theologians say, the felt experience of many, perhaps most, Christians in the modern world is one of ambient desacralization. This is why, in a 2019 Pew poll, only 31 percent of US Catholics said that they believe the Eucharist is actually the body and blood of Jesus Christ[3]—one of the most fundamental teachings of the Catholic faith. Liquid modernity is leaching the sense of the numinous and the mysterious out of even the sacramental faiths.

There is fresh hope coming from unusual sources. According to Pageau, new findings in various disciplines are starting to reveal that consciousness does, in fact, interact with matter in ways that refute the old model of matter as nothing more than dead stuff. And now, as our cultural systems and frameworks of meaning-making disintegrate, the older belief that life organizes and manifests itself in patterns not made by humans but perceptible by them has taken on new importance.

Orthodoxy, he says, never lost sight of these truths, which went into eclipse in the West beginning with the Renaissance. Now that the West has run its nominalist experiment to its nihilist end, perhaps Western people (as well as Eastern ones ignorant of or alienated from the Orthodox faith) will rediscover these ancient truths.

"Materialism has played itself out," Pageau tells me. "After World

War II, the philosophical materialists and reductionists claimed they could explain everything in terms of purely material reasons. But you can't do that with consciousness. People have begun to see that there is a necessary patterning to reality, a patterning that seems to have something to do with our capacity to perceive reality and to participate in it consciously."

For all its gifts, science alone can't offer any of us a reason to live, or the patterns by which we must live, if we are to flourish. In Pageau's view, much of contemporary Christianity (he came to Orthodoxy from evangelicalism) lacks the mythological depth to be an island of meaning in the storm-tossed sea of liquid modernity. On the other hand, ancient Orthodoxy has preserved a framework of imagination and practices through which time and place are patterned and made sacred. In the twenty-first century, Orthodox Christianity resembles the primitive forms of faith discussed by Mircea Eliade—and therein lies its particular power to speak to the post-Christian modern world.

This, says Pageau, offers a lifeline to moderns who are tossed around by their passions, told they are free to choose everything—but have no idea what to choose. In Orthodoxy, they can find not merely a story and a set of moral and theological beliefs but also a profound description of how reality works. This includes patterns, hierarchies of patterns, and patterns embedded in Scripture, mythology, the natural world, ritual, and elsewhere.

This is a coherent reality that people don't create but rather discover, if they can escape their radical subjectivity—the prison inside their own heads.

"We have to be in some ways patterned beings that have a coherent, functional approach to reality, or else we'll die," Pageau says. "Saint Maximus the Confessor is helpful here. He says that true freedom is not the capacity to do whatever you want. Freedom is aligning yourself with the truth. If you don't, you're a slave. Freedom means moving toward goodness, truth, and beauty, not being enslaved to your passions, your whims, and your will."

He goes on: "You discover that these patterns all interact with each other, holding everything together like a dance in which we all participate. We're not talking about religion as feelings or morality but as the thing that ties all of reality together, in God. It's all there in the fathers of the church."

It's no accident that people today, especially young people, are making their way to more fringe forms of Christianity, says Pageau, including some sterner varieties of Protestantism (Calvinism in particular), Latin Mass Catholicism, and, of course, Orthodoxy.

"How is it that people becoming Orthodox have become the avant-garde?" the former Baptist asks, laughing. "Everything that's happening now happened to me a long time ago. The questions people are asking now about meaning, about the fractal nature of reality, these are questions that my brother, Matthieu, and I were asking ourselves in our twenties. I knew that I was a Christian, but I thought, 'What do I do?' I was reading Hindu texts and Sufi texts and wondering why we Christians don't have anything like these transformational approaches to faith.

"It was only later, when I started reading the church fathers, especially Saint Gregory of Nyssa, that I began to open my eyes and realize that Christians do have it," he continues. "I started by loving the Middle Ages, and crying because there was nothing like it anymore, nothing like that art. And then I discovered Orthodoxy and realized that it's all still here."

Pageau makes his living carving icons out of wood and has established himself as a successful sacred artist, working in the Orthodox tradition. Yet his YouTube interviews and presentations draw a large number of nonbelievers—some of whom later turn up at Orthodox churches seeking catechesis and baptism, according to parish priests, who say Pageau is a gateway. Why do atheists and agnostics listen to him?

"It has to do with the New Atheists making religions look so arbitrary and alien that when you show some people just a little of the beauty in religion, and of the patterning there, they get so surprised that they're willing to start paying attention," he says. "These people are starting to face the problems of emergence"—the area of thought dealing with new phenomena arising from the interaction of complex systems—"the problem of consciousness, and the relationship between mind and matter, all of these challenges, and they look around to hear what people are saying about it. They're used to hearing Buddhists talk about this stuff, but they're surprised to find a Christian like me who is willing to engage these questions and to point out that the answers are in the church fathers."

If people today—Christians and otherwise—want to live in a re-enchanted world, Pageau says they will have to fight for it.

"It starts with our own lives, with our belief that praying has value," he says. "We all struggle, standing still and saying psalms, but that's valuable, not just for our souls, but also for the basic building blocks of our world. It scales up. That total attention you are able to give to God will leak out into all aspects of reality."

You have to have families that are connected and communities of connected families. Pageau says that we have to take the Benedict Option in the sense that we must deliberately live in rooted religious ways that were second nature to medieval people. That's the only way to resist the fragmentation and scattering of postmodern life.

"There are young people in my parish that are actually doing it," he says. "They started a work co-op, and they're trying to involve as many people in our parish and other parishes in this work co-op. They say their morning prayers, they work together, then want to live in the same place. They want to get a common space that they can rent or buy where they can meet informally. It sounds so boring, so normal, but we are at a point where this is the way to renewing the life of the church. This is the way it's done."

The particular gift Orthodoxy brings to the search for re-enchantment is the teaching that to pattern our world in fruitful ways we have to first pattern our own lives, and our relationship to God, in fruitful ways. You don't have to be a theological genius to grasp how to do this; you only have to show up, and keep showing up, fasting and bowing and living according to this pattern the Orthodox Church has produced over two millennia. Through participation, over time you will find things falling into place. You will discover brokenness beginning to heal.

"It's a cure that's not just intellectual," Pageau points out. "People propose solutions to the meaning crisis that are fragmentary. Political solutions, philosophical solutions, they will fail because they don't reach all the way down, or all the way up. I mean, they don't talk about daily practices, like bowing when you pray, and they don't talk about focused attention on the higher good that draws it all together."

The collapse of the WEIRD model, and the breakdown of normative Christianity in the West, is unavoidable, warns Pageau. Therefore, we should not be surprised by the violence breaking out around us, by the radical instability of the self, by the emergence of technological efforts to control a collapsing society, and so forth. Nor, he says, should we be shocked by the normalization of the occult in American popular culture. You can't have Christian re-enchantment without having a parallel re-enchantment from the dark side.

"Re-enchantment is happening—we're not making it happen, it's happening on its own. We're going to see things that we haven't seen in a thousand years. We're already seeing it," he says. "We see demon-possessed people. They're coming out in public. They have power. It's going to become inevitable as things go back to that world."

Many people today are drawn to the occult because it promises mystery and magic, and also because it is often built around self-gratification. Says Pageau, "It's Luciferian in its structure because it has to do with myself, in terms of my will, my experience, and it has to do with the sense that I am the highest point of that."

I mention to Pageau that an Orthodox friend at a booming parish in the American South tells me that they are swamped by young converts coming out of neo-paganism—and that this presents a huge challenge to clergy unprepared for it. I also mention two Orthodox priests I know who believe in the demonic but who were either too afraid or too proud to take it seriously when it showed up in their parishes.

"Priests and pastors are going to have to deal with it, because people have been living in that world," he replies. "You are going to have people come to your church and say that they want to be Christian, and they have been worshiping Odin and sacrificing animals. You are going to have people who have taken massive amounts of psychedelics and had encounters with beings that have ruined them. Those are the kinds of people who are going to be coming to the church—and we aren't ready for it."

THE *URGENCY* OF THE *MYSTICAL*

> *The devout Christian of the future will either be a
> "mystic," one who has experienced "something,"
> or he will cease to be anything at all.*
>
> —Karl Rahner

Why should anybody want to sail into the mystic?

First, because it's real and true. The received narrative of the modern world—that mind and body are separated, that the spirit has nothing to do with materiality, and that there is no intrinsic meaning to matter—is a lie. That is not how the world works. We live not in an impersonal universe but in a divinely ordered cosmos permeated by Logos. Christians know from Scripture that this Logos is not merely a rational organizing principle, it is Jesus Christ, the second person of the Trinity.

Far too many Christians have forgotten this truth and absorbed instead one of the defining ideas of modernity—a lie that has made us rich and strong but also unhappy and alienated from the world around us, even our own flesh. The lie is this: There is no connection between spirit and matter. Matter has no intrinsic meaning.

It has turned us from a flock of pilgrims on a journey of ultimate meaning into lonely tourists flitting around from place to place, madly trying to stay one step ahead of boredom. We were not made to live in such a world—but if we accept the philosophical and metaphysical principles of modernity, it is hard to do otherwise. The bottom line: if we want to live, we have to turn our lives around and walk away from the false parts of the Enlightenment and toward the true Light.

The second reason is that living in disenchantment is killing us and destroying our civilization. We have lost a sense of meaning and purpose. We are alienated from the natural world, one another, ourselves, and our bodies. This can't go on, and it won't go on. Either we will stop it or it will stop us. A disenchanted world is a hopeless world. And it's a world that will look to politics, the occult, sex, pornography, technology, drugs, and other false means of escape from hopelessness.

The Christian faith does offer moral order, political and social action to help the weak and oppressed, and therapeutic comfort for broken individuals. But if a church or denomination offers only moralism, politics and social activism, or emotionally exciting therapeutic uplift disconnected from deep prayer, sacrificial commitment, and authentic change of life, it is useless. It is worse than useless, because it convinces the world that Christianity is counterfeit.

Plus, no matter how intellectually satisfying the theological treasures within a particular Christian tradition may be, if they do not lead to an ongoing personal relationship with Jesus Christ, what good are they? In the post-Christian world, people—especially young people—are not looking for powerful exegesis of papal encyclicals, erudite sermons about the mechanics of salvation, five killer apologetic arguments to use against atheists, or any other canned strategy. They want to know whether life has any meaning or this is all there is. They don't want to know *about* God; they want to know God. Heaven knows he isn't much of a theologian, but Mick Jagger, of all people, had it right when he sang, in an obscure blues cut from an early seventies album, "Don't want to talk about Jesus; just want to see his face."

Marshall McLuhan, you will recall, insisted on the difference between percept and concept. A percept is immediate awareness of a thing; a concept is awareness of the thing made abstract. Faith is primarily a spiritual percept, not a concept, which is an act of the mind. When asked whether the incarnation was a percept or a concept, McLuhan responded, "It is a percept because, as Christ said over and over again, it is visible to babes, but not to sophisticates. The sophisticated, the conceptualizers, the Scribes and the Pharisees—these had too many theories to be able to perceive anything. Concepts are wonderful buffers for preventing people from confronting any form of percept."[1]

The death of Christianity happens, he said, when Christians start to act as if the faith is primarily about ideas and logical arguments, not direct perception of the living God. As a Catholic, McLuhan believed that authoritative doctrine served as the framework within which to comprehend and interpret that experience, but it could never be anything more than the map that pointed the way to the territory. He also said that everyone he knew who had left the faith began their defection by ceasing to pray. Prayer is the main way the Christian experiences faith as percept, not concept. But as you have seen in this book, it is not the only way to perceive the presence of God filling all things.

We should also seek enchantment and wonder because it keeps our eyes on God, in whom we live and move and have our being, and our hearts aflame with love for him. The Bible teaches that human beings are made in the image of God and for loving communion with him. Being finite and fallen, it is not easy for us to maintain this connection at all times. Experiences of wonder remind us that God is present at all times and is calling out to us, in love, to return to him and dwell in the blessedness for which we were created. Ian Norton, whose account of his miraculous deliverance from heroin addiction began our story, is an especially vivid example, as is Martin Shaw's rainbow arrow shooting down in the night sky. But there are many others.

A final reason to live oriented toward wonder is because it gives us the strength we need to persevere resiliently in times of suffering. Alexander Ogorodnikov told me how he regained his faith and sense of purpose after God sent angels to him at night as he languished in solitary confinement. Romanian priest Gheorghe Calciu testified to how the otherworldly sanctity of a dying Christian cellmate in his country's gulag inspired his perseverance. As you read earlier in this book, Jewish doctor Viktor Frankl found the strength to carry on inside a Nazi concentration camp when life-giving thoughts about his wife coincided with the sun's rays illuminating German farmhouses at just the right moment.

AN ENCHANTED VIA DOLOROSA

And then there is what happened to me. I tell you what follows to show you what it means to live inside Christian enchantment and how it provides even ordinary people—people who aren't heroic anti-Soviet Christian dissidents but everyday bumblers like me—the power to persevere despite facing the intense headwinds of personal suffering. It's how this book you're reading began its life.

In the fall of 2018, I was in Italy on a tour to promote the Italian edition of one of my books. My final lecture was in an oratory church in Genoa. After the talk, a man pushed through the exiting crowd to reach me at the podium. He had a thick build and scruffy white hair. His name was Luca Daum, and he introduced himself as an artist. Apologizing for his bad English, he said he had been praying that very afternoon when the Holy Spirit told him to come to my lecture and give me a particular engraving he had made, nested in a folder. I opened it and saw the image it contained.

Its title is *The Temptation of St. Galgano*. I had no idea who Saint Galgano was, but the engraving was beautiful, and I thanked the stranger for it.

That night in my Milan airport hotel room, I googled Saint Galgano. It

Luca Daum, The Temptation of St. Galgano (2018).
Reprinted with the kind permission of the artist.

turns out that Galgano Guidotti was a young Tuscan nobleman of the twelfth century who had a reputation for violence. His mother prayed fervently for his conversion and especially petitioned Saint Michael the Archangel to help lead her son to Christ. Galgano had a vision of Saint Michael, who told him that God was calling him to leave the world and serve him.

The next day, Galgano was riding his horse near a steep hill in the countryside when his horse reared and threw him. A voice told Galgano to look at the top of the hill, where he saw Jesus Christ, the Virgin Mary, and the twelve apostles standing outside a round church. A force seemed to carry him to the hilltop, where the vision disappeared. As he stood there, Galgano heard a voice tell him to leave his sinful life and serve God. Galgano said it would be easier for him to stick his sword into the stone in front of him than to do that.

The young feudal lord brought his sword down onto the stone—and it went in, almost up to the hilt! Galgano built a hut there, next to the sword in the stone, and lived there as a holy hermit atop the hill, called Montesiepi. He died almost one year later at the age of thirty-three. By then his reputation for holiness was so great that bishops and abbots came to Galgano's funeral. His own bishop ordered a round chapel built over the sword in the stone, just like in Galgano's vision.

Galgano was canonized in 1185, only four years after his death. His was the first cause for canonization taken up by the Catholic Church under new rules that required investigation of the putative saint's life. A cardinal came to Chiusdino, Galgano's hometown, and interviewed Galgano's mother, others who had known him, and people who reported miracles after visiting the sword in the stone and asking Galgano to pray for them. All of these testimonies remain today in the Vatican's archives.

And there's this: in the year 2000, Italian scientists investigated the sword in the stone. A ground-penetrating radar found that the unseen part of the blade penetrates unbroken through the rock. Metallurgical testing proved that the sword's metal dates to the twelfth century, just as the legend says.

I sat in my hotel room bed taking all this in and thought it was a marvelous story. But what did it have to do with me? I packed Luca Daum's engraving carefully into my suitcase and set my alarm to catch the early flight back to America.

Two years later, in the late spring of 2020, I sat on my couch at home deep in a funk. The country was well into the first round of COVID, which weighed heavily on my mind. Worse, I had fallen once again into the trap of brooding over my failed marriage. My marriage had begun to fall apart in 2012, shortly after my wife and I moved with our kids back to my Louisiana hometown. Long-buried conflicts within my birth family emerged, triggering a debilitating chronic illness and later an avalanche of problems between my wife and me.

Having spent almost a decade burning through therapists, with our relationship growing worse and worse, I had given up. I hung on because I did not want our children to experience divorce, but I was depressed, isolated, and internally paralyzed. I had not been to confession in a long time, which in the Orthodox Church meant that I could not receive Communion, with its healing graces.

One night, I somehow found the will to force myself to get off the couch, put on my shoes, find a priest, and go to confession. Back home, I felt exhilarated. Everyone else at home was asleep, so I decided to watch a movie. That spring, I was exploring the work of the late Russian filmmaker Andrei Tarkovsky. His movie *Nostalghia* was one I had not yet seen, and it was available online.

Nostalghia, which I have mentioned before in this narrative, is the story of a Russian poet, Gorchakov, who has been in Italy for a long time researching a biography of a Russian composer who once lived there. When the movie opens, Gorchakov is so consumed by missing Russia that he has become blind to all the beauties of Italy. He is trapped inside his head and living like a miserable ghost who can't leave Russia behind and can't accept Italy. In an early, wordless scene, the poet settles down in his Tuscan hotel room; the way he moves through the room conveys his depression and abstraction from the world around him.

My God, I thought, *that's me.*

As the drama unspooled, I felt more and more in common with Gorchakov, trapped in the quicksand of his memories. In a dream sequence late in the film, we see him walking across the nave of a large ruined church gazing anxiously down at the ground. A woman's voice—Saint Catherine of Siena's—says, "Lord, do you see how he's asking? Say something to him."

And the Lord answers, "But what would happen if he heard my voice?"

Saint Catherine pleads, "Let him feel your presence."

The Lord replies, "I always do, but he's not aware of it."

I thought, *That's me for sure!* I ask God for direction all the time, but would I follow his words if he spoke to me? Perhaps there is something within me that doesn't want to hear. And I know by faith that God is there, but why don't I feel him? Am I not aware of it? Am I so lost in my own head, and my own habit of brooding, that I am missing God's revelations to me every day?

Yes, I thought, *this must be true.* I couldn't deny it. I believed in God and in an "enchanted" version of Christianity, but I had fallen into despair, captured by my brooding and my grief such that I was insensible to God's calling.

One message of *Nostalghia* is that you cannot find bliss and harmony unless you are willing to sacrifice for it—and that might mean sacrificing your own happiness out of love for another. It also means sacrificing the control that you have when you stay inside your head, stuck in a rut that might be agonizing but at least familiar. And it means not only changing the way you think about the world but the way you move through it. This was not an easy message to hear, but one that resonated deeply within my heart. When the movie ended, I googled around to see where that gorgeous ruined church from the dream sequence was.

I gasped. It was the Abbey of Saint Galgano, on the plain near Montesiepi, where the saint plunged his sword into the stone nine hundred years ago!

Now I knew I was onto something. Luca Daum was a messenger, but why did God send Saint Galgano into my life? I studied Daum's *The Temptation of St. Galgano* more closely. The temptation is a thought that emerges from the saint's head, a serpent disguising its true nature with a human face. The serpent appeals to Galgano to take his eyes off heaven and look to the earth. The symbolism is clear: Galgano's doubts threaten to distract his attention from God and to convince him to doubt his own calling.

What was my temptation, then? To dwell on all that is imperfect and lacking in my life instead of fixing my eyes on God? To trap myself in my own head, where my attention fragments, instead of keeping watch on the world beyond? Yes, and yes—but surely there must be more.

I thought about Saint Galgano for more than a year. The entry of this minor medieval Tuscan holy man into my troubled life, through the art of an Italian engraver and a Russian filmmaker, was surely not by coincidence. I was onto something. But what?

In the late summer of 2021, I was back in Italy on another book tour. When it ended, I met Robert Duncan, an American Catholic friend, in Siena and we drove to rural Tuscany to see the sword in the stone. We arrived at Montesiepi, the steep hill that Galgano, rapt in a mystical vision, first climbed in 1180, and stopped halfway up to eat bruschetta, drink local wine, and prepare ourselves.

Then we walked the final leg of the journey. Wordlessly, Robert and I entered the cool of the round chapel. And there it was, under a thick plastic canopy: the sword in the stone. I kneeled by the thin iron fence around it and poured out my heart to the Lord God, asking for his will for my life. I prayed to Saint Galgano, too; Christians of the older traditions believe we can approach holy men and women who now dwell in heaven, asking them to help us by their prayers. I asked Galgano to pray with me that I would have eyes to see God's hand and ears to hear his voice—and a heart brave enough to say yes to him, whatever the cost.

I prayed for the courage to bury my own sword in the stone and to follow the will of God as Galgano did. Why was the sign of Galgano sent to me? I could not say at the time. But I had to follow where it pointed, come what may. These were synchronicities—Carl Jung's word for meaningful coincidences—that I took for signs drawing me deeper into mystery.

As I was writing this book, I discovered the meaning of Luca Daum's rendering of Saint Galgano as an iconic message for the postmodern world. But I also discovered its meaning for me.

On a cool late spring Saturday in Budapest, where I was doing a three-month fellowship (as much to escape the pain of a broken marriage as for anything else), I woke up, made coffee, and sat down to check my email. There was a note from my wife. It said that she had filed for divorce the day before. This was how I found out that my twenty-five-year marriage was coming to an end.

It was not surprising—again, the marriage had been in crisis for ten years—but it was shocking, as we had never discussed divorce.

The news that upended my life came a day before Palm Sunday for Orthodox Christians. In my emotionally bedraggled state, I kept my plans to fly the next day to Jerusalem for Holy Week. I set my bags down in my hotel room in the Old City, then made my way through its rabbit warren of medieval streets to the Church of the Holy Sepulchre. The original version of that vast old pile was built by Emperor Constantine in the fourth century, though it has been damaged and rebuilt over the centuries. The church encompasses the hill on which Jesus died and the tomb from which he rose from the dead. I ambled into the church and up the staircase to the chapel on top of Golgotha, fell on my face before the altar, and begged God for mercy for me, my wife, and my children.

That's how one of the most intense and spiritually charged weeks of my life began: with a desperate plea from a broken man.

I spent the early part of the week doing research and returning over and over to the Church of the Holy Sepulchre to pray at Golgotha. You can actually touch the rock through a hole under the altar. It can be overwhelming to face the fact that the story on which you have based your life happened here, in this place, and no other. That the eternal destiny of every man, woman, and child who ever lived and who ever will live was decided in the relatively short space between the hilltop site of execution and the tomb in a cave. But that's Jerusalem. There is nowhere like it on earth. It is the thinnest of thin places. And there I was, during the worst week of my life, walking in the steps of Christ's passion.

So many things happened that week to remind me that God was watching and had his hand on me. For example, on Good Friday, the most mournful day of the Christian year, I emerged from my hotel room and saw a Palestinian chambermaid vacuuming the hallway. She was a woman about my age and had a kind face. I saw a simple choker cross made of black yarn around her neck and told her it was beautiful.

She looked at me with eyes full of compassion. "It's yours," she said, then took it off and placed it over my head. I burst into tears and she jumped back.

"I'm so sorry," I said. "I'm having the worst week of my life. My wife just filed for divorce, and I don't know what to do. You showed me mercy. Thank you."

She hugged me and asked me to tell my story. When it was over, she stood back and said, "My name is Angela. Some people call me their angel. They tell me things, and I put them in here"—she placed her palms on her chest—"and that's where they stay."

You can call it a meaningless coincidence. I don't. I had been praying on my knees, with my head touching the ground in front of the altar built over where Jesus had died, begging for mercy. And then a humble cleaning lady named after the messengers of God touched me with mercy at the start of the darkest of all days. Angela's gift was a candle lit against the darkness enveloping me.

The next day, Holy Saturday, I went back to the church for the Holy Fire ceremony. All but unknown in the West, this is one of the most important events of the year for Orthodox Christians, especially the Arabs. Since at least the fourth century, Christians have gathered around the tomb of Jesus on this day. The patriarch ritually enters the aedicule, the small chamber built over Christ's tomb, and prays with two candles before him. A mysterious blue light enters the darkness and lights the candles. This is the miracle of the Holy Fire. The patriarch emerges to general clamor in the basilica and passes the fire to the faithful, all of whom are holding candles and singing hymns. The Orthodox see this as the first light of the resurrection.

A former Orthodox patriarch of Jerusalem, Diodoros, who served from 1981 to 2000, described what happens after he enters the tomb in the darkness:

> In the tomb, I say particular prayers that have been handed down to us through the centuries and, having said them, I wait. Sometimes I may wait a few minutes, but normally the miracle happens immediately after I have said the prayers. From the core of the very stone on which Jesus lay an indefinable light pours forth. It usually has a blue tint, but the colour may change and take on many different hues. It cannot be described in human terms. The light rises out of the stone as mist may rise out of a lake—it almost looks as if the stone is covered by a moist cloud, but it is light. . . .
>
> At a certain point the light rises and forms a column in which the fire is of a different nature, so that I am able to light my candles from it. When I thus have received the flame on my candles, I go out and give the fire first to the Armenian Patriarch and then to the Coptic. Thereafter I give the flame to all the people present in the Church.[2]

So, look, I'm Orthodox, I believe in miracles, and I have seen lots of videos of the Holy Fire on YouTube. The fire doesn't behave like normal flame. You can see clips online of people holding their hands in the flame and not being burned. This effect lasts for the first half hour or so, after which it becomes like normal fire—or so they say. Besides, the Israelis search the patriarch before he enters the aedicule to make sure he's not carrying matches or a lighter.

Despite all of that, I was skeptical. How could one not be? There have even been some Orthodox clerics in Jerusalem over the years admitting it's a fake. I expressed my doubts to an Arab Christian woman I had met. She scowled and said, "You'll see."

Standing in the crowd of thousands packed inside the ancient church, I watched a joyful mob of Arab Christian men proceed in, some riding the shoulders of others, chanting, "We are the Arab Christians! We have always been Christian, and we always will be!" Monks paraded by, and priests, and, finally, Patriarch Theophilos, the Greek Orthodox bishop of Jerusalem, and the 140th one in a direct line of succession from James, the stepbrother of Christ. All of this history marched by in a frenzy of jostle and acclamation.

And then the patriarch entered the aedicule. The air in the basilica was thick and electric with anticipation. When he emerged bearing the fire in his hands, a bell sounded urgently and the crowd erupted in praise.

The fire passed quickly among the faithful, from candle to candle, each pilgrim's sheaf of thirty-three blazing up with a thick flame several inches high. I held out my candles when the flame passed me, and with fire four or five inches tall blazing in front of my face, I brought my right hand to the fire, then moved it through slowly.

I felt nothing.

I did it again. Nothing.

Nothing.

Around me, everyone was experiencing the same thing. A Serbian pilgrim from London standing next to me held his lighted candles under his chin, with the flames bathing both of his cheeks. His eyes were wide. He felt nothing. He was not burned. Nobody was.

I kept returning my hands to the fire of my candles—not rushing my palms through, but moving them slowly—and it did not burn. At last I knew that, whatever the debunkers say, this was a true miracle. A Swedish woman in our group took a photo of me holding an icon of the resurrection in one hand, the Holy Fire in the other. In the photo my face looks as bright as the sun, such was my joy. In that moment, the miracle of the Holy Fire burned away all my sorrow in the light of the resurrection.*

I keep the photo from the Holy Fire ceremony on my smartphone to revisit now and then when I am feeling down. Yes, the man in the photo is in defeat and disgrace, but you wouldn't know it to look at him. You would never know that his marriage had failed. You would never know that he feels

---

* And, yes, after some minutes, as we were told would happen, the flames on our candles were normal again: you could not stand to touch them. To foreclose the idea that the candles, which the faithful buy in little shops throughout the Old City, had been specially treated with chemicals, I bought an extra sheaf to take home to America. Back in Louisiana, I lit it with matches—and the flame was impossible to touch from the start.

crushed by the prospect of returning to America to unwind his life. You would never know that, for a very long time, that man would have preferred to die than to keep living in this grinding way.

No, you see in that photo a blessed man—a man who has just beheld a great miracle in the holiest place on the planet. That man knows that God exists, that Christ is risen, and that he is loved. He is confident that life remains a blessing, although he cannot bless. But he thinks maybe he can bless others, if he tells them the story of how Jesus the Lord is at work making things new and turning suffering to his glory for those who are willing to share in his passion.

This is what the experience of holy wonder can do for you.

There is more. On that same day, the paschal ceremony began near midnight. I made my way through the darkened paths of the Old City toward the church built over the site of the resurrection but became lost. I turned down one very dark street but could tell it wasn't the way. "Lord, send me an angel to help me find the church," I prayed, then turned back to the lighted street. I laughed at myself for expecting a miracle.

When I emerged from the darkness, who should be rounding the corner but Angela, the chambermaid! She was accompanied by a man.

"Rod!" she said.

"Angela!" I replied.

"How are you?" she asked.

"Very good, thanks to you."

"No, thanks to God." Then we embraced and she introduced me to her brother.

After some small talk, I asked her for directions to the Church of the Holy Sepulchre. "Take this right, then the next right, and you will be there," she said. I did, and I was. And that was the flesh-and-blood angel the Lord sent to me on the holiest night of the year.

I stood in the basilica for the next five hours as the patriarch and his priests observed the ritual marking the greatest miracle of all, which happened on that very site almost two thousand years ago. Heaven and earth meet in Jerusalem in a way unlike anywhere else on earth—and on this night of nights, believers dwelled in the heart of the Light that death's darkness could not overcome.

I was at peace.

THE PILGRIM RETURNS TO THE WORLD

After that Easter journey, I began to look even more intently for signs of God's presence and love everywhere. When I would experience hardship—something serious or something trivial—I now framed it as an opportunity to grow closer to him. And I practiced the presence of God by talking to him throughout the day more often than before.

I noticed, too, that the things I had learned about focused attention, particularly the strategies from Orthodox priests about refusing logismoi, any bad or distracting thoughts, helped me avoid being drawn again into the trap of nostalgia for a lost golden past. Whenever I was tempted to feel anger or self-pity, I thought about Saint Galgano in Luca Daum's drawing and compelled myself to stay focused on Christ. *God has not abandoned me*, I would tell myself. *This is all happening as a test of faith.*

There are people who would say, "If God is real, why didn't he save your marriage? Why does he let children die? Why do the wicked prosper and the just suffer?" This is the wrong approach. My friend Marco Sermarini, whose bereavement of his wife did nothing to dim his bright shining joy, says that the existence of suffering in the world calls us to perform "the spiritual exercise of wonder."

"If you read the book of Job, there is a question recurring, 'Where were you when I laid the earth's foundation?' and so forth," says Marco. "I think this is a program, not just something random."

This is an important point. It is true that we can't force the awesome and wonderful to manifest themselves to us; the best we can do is to keep ourselves in a state of watchful waiting. But it is also true that we can practice wonder, in the sense that we can meet our doubts with an exercise of faith in the unfathomable mysteries of God, who is all good. When the tide of the Holy Spirit seems to have gone out, we have a responsibility to trust that it will return in time. Having seen the wonder of God once, we practice it in our prayers, our prostrations, and our liturgies of the everyday. That's how we make it real and ever present.

How do we begin to live out Christian enchantment? If you are not a believer, or if you are a weak one, start by accepting that the contemporary story about how Christianity is a thing of the past, whose claims cannot be believed by modern people, is just one take among many. If you believe the secular materialist narrative, you are saying that the overwhelming majority of people who have ever lived, and the majority of people alive today, are wrong. It is possible that you are right—but the odds are not in your favor. Shouldn't you at least consider that you are wrong?

Then you can face seriously the task of changing your mind to become more open to the reality of God and the presence of mystery, meaning, and miracle in this world. True, God cannot be commanded to show himself, but that does not relieve us from the responsibility to open ourselves to him. After all, you will never find if you don't first seek. You will never experience re-enchantment without metanoia—a radical change of mind. Iain McGilchrist explains how and why the left-brain vision that made the modern world is a distortion of the truth—and why those who seek the truth must not abandon it but rather should balance it with the intuitive way of knowing from the brain's right hemisphere.

This is not a matter of accepting an illusion because it might make you feel better. This is about learning to see the truth, to access the really real, which has been denied to you by the flawed way of perception the modern world has falsely claimed is the whole truth. The harder we cling to the modern idea that the material world is nothing more than stuff that we are free to manipulate, the more difficult it will be to experience a resonant sense of connection with it.

Because the way we pay attention to the world has a lot to do with what we perceive, you can endeavor to shed distractions in life that get in the way of focus. And you can take on prayer disciplines that help still the mind, cleanse the nous, and repair the fragmented attention that makes it hard to relate to God.

Then lean, and lean hard, into beauty. Beauty—the moral beauty of good and holy people and the aesthetic beauty of art, music, and architecture, as well as the natural world—is a portal through which enchantment passes to us. Stop thinking of it as merely something admirable or decorative. True beauty reveals to us something of God's nature, and truth. It shows us that the world has meaning and that we are part of that world. Beauty offers us those moments of epiphany in which the fundamental unity and purpose of the world appear to us. It is also a bridge to the world of the transcendent and ultimately to God.

Cultivate a real appreciation for beauty by reading, listening to, and looking at works of art, music, and architecture that have stood the test of time. Go out into nature and see and feel it for meaning. Read the lives of the saints and meditate on the lives of holy people in our world today. The beauty present in all of these people, places, and things is a sign telling us all where we need to go if we want to live.

Take stories of miracles and encounters with the numinous seriously. Don't be credulous; not every miracle story is true. But many of them are. You might not experience one, and if not, that doesn't mean you are unworthy. Still, they really do happen to people, even today. This fact should humble us all and remind us that anything is possible. None of us knows if a miracle awaits us, but we have the responsibility to prepare ourselves for that possibility. We don't want to be the kind of people who, when confronted by a miracle, react with fear or reflexive disbelief because we don't want to change our lives.

You can also educate yourself about the realities of the dark side—of black magic and the occult. Modern secularists and rationalist Christians laugh, but demonic possession is real. If you've seen it, you don't need convincing. Demons can work apparent miracles, too, for the sake of deceiving us. Remember that occultists want false enchantment—that is, to experience and access the power of the spirit world—but only for the sake of learning to control it, to compel demons to do things for them. This is the way of destruction. More and more people are choosing it. You must learn why it is evil and turn away from it in all its forms—psychedelics, occult practices, all of it.

It is frankly depressing to look at the state of the churches today and to take stock of the overall quality of leadership, both clerical and lay. Don't despair! God is raising up new voices to show his people the way forward. It will not do to complain about the very real failures of religious leaders and claim that as an excuse to abandon the faith. This is cowardice. How can you be sure that God won't use you to rally believers to repentance and return to a true and living faith, as he has done so often in ages past with other ordinary men and women?

To summarize: We Christians have a mission to focus our attention on Christ and to create the conditions for the flow of divine energy—of grace—to purify the eyes of our hearts so that we can see the holiness all around us and share in the life of God. To accomplish this, we have to learn how to sacrifice, die to ourselves, and fix our personal swords, as symbols of our will, into the stone of God as an act of faithful obedience.

We have to learn how to direct our attention rightly, pray more effectively, and reestablish resonance with the world beyond our heads. We have to discover how to open our eyes to beauty and allow it to work its magic on us, drawing us into a deeper relationship with reality.

We have to learn about the frightening facts of spiritual warfare and dark enchantment and turn from its enticements. And we have to seek out the community of wise and faithful men and women with whom to share the pilgrim's journey.

We can't force enchantment to happen, but we can certainly do all of these things to prepare ourselves for it—even in the face of a world that says they are impossible and that offers us instead the false enchantments of sex, money, fame, technology, and even the occult. The means to do this are part of our past and part of our present. They can be part of our future, if we want them enough to make life-changing sacrifices. There is no other way. The more control you want to have over your life, the less enchantment you will experience. As Jesus said, "Whoever wants to save their life will lose it, but whoever loses their life for me will find it" (Matt. 16:25).

One more thing: we have to learn openness to synchronicity, seren-dipity, and signs—and to listen (with discernment) to them. Where would I be if that Genoese artist had not listened to what God told him that after-noon in his studio and come that night bearing a gift for the American writer? Where would I be if I had not made the connection between the artist's drawing of the obscure medieval saint and a little-known Russian film that just happened to pass before my sad and weary eyes on a warm spring night in Louisiana, offering me a way out of my despair?

I can tell you this much: you would not have the book you have just read. In fact, the image of Saint Galgano's temptation is a condensed sym-bol of this book's message: it is a portrait of a strong-willed man who, after refusing God's call, went to a mountaintop and saw God. In response to this revelation, which included a true miracle (which you can still see today), he sacrificed his life for Christ, before whom, in Daum's drawing, Galgano bows. Yet Galgano struggles to keep his eyes firmly fixed on heaven, despite the temptation of his own thoughts to attract his attention away from God.

There you have it: the core message of re-enchantment, in a single man's story, captured in a single image.

Listen for the Lord's calling with a heart willing to obey when the word comes.

Respond to the revelation of awe by sacrificing everything to serve God.

Pray without ceasing.

Keep your eyes on heaven, despite the many temptations to turn your eyes to the things of the earth.

Any seeds that this story has planted in your heart that bear good fruit can be traced first to Luca Daum's act of prayerful obedience and my own willingness to receive this strange grace and to act on it as if it were a mes-sage in a bottle.

I put the message into this book and have handed off the message to you. I pray that you open your mind and heart to receive it! For sooner or later, if you are standing in the right place, with your eyes wide open to the night sky, a great comet will come blazing by and invite you to hitch a ride.

RAHNER'S WARNING

What did the German Jesuit theologian Karl Rahner mean when he said the Christian of the future will have to be a mystic, in the sense that he has experienced "something," or he will cease to be anything at all? Rahner was born in 1904 and died in 1984, and he lived through a century in which Christianity dissolved into atheism. He did not live long enough to see that atheism was untenable and that post-Christian people would require a god of some kind.

With the wisdom of a postmodern experience that the great Jesuit did not live to have, let us improve on his warning: Christians of the future will have to be mystic or they will become anything.

The overwhelming power of modern global culture, and its narratives of liberation through the embrace of technology and personal autonomy, will be all but impossible to resist through familiar means. Reason as a guide to truth has also gone into eclipse in these postmodern times. A moralistic Christianity—one that foregrounds ethical action as the substance of faith—is powerless. Yes, to be a good Christian requires one to act morally, but that morality must derive from a life-changing inner experience with God. There is no substitute. In whatever way your Christian tradition understands the command, we are all bound to obey Christ when he said, "You must be born again" (John 3:7).

The churches and other once authoritative institutions have lost their power to bind and command. Moreover, to be a faithful Christian in the West today is to be an outsider, a dissident; there are no social pressures to accept Christianity and many to refuse it.

In my life, it was only the experience of awe at Chartres and the testimony of an elderly weeping monsignor of the miracles that changed his life that finally compelled me to walk away from my own desires and conformity to my social group and become a Christian. And it has been a variety of authentically mystical experiences over the years—some I've shared with you in this book, but there are others—that have kept me on the straight path when I have been tempted to stray.

Rahner was right: if I had not had those mystical experiences—some of them with God, and some with the demonic—it is easy to see how I could have been carried away by the cultural undertow of our era. These hierophanies, manifestations of the unseen realm, brought me back to reality. God is with us, no matter what, and he is sovereign. Our lives in this world require a spiritual struggle with what Paul calls principalities and powers. Like the New York businessman walking the streets of Manhattan, and the Vatican exorcist striding across Saint Peter's Square, I, too, have seen too much ever to believe that this world is what most people think it is.

It cannot be said often enough: mystical experience alone cannot suffice. This is the error that many charismatic Christians make: they take experience as authoritative. But mystical experience can only be interpreted within a doctrinal frame based on Scripture and authoritative church teaching. To step outside of that is to risk grave error. Yet to downplay or deny mystical experience is not only to risk dismissing reality but also to surrender a powerful source of strength and clarity during the fog of spiritual warfare.

So, a final confession, of a mystical event that has guided the entirety of my career as a writer. It makes me uncomfortable to talk about this, but then, I'm too old to care what people think.

In 1993, at the beginning of my Christian walk, I was praying for a believing friend having an intense spiritual crisis when I had a sudden quasi-apocalyptic vision. I saw a civilizational catastrophe that cast light on the test my stricken friend faced. At the conclusion of this strange fugue state, I heard God's voice say, "You will lose your reason," but, the voice continued, cling to Christ and "don't be afraid, for the Lion of the tribe of Judah, the Root of David has triumphed."

You will lose your reason. What? And what is this Lion and Root stuff?

I figured they must be messianic titles, but as a man new to the faith, I couldn't be sure. I phoned my friend, told him what had happened, and he thanked God for this sign, which he believed told him what to do. A few minutes later, shaken by what had happened to me—it was the first such episode and, as of this writing, the last—I sat on the couch of my Washington, DC, apartment reading one of the Gospels, which were all fresh to me then.

Though it was the dead of winter outside, and the windows were closed, a puff of air blew softly across my left cheek and seemed—I know this is weird—to pass through my mind. It left the words "Revelation 5:5" there. Startled by this, I turned to that verse and read these words: "Then one of the elders said to me, 'Do not weep! See, the Lion of the tribe of Judah, the Root of David, has triumphed. He is able to open the scroll and its seven seals.'"

A surge of electricity shot up my spine! I could not have known that verse. This confirmed that the vision I had experienced while praying had not come from the overheated imagination of a new convert but had been real.

That was more than thirty years ago. I have lived to see specific things foretold in the vision come true. In recent years, as our common culture has gone morally insane, I believe now I understand God's warning about the loss of reason. He wasn't talking about me personally; he was talking about humanity. It was only in completing this book that I came to grasp the purpose of that prophecy. In a time of general madness and perhaps coming persecution, our last and best hope is found only through a strong and robustly countercultural faith, one rooted deeply in the Christian tradition and a creed that roars out the good news, and in defiance of the world's wisdom: that the Lion of the tribe of Judah has already won the victory.

Maybe, then, by writing this book, the seeds the Holy Spirit planted within a young journalist, shaken more than three decades ago by a mystical experience at the beginning of his career—one that he never dared to make public until now—has come to fruition with this book. I don't know if we are at the end of *the* world, but we are undoubtedly at the end of *a* world—and if Christians are going to make it through this long dark winter without losing our faith, we must become practical mystics.

If we prefer to rely on the fragility of both secular rationalism and a Christianity whose once strong God has been reduced to a mere moralist or political activist, or relegated to the status of cosmic butler or genial grandfather, we're not going to stay Christian. Even worse, if we allow the gods of AI and related technologies to possess us, we will in time cease to be human.

This book has shown you how to open your mind and your eyes to real reality—if you have the courage. Seek the living God and the experience of him, in the ways of our faithful ancestors, while you may. The hour is late, the times are dark, the heavens full of signs and portents are wheeling about us— and the stakes could not be higher.

ACKNOWLEDGMENTS

My friend Ross Douthat, though a more cerebral Christian than I, has always been a receptive listener to my mystical tales. Some years back, he urged me to "write your woo book." And so I have. I appreciate his encouragement and support.

This book emerged from a period of pain and loss, though I now see that the unsought sacrifice by the messenger was part of the message. I can never thank enough the friends who stood by me through the grief of the loss of my marriage. I'm thinking in particular of Frederica Mathewes-Green, Kale Zelden, Ed Grier, Matt Burford, Lee Burnett, James Card, Luca Salis, Pierre Valentin, Jason McCrory, Gavin Ashenden, and Marco Sermarini, but there were others. I think with gratitude and affection also of the Hungarians that welcomed me and my son Matthew and gave us a place to settle: John and Melissa O'Sullivan, Anna Salyi, Balazs Orban, Istvan Kiss, Loretta Toth, and the entire crew at the Danube Institute. James and Helen Orr and their children are dear friends who offered gracious hospitality and friendship. Father Eben Treviño has been a confidant and a strong spiritual support. Dale Brantner was an invaluable help in Jerusalem. I'll never meet most in the community of readers I've built up with my Substack newsletter, but so many have prayed for me and my family and consoled me privately. Thank you all. It means more than I can say.

This book has had a rocky and lengthy gestation, owing to personal crisis. I thank my ace literary agent Gary Morris for shepherding the manuscript through its trials, and Paul Pastor for being just the editor this strange book needed. Thanks to Robert Duncan for accompanying me to Montesiepi to see the sword in the stone. Motoring through Tuscany with a fellow Christian dude from the American South, listening to the Rolling Stones with the windows down and the warm wind in our faces, was a particular grace. Many thanks to Ramon and Anita Tancinco for their warm welcome and stories at their farm outside of Krakow. I also thank the many people who shared their stories of the numinous and the miraculous with me, especially those who asked to be anonymous in print but wanted to bear witness to what happened to them anyway, for the greater glory of God. It is not easy to talk about such things, and I cherish their trust. I am only sorry that I did not have room in these pages to tell everything folks shared with me. Maybe some will be motivated to write books of their own, no longer intimidated by the prospect of mockery. Sooner or later, the taboo will be broken; I hope this book plays a role in that.

Finally, I thank my son Matthew. He knows why. May we both see better days.

NOTES

CHAPTER 1: TO SEE INTO THE LIFE OF THINGS

1. C. S. Lewis, *The Discarded Image* (1964; repr., Cambridge: Cambridge Univ. Press, 2012).
2. Charles Taylor, *A Secular Age* (Cambridge, MA: Belknap Press, 2007), page 5 of 874, Kindle.
3. Viktor Frankl, *Man's Search for Meaning* (Boston: Beacon Press, 2006), page 41 of 166, Kindle.
4. Whittaker Chambers, *Witness* (Washington: Regnery, 1969), 15–16.
5. Iain McGilchrist, *The Matter with Things* (London: Perspectiva Press, 2021), loc. 2041 of 50425, Kindle.
6. Joshua Landy and Michael Saler, "Introduction: The Varieties of Modern Enchantment," in *The Re-Enchantment of the World*, ed. Joshua Landy and Michael Saler (Redwood City, CA: Stanford Univ. Press, 2009), 2.

CHAPTER 2: EXILE FROM THE ENCHANTED GARDEN

1. Daniel Everett, *Don't Sleep, There Are Snakes* (New York: Vintage, 2008), xvii.
2. Joseph Henrich, *The WEIRDest People in the World: How the West Became Psychologically Peculiar and Particularly Prosperous* (New York: Farrar, Straus and Giroux, 2020), 5.
3. Mircea Eliade, *The Sacred and the Profane*, trans. Willard R. Trask (New York: Harcourt, 1959), 9.
4. Eliade, *Sacred and Profane*, 9.
5. Eliade, *Sacred and Profane*, 10.
6. Robert Knapp, *The Dawn of Christianity* (London: Profile Books, 2018), 12–13.
7. Knapp, *Dawn of Christianity*, 12.
8. Knapp, *Dawn of Christianity*, 200.
9. Knapp, *Dawn of Christianity*, 178.
10. Knapp, *Dawn of Christianity*, 180.

11. Origen, quoted in Knapp, *Dawn of Christianity*, 202.
12. Hans Boersma, *Heavenly Participation: The Weaving of a Sacramental Tapestry* (Grand Rapids: Eerdmans, 2011).
13. Michael Allen Gillespie, *The Theological Origins of Modernity* (Chicago: University of Chicago Press, 2009), 15.
14. Carlos Eire, *They Flew: A History of the Impossible* (New Haven, CT: Yale Univ. Press, 2024), loc. 502 of 11196, Kindle.
15. Eire, *They Flew*, loc. 513 of 11196, Kindle.
16. D. W. Pasulka, *American Cosmic: UFOs, Religion, Technology* (New York: Oxford Univ. Press, 2019), page 242 of 269, Kindle.
17. Michael Heiser, *The Unseen Realm: Recovering the Supernatural Worldview of the Bible* (Bellingham, WA: Lexham Press, 2015), page 17 of 384, Kindle.
18. Eugene McCarraher, *The Enchantments of Mammon: How Capitalism Became the Religion of Modernity* (Cambridge, MA: Belknap Press, 2019), page 5 of 799, Kindle.
19. McCarraher, *Enchantments of Mammon*, page 29 of 799, Kindle.
20. Marshall McLuhan, *Understanding Media* (New York: McGraw-Hill, 1964), 90.
21. Nicholas Carr, *The Shallows*, updated ed. (New York: Norton, 2020), loc. 44 of 6080, Kindle.
22. Carr, *The Shallows*, loc. 1870 of 6080, Kindle.
23. Paul Kingsnorth, "Blanched Sun, Blinded Man," *The Abbey of Misrule*, Substack, May 26, 2021, https://paulkingsnorth.substack.com/p/blanched-sun-blinded-man.

CHAPTER 3: ENCHANTED MIND, ENCHANTED MATTER

1. Iain McGilchrist, *The Matter with Things: Our Brains, Our Delusions, and the Unmaking of the World* (London: Perspectiva Press, 2021), loc. 135 of 50608, Kindle.
2. F. A. Hayek, *The Counter-Revolution of Science: Studies on the Abuse of Reason* (Glencoe, IL: Free Press, 1952), quoted in Jonathan Rauch, "Objections to These Unions," *Reason*, June 2004, https://reason.com/2004/06/01/objections-to-these-unions-2/.
3. Thomas Nagel, *Mind and Cosmos* (New York: Oxford Univ. Press, 2012), loc. 104 of 1831, Kindle.
4. Hartmut Rosa, *The Uncontrollability of the World*, trans. James C. Wagner (Medford, MA: Polity Press, 2020), page 2 of 133, Kindle.
5. Rosa, *Uncontrollability*, 2 of 133, Kindle.
6. Rosa, *Uncontrollability*, 28 of 133, Kindle.
7. Rosa, *Uncontrollability*, 44 of 133, Kindle.
8. Tobias Wolff, quoted in John Cornwell, *Powers of Darkness, Powers of Light* (New York: Viking, 1991), 255.
9. Wolff, quoted in Cornwell, *Powers of Darkness*.

10. Kenneth Clark, *The Other Half: A Self Portrait* (1977), quoted in Alex Rodger, "Moral, Spiritual, Religious—Are They Synonymous?" in *Spiritual and Religious Education*, ed. Mal Leicester, Celia Modgil, and Sohan Modgil (New York: Falmer Press, 2000), 5:10.
11. Marshall McLuhan, *The Medium and the Light: Reflections on Religion*, ed. Eric McLuhan and Jacek Szklarek (Eugene, OR: Wipf and Stock, 2010), 102.
12. McLuhan, *Medium and the Light*, 64.

CHAPTER 4: WHY DISENCHANTMENT MATTERS

1. Iain McGilchrist, "Dr Iain McGilchrist—The Intersection of Consciousness and Matter—Beyond the Brain 2023," Rupert Sheldrake, December 1, 2023, YouTube video, www.youtube.com/watch?v=KyNgE6RsGnw.
2. Jack Gould, "Lack of Responsibility Is Shown by TV in Exploiting Teenagers," *New York Times*, September 16, 1956, https://archive.nytimes.com/www.nytimes.com/partners/aol/special/elvis/early-elvis3.html.
3. Ari Shapiro and Taylor Crumpton, "Hip-Hop That Made the Grown-Ups Uncomfortable: The 'Controversy' Around 'WAP,'" *All Things Considered*, August 14, 2020, www.npr.org/2020/08/14/902659822/hip-hop-that-made-the-grown-ups-uncomfortable-the-controversy-around-wap.
4. Dan Witters, "U.S. Depression Rates Reach New Highs," *Gallup News*, May 17, 2023, https://news.gallup.com/poll/505745/depression-rates-reach-new-highs.aspx.
5. Witters, "U.S. Depression Rates."
6. Zygmunt Bauman, *Liquid Modernity* (Cambridge: Polity, 2000).
7. This is discussed in greater detail in my book *Live Not by Lies* (New York: Sentinel, 2020).
8. Ellyn Maese, "Almost a Quarter of the World Feels Lonely," Gallup, October 24, 2023, https://news.gallup.com/opinion/gallup/512618/almost-quarter-world-feels-lonely.aspx.
9. Lydia Saad, "Historically Low Faith in U.S. Institutions Continues," Gallup, July 6, 2023, https://news.gallup.com/poll/508169/historically-low-faith-institutions-continues.aspx.
10. PewResearch.org, "Public Trust in Government: 1958–2023," September 19, 2023, www.pewresearch.org/politics/2023/09/19/public-trust-in-government-1958-2023.
11. Carl Trueman, "The Desecration of Man," *First Things*, January 2024, www.firstthings.com/article/2024/01/the-desecration-of-man.
12. Michel Houellebecq, *The Possibility of an Island* (2007), quoted in Louis Betty, *Without God: Michel Houellebecq and Materialist Horror* (University Park, PA: Pennsylvania State Univ. Press, 2016), loc. 655 of 3480, Kindle.
13. Yuval Noah Harari, "Speech at World Economic Forum 2020," transcript published January 24, 2020, www.weforum.org/agenda/2020/01/yuval-hararis-warning-davos-speech-future-predications.

CHAPTER 5: THE DARK ENCHANTMENT OF THE OCCULT

1. Pew Research Center, "Religious 'Nones' in America: Who They Are and What They Believe," January 24, 2020, www.pewresearch.org/religion /2024/01/24/religious-nones-in-america-who-they-are-and-what-they-believe.
2. Stephen Bullivant, *Nonverts: The Making of Ex-Christian America* (New York: Oxford Univ. Press, 2022), 11.
3. Tara Isabella Burton, *Strange Rites: New Religions for a Godless World* (New York: Public Affairs, 2020), 146.
4. Robert Falconer, *The Others within Us: Internal Family Systems, Porous Mind, and Spirit Possession* (Self-published, 2023), page 295 of 696, Kindle.
5. Discussed by Rupert Sheldrake in his many YouTube videos, and at length in his book *Ways to Go Beyond and Why They Work: Seven Spiritual Practices in a Scientific Age* (Aurora, CO: Salix Press, 2019).
6. Charles Foster, "Mind Expanding: The Uses of Psychedelic Drugs," *Times Literary Supplement*, January 12, 2024, www.the-tls.co.uk/politics-society /social-cultural-studies/ten-trips-andy-mitchell-psychedelics-david-nutt-i -feel-love-rachel-nuwer-psychonauts-mike-jay-book-review-charles-foster.
7. Ed Prideaux, "Is the Psychedelic Industrial Complex Evil?" *UnHerd*, January 25, 2023, https://unherd.com/2023/01/the-psychedelic-industrial -complex-is-evil/.
8. Psalm 144:1.

CHAPTER 6: ALIENS AND THE SACRED MACHINE

1. Jacques Vallée, *Passport to Magonia: From Folklore to Flying Saucers* (Brisbane: Daily Grail Publishing, 2015), page 9 of 515, Kindle.
2. John Mack, interviewed for *Nova*, April 25, 1995, http://johnmackinstitute .org/1995/04/nova-interviews-john-mack-psychiatrist-harvard-university.
3. Jeffrey Kripal, *Authors of the Impossible: The Paranormal and the Sacred* (Chicago and London: Univ. of Chicago Press, 2010), 109.
4. Diana Pasulka, *American Cosmic* (New York: Oxford Univ. Press, 2019), page 9 of 269, Kindle.
5. Pasulka, *American Cosmic*, page 11 of 269, Kindle.
6. Pasulka, *American Cosmic*, page 38 of 269, Kindle.
7. Jacques Vallée, *Messengers of Deception: UFO Contacts and Cults* (Brisbane: Daily Grail Publishing, 2008), 251.
8. Steven Dick, "The Postbiological Universe" (paper, 57th International Astronautical Congress, Washington, DC, 2006), http://resources.iaaseti .org/abst2006/IAC-06-A4.2.01.pdf.
9. Charles Taylor uses the term throughout *A Secular Age* (Cambridge, MA: Belknap Press of Harvard Univ. Press, 2007).
10. Taylor, *A Secular Age*, page 76 of 874, Kindle.
11. Jacques Ellul, *The Technological Society*, trans. John Wilkinson (New York: Vintage, 1964), xxv.

12. Ellul, *Technological Society*, 4.
13. Ellul, *Technological Society*, 6.
14. Ellul, *Technological Society*, 12.
15. Yuval Noah Harari, "Historian: When Computers and Biology Converge, Organisms Become Algorithms," interview by Daniel A. Bell, *HuffPost*, May 11, 2016, www.huffpost.com/entry/computers-biology-algorithms -yuval-harari_b_9999150.
16. Tara Isabella Burton, "Of Memes and Magick," *Aeon*, December 14, 2023, https://aeon.co/essays/how-the-internet-became-the-modern-purveyor -of-ancient-magic.
17. Blake Lemoine, "Is AI a 'Catastrophic' Danger to Humanity?" Michael Sandler's Inspire Nation, October 19, 2023, YouTube video, www.youtube .com/watch?v=KQQaaX4rkr8.
18. Burton, "Of Memes and Magick."
19. Marshall McLuhan, *The Medium and the Light: Reflections on Religion* (Eugene, OR: Wipf and Stock, 2010), 209.
20. McLuhan, *Medium and the Light*, 209.
21. Christopher Laursen, "Plurality through Imagination: The Emergence of Online Tulpa Communities in the Making of New Identities," in *Believing in Bits*, ed. Simone Natale and D. W. Pasulka (New York: Oxford Univ. Press, 2019), 164.
22. Antón Barba-Kay, *A Web of Our Own Making* (Cambridge: Cambridge Univ. Press, 2023), page 8 of 295, Kindle.
23. Barba-Kay, *Web of Our Own Making*, page 240 of 295, Kindle.
24. Emma Loffhagen, "'I'm Sick and Tired of Dating Actual People'—Meet the Men Falling in Love with Their A.I. Girlfriends," *Evening Standard*, August 8, 2023, www.standard.co.uk/lifestyle/rise-of-ai-chatbot-girlfriends -replika-b1098144.html.
25. Kevin Roose, "Bing's A.I. Chat: 'I Want to Be Alive,'" *New York Times*, February 16, 2023, www.nytimes.com/2023/02/16/technology/bing -chatbot-transcript.html.
26. Ellul, *Technological Society*, 411.
27. Leopold Aschenbrenner, *Situational Awareness: The Decade Ahead* (San Francisco: n.p., June 2024), 158, https://situational-awareness.ai/wp-content /uploads/2024/06/situationalawareness.pdf.
28. Neil McArthur, "Gods in the Machine? The Rise of Artificial Intelligence May Result in New Religions," *The Conversation*, March 15, 2023, https:// theconversation.com/gods-in-the-machine-the-rise-of-artificial-intelligence -may-result-in-new-religions-201068.
29. McArthur, "Gods in the Machine?"
30. Diana Pasulka, *Encounters: Experiences with Nonhuman Intelligences* (New York: St. Martin's Essentials, 2023), 14.
31. Jonathan Cahn, *The Return of the Gods* (Lake Mary, FL: FrontLine, 2022).

CHAPTER 7: ATTENTION AND PRAYER

1. Iain McGilchrist, *The Matter with Things* (London: Perspectiva Press, 2021), loc. 31 of 50608, Kindle.
2. Matthew B. Crawford, *The World beyond Your Head* (New York: Farrar, Straus and Giroux, 2015), page 25 of 308, Kindle.
3. Crawford, *World beyond Your Head*, page 28 of 308, Kindle.
4. T. M. Luhrmann, *How God Becomes Real* (Princeton, NJ: Princeton Univ. Press, 2020), pages xii–xiii of 235, Kindle.
5. Luhrmann, *How God Becomes Real*, page 134 of 235, Kindle.
6. Frederica Mathewes-Green, *Welcome to the Orthodox Church: An Introduction to Eastern Christianity* (Brewster, MA: Paraclete, 2015), 194.
7. McGilchrist, *Matter with Things*, loc. 8440 of 50608, Kindle.
8. McGilchrist, *Matter with Things*, page 1487 of 2998, Kindle.
9. McGilchrist, *Matter with Things*, loc. 8674 of 50608, Kindle.
10. C. S. Lewis, *Perelandra* (1943), in *The Space Trilogy Omnibus* (New York: HarperOne, 2014), page 445 of 944, Kindle.
11. Lewis, *Perelandra*, page 445 of 944, Kindle.
12. Lewis, *Perelandra*, page 446 of 944, Kindle.
13. Mihaly Csikszentmihalyi, *Flow: The Psychology of Optimal Experience* (New York: HarperCollins E-books, 2008), page 4 of 304, Kindle.
14. Csikszentmihalyi, *Flow*, page 2 of 304, Kindle.
15. Csikszentmihalyi, *Flow*, page 6 of 304, Kindle.
16. Csikszentmihalyi, *Flow*, page 21 of 304, Kindle.
17. Csikszentmihalyi, *Flow*, page 31 of 304, Kindle.
18. Csikszentmihalyi, *Flow*, page 76 of 304, Kindle.
19. Csikszentmihalyi, *Flow*, page 235 of 304, Kindle.
20. Mathewes-Green, *Welcome to the Orthodox Church*, 202–3.
21. Gabriel Bunge, *Earthen Vessels: The Practice of Personal Prayer* (San Francisco: Ignatius Press, 2010), loc. 1755 of 3120, Kindle.
22. Luhrmann, *How God Becomes Real*, page xi of 235, Kindle.
23. Luhrmann, *When God Talks Back* (New York: Knopf, 2012), loc. 259 of 8674, Kindle.
24. Luhrmann, *How God Becomes Real*, page 67 of 235, Kindle.
25. Marshall McLuhan, *The Medium and the Light: Reflections on Religion* (Eugene, OR: Wipf and Stock, 2010), 209.

CHAPTER 8: LEARNING HOW TO SEE

1. Aleksandr Solzhenitsyn, Nobel Lecture in Literature, 1970, www.solzhenitsyncenter.org/nobel-lecture.
2. Andrei Tarkovsky, *Sculpting in Time: Reflections on the Cinema*, trans. Kitty Hunter-Blair (Austin, TX: University of Texas Press, 1986), 43.
3. Charles Williams, *The Figure of Beatrice: A Study in Dante* (1943; Brooklyn: Angelico Press, 2021), 22.

4. Williams, *Figure of Beatrice*, 26.

5. Dante Alighieri, *The Divine Comedy*, trans. Allen Mandelbaum, Digital Dante, Columbia University Libraries, accessed June 3, 2024, https:// digitaldante.columbia.edu/dante/divine-comedy/paradiso/paradiso-18/.

6. Williams, *Figure of Beatrice*, 123.

7. I tell this story in detail in my book *How Dante Can Save Your Life* (New York: Regan Books, 2015).

8. Patrick Curry, *Art and Enchantment: How Wonder Works* (New York: Routledge, 2023), 4.

9. Curry, *Art and Enchantment*, 4.

10. Curry, *Art and Enchantment*, 15.

11. Athanasius, "On the Incarnation," trans. "a religious of C.S.M.V.," quoted in *Medieval Philosophy: A Multicultural Reader*, gen. ed. Bruce V. Foltz (London: Bloomsbury Academic, 2019), 115.

12. Umberto Eco, *Art and Beauty in the Middle Ages*, trans. Hugh Bredin (New Haven, CT: Yale Univ. Press, 2002), 57.

13. Dante Alighieri, *The Divine Comedy*, trans. Allen Mandelbaum.

14. Christopher Alexander, *The Nature of Order: An Essay on the Art of Building and the Nature of the Universe*, vol. 4, *The Luminous Ground* (Berkeley, CA: Center for Environmental Structure, 2004), 14.

15. Alexander, *Nature of Order*, 15.

16. Christopher Alexander, "Making the Garden," *First Things*, February 2016, www.firstthings.com/article/2016/02/making-the-garden.

17. Alexander, "Making the Garden."

18. Alexander, "Making the Garden."

19. Alexander, "Making the Garden."

20. Iain McGilchrist, *The Master and His Emissary: The Divided Brain and the Making of the Western World*, expanded ed. (New Haven, CT: Yale Univ. Press, 2019), 445.

21. McGilchrist, *Master and His Emissary*, page 29 of 585, Kindle.

22. Benedict XVI, *Encyclical Deus caritas est*, December 25, 2005, www.vatican .va/content/benedict-xvi/en/encyclicals/documents/hf_ben-xvi_enc _20051225_deus-caritas-est.html.

23. Timothy G. Patitsas, *The Ethics of Beauty* (Maysville, MO: St. Nicholas Press, 2019), 54.

24. Patitsas, *Ethics of Beauty*, 159.

CHAPTER 9: SIGNS AND WONDERS

1. Dionysios Farasiotis, *The Gurus, the Young Man, and Elder Paisios*, ed. Philip Navarro, trans. Hieromonk Alexis Trader (Platina, CA: St. Herman of Alaska Brotherhood, 2008, 2011), page 77 of 312, Kindle.

2. Farasiotis, *Elder Paisios*, page 80 of 312, Kindle.

3. Farasiotis, *Elder Paisios*, page 287 of 312, Kindle.

4. Kenneth L. Woodward, "Graham Greene and the Stigmata," letter to the editor of the *New York Review of Books*, February 10, 2005, www.nybooks .com/articles/2005/02/10/graham-greene-the-stigmata/.

CHAPTER 10: THREE PROPHETS OF THE REAL

1. John Vervaeke, "Awakening from the Meaning Crisis," YouTube lecture series, undated, https://johnvervaeke.com/series/awakening-from-the -meaning-crisis.
2. Yuval Noah Harari, *Homo Deus: A Brief History of Tomorrow* (New York: Harper, 2017), 200–202.
3. Gregory A. Smith, "Just One-third of U.S. Catholics Agree with Their Church That Eucharist Is Body, Blood of Christ," PewResearch, August 5, 2019, www.pewresearch.org/short-reads/2019/08/05/transubstantiation -eucharist-u-s-catholics/.

CHAPTER 11: THE URGENCY OF THE MYSTICAL

1. Marshall McLuhan, *The Medium and the Light: Reflections on Religion* (Eugene, OR: Wipf and Stock, 2010), 82–83.
2. Niels Christian Hvidt, "Interview with Patriarch Diodoros I of Jerusalem on the Miracle of the Holy Light," *Orthodox Christianity Then and Now* (blog), May 10, 2022, www.johnsanidopoulos.com/2022/05/interview-with -patriarch-diodoros-i-of.html#:~:text=At%20a%20certain%20point%20 the,and%20then%20to%20the%20Coptic.